Expecting Trouble

Expecting Trouble

Surrogacy, Fetal Abuse, & New Reproductive Technologies

edited by
Patricia Boling

with a Foreword by Nancy Hartsock

Westview Press
Boulder • San Francisco • Oxford

Copyright © 1995 by Westview Press, Inc.

Published in 1995 in the United States of America by Westview Press, Inc., 5500 Central Avenue, Boulder, Colorado 80301-2877, and in the United Kingdom by Westview Press, 12 Hid's Copse Road, Cumnor Hill, Oxford OX2 9JJ

A CIP catalog record for this book is available from the Library of Congress.
ISBN 0-8133-2002-X(HC); 0-8133-2003-8(PB)

Printed and bound in the United States of America

The paper used in this publication meets the requirements
of the American National Standard for Permanence of Paper
for Printed Library Materials Z39.48-1984.

10   9   8   7   6   5   4   3   2   1

Contents

Foreword

THE THOUGHTFUL ESSAYS in this book mark what I would characterize as an important advance in feminist political theory: feminist theory that focuses on politics and policy issues. The issues taken up here promise to be more and more prominent in feminist debates, and in public policy debates generally, as changes in technology spur changes in the way we think about fetuses and pregnant women. The debate over abortion that took place during the 1970s and 1980s is shifting and expanding. Rather than being framed in terms of women's choice and fetuses' right to life, current discussions are more about protecting fetuses from their mothers' drug and alcohol abuse, issues of maternal responsibility and fault, and the alienability of "services" women perform as birth mothers.

In some ways the concerns of the authors in this book represent the "traditional" concerns of feminist theory. They focus on the "private sphere," on the situation of women in the context of reproduction. The authors demonstrate, however, that pregnancy has become an increasing preoccupation of "public" policies and the focus of public attention and pressure. This book makes an important contribution by examining how these invasions take place. Some of the authors concentrate on the increasing commodification of life in late capitalism, for example in the case of surrogacy. Several suggest that surrogacy contracts represent the intrusion of the market and of contract law into human reproduction and the relationship between mother and fetus, two subjects formerly viewed as intimate, emotionally charged, and not for sale (see the essays by Shanley and Narayan). Others point out that maternal nurturance has always taken place under patriarchal pressures, suggesting that the gulf between reproduction under a surrogacy contract and that within a traditional marriage may not be as wide as we might like to believe (Narayan). Thus, in an extension of the logic of late capitalism, the fetus can be seen as an object of property subject to contract laws or as a consumer good to be engineered to ensure the best possible "product" (see Richard's essay). Other authors trace the emergence of legal obligations to the unborn as well as the beginnings of a redefinition of pregnancy as an adversarial relation in which both parties have rights that may conflict (see essays by Condit, Strickland and Whicker, Johnson, and Bower). In their discussions, however, these authors raise questions that move beyond how state actions and policies affect pregnant women; these essays illuminate more general questions about the ways we have chosen to think about individuals and state policies.

For example, they raise questions about whether the discourse of privacy and individualism is the best way to think about the ways public policies affect people. The shared, socially and institutionally located character of pregnant women's experiences, as well as the possibility of empowering women through community-based group discussion and action, are absent from these discussions (see Young). Nor does the specific situation of pregnant women as both one and not-one (to paraphrase Adrienne Rich) fit within these terms (Shanley). At the same time, the language of individualism and rights has served important purposes for women. Our "birth" as legal persons marked an important step forward and opened many new opportunities; it can only be a difficult balancing act. These sophisticated and thoughtful essays encourage us to think about the contexts within which individuals make choices, contexts structured by men's power over women and by axes of domination structured by race and the unmentionable category of class.

Public policies respond to general perceptions of women and their roles in society. Several essays in *Expecting Trouble* focus on the ways in which women are both systematically and differentially oppressed. Thus, Iris Young points to the special anger directed toward (pre)mothers should they fail in their special obligations toward fetuses and to the way pregnant drug abusers (especially the poor and women of color) are treated by law enforcement and therapeutic institutions. Similarly, Lisa Bower argues that the stereotyping of substance-abusing women of color within institutional settings such as medicine, law, and drug enforcement constructs a signifying chain that connects being black, poor, drug addicted, sexually promiscuous, and natally absent—functioning to reaffirm white maternal identities.

The essays in this book attend to a variety of different situations pregnant women face: the middle-class (often white) woman who is pressured to perform her prematernal obligations to have a tailor-made child; the poor (often African-American) woman who is imprisoned for fetal abuse; and the poor (often white) woman who has babies on contract.

Despite the different ways pregnancy is treated, depending on race and class, a commonality that women face is the increasing commodification of life in late capitalism. One can see this in the treatment of the fetus as a consumer good that needs to be engineered into the best possible product; in the enforcement of contract law over biological relationship in cases such as that of Baby M.; and in the increasing concern over legal obligations to the unborn resulting in charges of fetal abuse. All of these trends represent the logic of capitalism entering into thinking about pregnant women: The fetus is an individual and is therefore in competition with other individuals, preeminently its mother. At the same time, in a contradictory logical move, the fetus is a commodity: The fetus has legal rights against the mother, who has an obligation to produce the best possible commodity.

The essays in this book raise important questions. What should women do to empower themselves and to improve the lives of women more generally? How should women respond, individually and collectively, to the new technologies and the policing of women's bodies in the context of the expansion of commodification in late capitalism? And how should society treat and recognize the unique status of pregnant women? In dealing with these questions, the essays in *Expecting Trouble* contribute to feminist theorizing at its best: They are accessible, clearly written, and rooted in current political struggles.

Nancy Hartsock

Introduction

PATRICIA BOLING

THIS VOLUME GREW out of a panel on government control of reproduction at the American Political Science Association 1992 annual meeting. Like the original panel presenters, the contributors to *Expecting Trouble* convey the stark contrast between the promise of new ways to ensure healthier babies, help women and couples conceive and carry much-wanted pregnancies to term, and end the scourge of genetic defects and diseases versus the fear that new reproductive technologies will erode respect for pregnant women's rights and autonomy as doctors and the legal system redefine their responsiblities. Indeed, the essays seem to sketch the contours of a "pregnancy police state," where waiters refuse to serve pregnant women glasses of wine, children sue their mothers for harm caused before birth, surrogacy contracts are enforced even if the birth mother changes her mind, threats of prosecution force pregnant drug users, at least if they are black or poor, to attend drug rehabilitation centers, and police officers appear at hospitals to arrest women whose newborn babies have tested positive for drugs.

It is not simply its Manichaean quality that makes work in this area interesting. The conditions under which women get pregnant, gestate babies, and give birth are changing in fundamental ways as society spurs new medical techniques and procedures, commercial agreements that allow a woman to carry and give birth to a baby for others, and a sharpened sense of maternal responsibility for protecting fetuses from exposure to toxins and injuries. We are called upon to think about how new technologies, surrogacy arrangements, and addictions affect a crucial part of the human condition—the way our species reproduces itself.[1] How do they affect the sense of connection between pregnant woman and fetus? How do they affect women's experience of pregnancy as a medicalized and carefully managed process, as opposed to a cyclic, normal set

1

of physical and emotional changes available to women's control and understanding? Do they provide a cure for birth defects and women's worries about infertility, or does the availability of interventions such as in vitro fertilization, hormone treatment, and surrogacy add even more pressure to reproduce? Has the existence of new reproductive technologies altered our willingness to accept babies as genetic surprises, no matter what their sex, genetic diseases, birth defects, or other characteristics? Why are we more willing today to permit state intervention and use criminal sanctions to monitor and coerce pregnant women who smoke, drink, use drugs, or otherwise engage in behavior that might endanger their fetuses? How will this affect women's autonomy and equality? And how will our inventions be incorporated into and structured by social arrangements—gender roles and identities, differences in power between women and men, rich and poor, white and nonwhite—that already exist?

As Deirdre Condit argues, until the last few decades, pregnancy and birth have been woman-centered experiences. Most of what we knew about the changes in woman's body and the developing fetus was based on what women reported; midwives provided most of the care to women before and during birth. Modern science and technology have transformed human reproduction, for good and for ill. Contraception is far more reliable and abortion is safe and in many countries legal and accessible. The decision to give birth is more optional than ever before—women are no longer chained to the inescapable biological imperative of impregnation and birth. They are able to choose when and whether to have babies, and thus they have options and roles in the world other than being mothers and can pursue tasks and jobs that can be combined with motherhood.[2]

Recent medical breakthroughs such as ultrasound imaging and camera-mounted fetoscopes enable us to see the fetus developing in utero; test for genetic defects (and to a limited extent intervene medically to correct such defects); fertilize ova and clone embryos in laboratories; and perform surgical procedures on the fetus in utero. They have also greatly improved our knowledge of embryology and the deleterious effects of inadequate diet and of exposing embryos and fetuses to various teratogens and drugs. However, we are only beginning to consider the impacts of these innovations to our understanding of pregnancy as a unique relationship between a woman and the developing human life within her. As Condit demonstrates, older notions of connectedness and identity between the pregnant woman and the fetus are giving way to thinking of woman and fetus as separate beings with potentially antagonistic interests. Doctors and other experts are promoting state-of-the-art technology as the appropriate standard of care for their patients, both fetal and maternal. According to Patricia Richard, many concerned parents accept such prenatal interventions because they feel that they have to follow experts' advice and because they want to give their children the best possible start in life. As prosecution of pregnant drug abusers and coercion of pregnant women to undergo medical treatment become more acceptable, new roles for the state in defining and enforcing obligations to protect developing fetuses emerge. Gestation and birth are beginning to be thought of as services akin to babysitting that women can sell.

These new technologies are not written on a blank slate. Innovations in genetic testing, sonography, fetal care, in vitro fertilization, and improved knowledge about the effect of teratogens on fetal development are introduced into a society where, as Uma Narayan points out, motherhood is considered a major source of value and obligation for women. Thus women's ability to resist new pressures on the care they should seek and how they should behave during pregnancy is limited, both by the tendency to see women as "fetal containers" and by women's particular class and race positions.

"[How] we wish to use our new scientific and technical knowledge," Hannah Arendt wrote, is not a narrow technical question but "a political question of the first order and therefore can hardly be left to the decision of professional scientists or professional politicians."[3] The essays in this book are interesting and important because they struggle to make sense of emerging reproductive techniques and practices and because they contribute not just to our knowledge, but to our thinking about crucial theoretical, policy, and political issues. For example, both Patricia Richard and Lisa Bower argue that "choice"—a core organizing idea in debates over abortion—is an inadequate framework either for thinking about the issues raised by new reproductive technologies or fetal abuse or for protecting women from pressures to ensure healthy babies. Richard sees the problem as one of choices that are shaped and constrained, causing pregnant women to end up wanting what society wants them to want without offering a vantage point for thinking critically about such constraints. Bower, however, argues that focusing on choice makes it difficult to address how class and race constrain women's choices and contributes to figuring responsible autonomous "choosers" as white and pregnant drug abusers as black. Both Bower and Young point to the inappropriateness of "choice" for describing problems of addiction; one does not simply choose to stop using cocaine, for example.

Much like Bower, Condit analyzes the power of cultural images to shape the debate over fetal abuse. She focuses on images that personify the fetus and how they contribute to seeing fetus and mother as having separate and antagonistic interests and rights.

Iris Young's essay reviewing three approaches to dealing with pregnant drug abusers—punishment, treatment, and empowerment—associates each with different philosophical arguments. Young links arguments for retribution to Benthamesque theories of punishment and also to deeply rooted fear and antagonism to the mother of early infancy, drawing on Dorothy Dinnerstein's psychoanalytic theory. She connects the rehabilitation approach to Carol Gilligan's ethic of care, which she sees as a distinct improvement over the punitive, victim-blaming approach but also criticizes its tendency to normalize notions of good mothering. Young proposes to empower pregnant addicts by having them par-

ticipate in community-based programs that are more democratic and egalitarian than conventional drug rehabilitation programs, rooting her approach (as
she has done elsewhere) in Foucault-influenced democratic theory.

Mary Shanley also makes important theoretical contributions. Her essay
moves from a critical view of permitting paid, enforceable contracts for
surrogacy to an insightful critique of liberalism's excessive individualism and inability to capture relationships that are not equal, chosen, or revocable, especially those that provide caretaking and nurture.

In sum, several authors whose essays appear in *Expecting Trouble* use reproductive issues as an occasion to reflect on issues with broad theoretical significance. Every contributor uses theoretical arguments and insights—whether
drawn from work on elites and agenda-setting (Schroedel and Peretz), thoughts
on the moral commitments of mothering and families (Johnson), or work on the
ethics of surrogacy arrangements (Narayan)—to illuminate timely discussions
of new reproductive issues.

The essays in this volume address three broad topics: the coercive character of
the promising new technologies of fetal medicine and assisted reproduction, the
debate over fetal abuse and how best to deal with pregnant substance abusers,
and the issues raised by surrogacy practices. Many of the essays deal with more
than one of these issues, so I have grouped them by the major issue on which
they focus. Chapters 2 and 3 take up issues related to new reproductive technologies; chapters 3 through 8 deal with fetal abuse, and chapters 9 and 10 discuss
surrogacy.

Patricia Richard's chapter, "The Tailor-Made Child," gives a detailed overview
of the kinds of reproductive technologies now or soon to be available. She
discusses the implications of technologies that make it possible to detect and
"weed out" defective or unwanted fetuses and suggests that we are moving toward increasing commodification of reproduction (having fewer and more "perfect" children) and greater social control over women, since the pursuit of
"high-quality" offspring often requires monitoring the woman or even surgical
intervention into her body. Richard points out that new reproductive technologies are attractive to many because they appeal to our national penchant for
technological quick fixes and allow us to focus on individual responsibility for
ensuring healthy babies rather than our social responsibility for providing de-
cent universal health care. Richard argues that the coercive character of new reproductive technologies may have more to do with women's own anxious desire
to ensure they have healthy children than with external state control or pressure.
She ends by questioning choice as a framework for guaranteeing women's reproductive freedoms because it ignores the pressures on women's choices, the serious differences in power among social groups, and the class character of access
to different reproductive technologies.

Deirdre Condit's chapter, "Fetal Personhood: Political Identity Under Construction," addresses both the impact of new reproductive technologies and fe-

tal abuse. Condit first examines the recent shift from the age-old understanding of the fetus as shy recluse—unseen and mysterious inside the pregnant woman's body—to the widely viewed "baby persons" of the pro-life movement, sonograms, fetoscopy, and popular culture. She shows how most viewers of such images—which are almost always divorced from the pregnant woman's body—accept the fetus as a separate, independent entity. This predisposes people to accept the idea of fetal rights and protections, since viewing fetuses and pregnant women as autonomous beings leads us to think of their interests as antagonistic. Condit then reviews developments in tort and criminal law, the movement to legislate fetal identity after *Webster v. Reproductive Health Services,* and the increasing use of guardians ad litem to represent the fetus's interests in legal proceedings where those interests are presumed to conflict with the mother's. The last part of her chapter, dealing with the divergence between fetal interests and pregnant women's rights, offers an overview of cases dealing with forced medical care and prosecutions of pregnant substance abusers. She closes by arguing that we need to re-embed the fetus in the woman's body and find a better balance between our protective impulses toward fetuses and the rights of pregnant women.

Chapter 4, "Fetal Endangerment Versus Fetal Welfare: Discretion of Prosecutors in Determining Criminal Liability" by Ruth Ann Strickland and Marcia Lynn Whicker, is rich in descriptive detail. The chapter begins with a dozen stories of women prosecuted for fetal abuse in various states for various reasons. Then the authors provide an evenhanded overview of the arguments for and against prosecuting pregnant drug abusers. They conclude by presenting the results of their survey of state attorney general offices and a brief discussion of the problem of prosecutorial discretion in a system where local prosecutors often receive little or no supervision from the state level.

Jean Schroedel and Paul Peretz's "A Gender Analysis of Policy Formation: The Case of Fetal Abuse" (Chapter 5) is an analysis of how fetal abuse has come to be defined in terms of *maternal* actions and remissness, leading us to overlook the equally important way men's actions can harm fetuses. Because the media, scientific community, and prosecutors, responding to deeply embedded patriarchal values in our society, reinforce the story that fetal abuse is caused by women, we have paid almost no attention to the damage caused by defective sperm (resulting from male exposure to smoking, alcohol, drugs, and environmental teratogens) and male battering of pregnant women.

Iris Young's "Punishment, Treatment, Empowerment: Three Approaches to Policy for Pregnant Addicts" (Chapter 6) uses theoretical analysis of three approaches to pregnant drug addicts in order to generate specific suggestions for social workers and care providers who work with these women. Young is critical of the punishment approach on a number of grounds. She thinks the passion behind the desire to punish pregnant drug users stems from anger directed at mothers who refuse to be self-sacrificing and do anything necessary to nurture and preserve their babies; it is not just *anyone* who's harming the baby, but its mother, which at a subconscious level strikes most of us as monstrous. Young surveys three possible justifications for a punishment approach: deterrence, using it as a stick to force women into treatment programs, and retribution. Of these, the only one she thinks plausible is retribution. However, since retribution is premised on the assumption that those being punished are members of the social compact, Young rejects it since in her view most poor and working class women who end up being prosecuted for drug use during pregnancy are not equal citizens.

Young then examines a treatment approach to drug-addicted pregnant women, which she thinks consonant with a feminist ethic of care. But she rejects this as well because of its normalizing tendencies. She proposes an approach that uses dialogue and consciousness-raising to help pregnant drug users understand the social sources of their powerlessness, which helps them feel both personally and collectively empowered.

In Chapter 7, "The ACLU Philosophy and the Right to Abuse the Unborn," Phillip Johnson is sharply critical of several authors' approaches to thinking about state interference with pregnant women's lifestyles and behaviors, especially prosecution of those who use illegal drugs while pregnant. He and Iris Young agree that punishing pregnant addicts does nothing to prevent the birth of babies harmed by the chronic drug use of their mothers; beyond that their views diverge. Johnson criticizes the position that any attempt to interfere with the liberty of pregnant women must fail as too intrusive on their rights. He frames his reflections in terms of the distinction "between what is moral and what is merely legal," suggesting that even though prosecuting pregnant drug users is untenable, the crack-mother prosecutions reveal a lot about the decline in family morality, which we as a society have long valued and taken for granted.

In a curious way, Lisa Bower's essay "The Trope of the Dark Continent in the Fetal Harm Debates: 'Africanism' and the Right to Choice" (Chapter 8) echoes Johnson's views. Bower argues that defending reproductive choice in the debate over prosecuting pregnant drug abusers reflects a desire to reaffirm a besieged white middle-class notion of morality and maternal responsibility. Bower thinks this problematic for two reasons. Rhetorically, we associate poverty, addiction, bad mothering, rampant sexuality, fecundity, and dependency with being black in order to associate being white with independence, freedom, good mothering, and so on. Such a strategy is powerful because racial stereotypes and generalizations continue to conjure such associations. Further, Bower believes that using choice to defend pregnant drug users from prosecution is inadequate because it gives us no way to see that race and class are crucial categories for understanding constraints on reproductive decisions.

The last two essays in the book deal with surrogacy. Mary Shanley's " 'Surrogate Mothering' and Women's Freedom: A Critique of Contracts for Human Reproduction" begins by canvasing the arguments in favor of surrogacy contracts, then explains why they are inadequate given the unique relationship between mothers and the fetuses they carry and give birth to. She argues for allowing women to voluntarily bear a child for someone else, so long as there is no pay or contractual enforceability. Shanley's essay next moves beyond surrogacy issues to challenge the narrowly libertarian version of liberalism that ignores social relationships of interdependence and dependence and supposes that we all enter and leave relationships freely, the way we make contracts. She argues that the relationships between mother and fetus and mother and baby call into question the market model of freely made, revocable agreements between self-possessing individuals.

Uma Narayan's essay, "The 'Gift' of a Child: Commercial Surrogacy, Gift Surrogacy, and Motherhood" (Chapter 10), finds that many of the objections commentators have raised with regard to commercial surrogacy also apply to situations where surrogacy is carried out altruistically, for example on behalf of family members. Narayan thinks reproduction in the various contexts of heterosexual marriage, gift surrogacy, and commercial surrogacy have a lot in common: often women are dependent emotionally and financially, look to motherhood to validate themselves as persons, and have few other options for meaningful work and roles. Turning to legal regulation of surrogacy, Narayan considers various alternatives and ends up arguing for permitting both gift and commercial surrogacy and treating all disputes over children who result from such arrangements as custody disputes. She defends this approach on the grounds that it will help empower women and protect the multiplicity of interests—those of the birth mother, the contracting parents, and the child—that are at stake in surrogacy arrangements.

Expecting Trouble focuses on the "reproductive rights" issues of the 1990s and is a crucial outgrowth of and addition to earlier work done on abortion[4] and the problems posed by contraception and sterilization abuse.[5] The essays provide a range of different theoretical sensibilities and concerns and are grounded in recent developments in the issue areas treated here. This book should prove an excellent resource, either in the classroom or for research, for those interested in learning about the policy debates being generated by reproductive technologies, fetal abuse, surrogacy, approaches courts have taken thus far in prosecutions of substance-abusing pregnant women, and the moral, philosophical, and theoretical dimensions of differing approaches to these political and policy issues.

Notes

1. For an insightful discussion of the need to understand technologies that speak to a desire to help us escape the human condition of embodied life on earth, see Hannah Arendt's discussion of Sputnik and other technological breakthroughs in the Preface to *The Human Condition* (Chicago: University of Chicago Press, 1958).

2. See Joan Huber, "A Theory of Gender Stratification," reprinted in Laurel Richardson and Verta Taylor, eds., *Feminist Frontiers III* (New York: McGraw-Hill, 1993).

3. Arendt, *Human Condition*, 3.

4. See Rosalind Petchesky, *Abortion and Woman's Choice* (New York: Longman, 1984); Kristin Luker, *Abortion and the Politics of Motherhood* (Berkeley, University of California Press, 1984); Mary O'Brien, *The Politics of Reproduction* (Boston: Routledge and Kegan Paul, 1981).

5. See for example Linda Gordon, *Woman's Body, Woman's Right: Birth Control in America* (New York: Penguin, 1976); Gena Corea, *The Hidden Malpractice* (New York: Jove, 1977); Angela Davis, *Women, Race and Class* (New York: Random House, 1981).

The Tailor-Made Child: Implications for Women and the State

PATRICIA BAYER RICHARD

FOR MOST OF HUMAN HISTORY, reproduction was little understood. As a consequence, women had babies without any notion of choice. Pregnancy happened and a baby arrived. With increased knowledge, however, people gained significant control over their fertility—over whether, when, and how they would have children. Now we near a threshold at which we confront other reproductive choices. Soon we may be able to opt for a boy or a girl that is screened for defects, treated and improved before birth: the tailor-made child. This chapter reviews developments bearing on this possibility and suggests implications for women and the state.

Reproductive Knowledge, the Fetus, and Women's Rights

In general, increased control over and intervention in reproduction stem from new scientific knowledge and related technology. Research in molecular and reproductive biology has improved our understanding of genes and prenatal development. New reproductive technologies (NRTs) such as genetic screening and in vitro fertilization (IVF) have both benefited from such research and contributed to it. These developments influence the status of the fetus and widen the possibilities for "designer children."

Fetal Rights

The ability to prenatally influence the "quality" of offspring directs attention to the fetus and its rights. On the one hand, a broadened arena for prenatal intervention may heighten the pregnant woman's obligations to the fetus. On the other hand, interest in quality suggests only a conditional acceptance of the fetus. These conflicting pulls reflect the underlying dimension of the abortion debate. That debate is entangled with virtually every aspect of reproduction, especially questions of fetal rights. Those opposed to legal abortion have attempted to frame the issue in terms of a fetus's right to life. Those in favor of legal abortion have sought to define the issue in terms of a woman's right to choose whether to have a child. The former definition tilts the scale toward the fetus as a person with rights, whereas the latter weights the issue in favor of women's autonomy.

The rhetoric of the abortion debate has helped shape perceptions of the fetus. Interest groups on both sides use abortion as a condensational symbol, encouraging intense, emotional, and personal responses.[1] The images and symbols utilized by opponents of abortion provide linguistic and visual underpinning for fetal rights. For example, pro-life groups call the fetus a person and a baby and label abortion as murder and a collective holocaust. They employ selected pictures of fetuses and use other techniques to compel our assent to these claims. Through these devices, they collapse the blastocyst, embryo, and fetus into a single entity in order to create a single vision—the "unborn baby."[2]

Such groups attempt to fuse fetus and baby not only in our understanding but also in the law. Historically, our legal system has treated the fetus as part of the woman bearing it and has afforded it no rights as an entity separate from her (the only exceptions being those necessary to protect the interests of born individuals).[3] Advances in reproductive technology bolster pro-life efforts to alter this.

Perhaps nothing has changed perceptions of the fetus more than the ability to see it in utero. Ultrasonography permits images of the fetus both in real time and in hard copy. This so-called "kangaroo pregnancy"[4] makes the fetus visible by obscuring the pregnant woman; sonograms show the fetus through the woman's body. Thus Bernard Nathanson describes the fetus as "the little aquanaut" in "intra-uterine exile" in the "uterine capsule" or "mother ship,"[5] and a well-known medical text on the fetal patient conjures fetal personality and an invisible woman: "The prying eye of the ultrasonographer [has] rendered the once opaque womb transparent, letting the light of scientific observation fall on the shy and secretive fetus."[6] The fetus has increasingly come to be viewed in medicine and law as a second patient.[7] As such, it may have interests inconsistent with those of the pregnant woman.

Of the various arguments for fetal rights, those based on scientific and technical developments appear the most secular and, probably for this reason, are the most popular. But, as Janet Gallagher suggests, they provide "contemporary scientific rhetoric for reassertion of an enduring set of deeply patriarchal beliefs" and have spurred "a resurgence of powerful, largely unacknowledged social attitudes in which pregnant women are viewed and treated as vessels."[8] When workplace policies that remove women from reproductive hazards are called "fetal protection" rather than exclusionary policies they similarly render women "mere vessels that may contain a fetus."[9] As with ultrasound pictures that give visibility to the fetus but hide the pregnant woman, fetal needs gain stature at the expense of the needs of those who bear them.

Thus far, the most dramatic claims of fetal rights have been made in the context of court-ordered cesarean deliveries. But greater knowledge about environmental threats to fetal health, along with genetic therapy and fetal surgery, create a growing arena in which to assert fetal rights.[10] If research in teratology (the study of abnormal development and congenital malformations in embryos and fetuses)[11] establishes links between certain practices or exposures and increased risk of fetal harm, women may be charged with negligence if they bear offspring with defects. Moreover, women may be asked to yield their bodies to the fetal patient. With the advent of active fetal intervention comes the first attempts to outline appropriate courses of action for the fetus with a correctable congenital defect.[12] Given precedents for violating bodily integrity when very important interests are at stake, John Robertson argues that legislation authorizing courts to order pregnant women to undertake some actions necessary to preserve the fetus's life would probably be found constitutional. In his view, limits on coercive treatment rest primarily on risk to the woman.[13]

At this point, the legal delineation of "prematernal duty" remains uncertain.[14] In some analyses, the option of abortion influences the pregnant woman's obligations to the fetus. According to Robertson, once a woman decides not to abort and, thus, "to use her body to procreate, [she] loses some bodily freedom during pregnancy in order to ensure the health of a child that she has chosen to birth."[15] Other scholars find support for prematernal duty in such decisions as *Jefferson v. Griffin Spalding County Hospital Authority*, 247 Ga. 86, 272 S.E. 457 (1981), in which the Georgia Supreme Court compelled a woman to have a cesarean birth. Eric Finamore, for example, argues that these cases establish a pregnant woman's "affirmative duty to take steps necessary to ensure the health and birth of the unborn child."[16] Although some commentators do not accept these interpretations of a pregnant woman's obligations, they suggest how the tailor-made child, the child who meets quality-control standards, could become a matter of legal obligation.

Fetal Abuse

The developing legal concept of fetal abuse provides another avenue toward prematernal legal obligations. Whether the fetus is seen as an entity capable of being abused bears critically on what duties pregnant women incur. In general, abuse statutes do not charge parents with providing the perfect environment but rather mandate that parents follow reasonable standards of care. Yet requirements for prenatal care remain in flux. Maternal rights and duties have been challenged in a variety of contexts, for instance those in which pregnant women have taken illegal drugs. (See Chapters 4 and 6.) These cases appear to be on the rise. By 1990 more than fifty fetal endangerment cases had been brought against pregnant women,[17] and there were more than sixty criminal prosecutions against women for drug use during pregnancy between 1987 and 1991.[18] Twelve states have expanded their definition of child abuse to include fetal drug exposure.

At the extreme of fetal abuse charges lie wrongful life suits. Here, affected children claim they were wrongly allowed to come to term in some adverse state, thus suggesting that the fetus has a right to be delivered in a reasonable state of health. As early as 1980, the courts had begun to look favorably on wrongful life torts, and at least three states recognize the rights of infants with birth defects to collect damages for such torts.[19]

The range of behaviors a woman must undertake or eschew to avoid charges of fetal abuse raises a specter: the classic "slippery slope." As a Note in the *Harvard Law Review* points out, in the fetal abuse context the state's interest is the enhancement of the new child's quality of life through the protection of the fetus from reckless or negligent harm.[20] The question is: How far should the state go to protect the fetus? Some writers (such as Margery Shaw, who is both a physician and a tort specialist), claim that women could be held criminally liable for prenatal harm caused by "negligent fetal abuse" and subject to tortious lawsuits by children "if they knowingly and willfully choose to transmit deleterious genes."[21] Taken to the extreme, women could be treated not only as "fetal containers" to be managed and monitored but also as negligent reproducers if they fail to correct genetic defects.[22]

Although there is the potential for a collision of interests, the image of the pregnant woman as antagonist to the fetus distorts reality. For the most part, women want to do what they can to provide their offspring with the best life chances possible. In fact, the desire of pregnant women to maximize their children's potential has encouraged the development of many reproductive technologies and constitutes a main impulse toward the tailor-made child.

New Reproductive Technologies and "Quality Control"

Research has transformed many aspects of reproduction. In Robert Blank's vivid phrase, two revolutions in reproduction have occurred, the first removing reproduction from sex and the second removing sex from reproduction.[23] The first revolution permitted control of fertility, which increased interest in technologies capable of producing the healthiest and "best" children possible, that is, the new reproductive technologies of the second revolution. Among the NRTs, sometimes termed "assisted" or "mediated" reproduction, are prenatal screening, artificial insemination, in vitro fertilization, embryo transfer, cloning, and cryopreservation techniques. Many of these techniques permit the tailoring of one's offspring. More generally, knowledge about conception, coupled with genetic analysis and engineering, permit medical researchers to investigate specific hereditary characteristics and potentially to eradicate genetically based disease and abnormality and to alter other genetic traits.

Prenatal Screening

Reproductive science and technology may soon yield very early screening of potential fetuses. For instance, the four-cell conceptus can be artificially twinned or quadrupled by taking advantage of the fact that the individual cells in the conceptus are "totipotent," that is, each cell is capable of forming a complete individual. Thus, if separated, each cell or two-cell group placed in an empty zona pellucida develops into an individual. One of the two or four conceptuses so created could then be used to check for suspected defects or genetic abnormalities by examining chromosomes and genes. The conceptus so examined does not survive, but whatever is found to exist in the twin or quadruple conceptus is an identical copy of that present in the remaining conceptus(es).[24] After this screening, the identical copies could be implanted, cryopreserved for later use, or discarded. Recently reported research at George Washington University used an artificial substitute for the zona pellucida (sodium alginate, a seaweed derivative) to clone abnormal embryos, or eggs fertilized by more than one sperm that do not survive past early development.[25] The coverage of this research raises renewed concerns about technological possibilities for human eugenics.

The superovulation induced by fertility drugs when "harvesting" ova for IVF offers similar possibilities. Generally, more fertilized eggs are produced than are implanted. The "extra" supernumerary conceptuses could be tested before or after cryopreservation. Additionally, testing of early embryos can be accomplished through IVF or flushing of embryos from the uterus with a procedure called blastomere analysis prior to implantation[26] or through preimplantation genetic diagnosis.[27] In this case, one or two cells are removed, cloned, and tested and the remaining embryo is frozen and stored. If it passes genetic inspection, the embryo is thawed and introduced through the cervix of the woman who provided the egg or of another woman.[28]

In the future, embryos may also undergo genetic correction or modification following inspection. An experimental technique, embryoscopy, allows direct optical viewing of first trimester fetuses. Fetal medicine experts see this method as a potential new tool in diagnosing abnormalities in embryos and fetuses early in pregnancy and, eventually, in treating or even performing surgery on them.[29]

Mary D'Alton and Alan DeCherney speculate that with the completion of mapping of the human genome in the next decade or so, precise diagnosis before implantation may be possible, allowing for corrective fetal treatment at very early developmental stages.[30]

Whereas these means of prenatal testing and genetic intervention are speculative and uncommon today, other forms of prenatal diagnosis, such as amniocentesis, chorionic villus sampling, and ultrasonography, as well as percutaneous umbilical blood sampling and fetal biopsy, are currently in use.[31] Widespread prenatal testing began in the early 1970s following the discovery that cells floating in the amniotic fluid surrounding a fetus could be used to detect major chromosomal abnormalities and selected biochemical defects. Now, various diagnostic techniques have been developed, including several procedures for collecting fetal cells, a variety of analytic techniques, precise methods for assessing fetal structural abnormalities, and a maternal blood test that classifies risk for major central nervous system disorders.[32]

The availability of prenatal diagnosis, along with genetic counseling, is likely to intensify parental concerns over possible defects. Many potential parents enthusiastically seek screening for the assurance that their babies will be "perfectly" healthy. Although there is a consumer-driven aspect to this growth in screening, medical providers who fear malpractice suits also feel pressure to routinely conduct such procedures.[33] Both parents and physicians want to better the odds of unflawed children.

For some prospective parents, male or, more commonly, female sex constitutes a flaw.[34] Since prenatal screening reveals fetal sex, it (along with sex-selective abortion) allows for the complete determination of sex of offspring. Sex selection has the potential to influence fertility rates, sex ratios, and birth order[35] and opens the door to tailor-made children and families.

As Andrea Bonnicksen observes, with more genetic knowledge comes a widening of those deemed "at risk," which in turn leads to more needs to diagnose and "fix."[36] For example, recent research, based upon the Human Genome Project's mapping of the X chromosome, found that a region on that chromosome sometimes carries a genetic influence for homosexuality in males.[37] Although researchers conclude that "it would be fundamentally unethical to use such information to try to assess or alter a person's current or future orientation,"[38] gay groups already have raised the specter of interventions to "correct" homosexuality, or detection, to allow for abortion.[39]

Prenatal Interventions

The number of interventions to correct or improve the fetus prenatally is increasing. Fetal surgery has been practiced since 1981, primarily to deal with obstructed urinary tracts and hydrocephalus.[40] In the future, however, craniofacial surgery may be performed to correct such defects as cleft lips or palates, conditions detectable before birth with ultrasound.[41] Prenatal therapies such as fetal plastic surgery and fetal wound healing offer advantages over postnatal op-erations because they leave no scars (on the fetus). Other techniques will likely mature as well. Recently, a French doctor transplanted fetal tissue into a fetus with genetic immune deficiency disease in a technique with applications for other inherited disorders.[42]

In addition to these heroic interventions to improve the child-to-be, in-creased knowledge about environmental factors influencing fetal development also has implications for "quality control." Because the fetus obtains all nourish-ment, even its oxygen, from the woman carrying it, the woman and her condi-tions create a fetal "lifestyle." Herein lies a rationale for seeking to affect women's behaviors and environments, especially during the period of greatest sensitivity and risk for the fetus—between seventeen and fifty-six days after conception, when the woman is least likely to be aware of her pregnancy.[43]

The Tailor-Made Child: Implications

The confluence of the trends discussed, the greater awareness of the fetus as an entity, the increased knowledge of reproductive biology, and the growth in re-productive technologies raise a number of concerns. By opening the possibility of producing the "optimal baby" or avoiding a "suboptimal" one, these trends speak to the commodification of reproduction already underway, the potential for increased social control over women, and the adequacy of using choice as the framework for safeguarding women's freedom and status.

Commodification of Reproduction

Some general societal tendencies support the commodification of reproduction. Among these are consumerism, the movement of more goods and services into the market, and belief in technological fixes.

In many parts of the world, trends are toward fewer and more perfect chil-dren. When people choose to raise only one or two children, they become more concerned that those children be healthy and normal.[44] Robert Blank reports studies indicating that many parents would consider termination of a preg-nancy for even moderate fetal defects and would use gene therapy to produce children to specification. Only 7 percent said they would not consider making genetic changes if it were possible. Blank believes that as the novelty of NRTs wears off and they become routine, the commodification of reproduction will accelerate.[45]

These trends represent commerce offered up as liberation and freedom. With assisted reproduction, potential parents buy eggs, sperm, and embryos from others. Thus reproductive products, as well as women as "gestational units," be-come fungible. Christine Overall envisions the fetus becoming a consumer good made to order and purchased on the open market, with parents becoming consumers of reproductive services designed to enhance the quality of the fetus-product.[46] Thus genetic screening and therapy become quality-control mechanisms by which to ensure customer satisfaction.[47] The idea that a direct correspondence between genes and traits exists only feeds the search for technological fixes. This sort of genetic reductionism creates inaccurate expectations that one can control an offspring's characteristics and heightens the demand for custom-made children.[48]

Increased Social Control

The demand for "perfect" babies makes women vulnerable to the technologies that promise results and to the people who control technologies and set standards. As Bonnie Steinbock observes, only through the body of the pregnant woman can a future child be "protected."[49] Similarly, gains in "quality" may require monitoring the woman or surgically intervening into her body.

The notion that babies are perfectible products encourages practices designed to ensure such outcomes. The President's Commission for the Study of Ethical Problems in Medicine and Biomedical and Behavioral Research worried that, with the commodification of reproduction, options can turn into requirements:

> The very idea that it is morally permissible to terminate pregnancy simply on the ground that a fetus of that sex is unwanted ... rests on the very dubious notion that virtually any characteristic of an expected child is an appropriate object of appraisal and selection. Taken to an extreme, this attitude treats the child as an artifact and the reproductive process as a chance to design and produce human beings according to parental standards of excellence, which over time are transformed into collective standards.[50]

Some would-be mothers, intent on maximizing their children's chances, might welcome intensive monitoring, genetic treatment, or even fetal surgery. Over time, community standards may shift toward expecting these practices and eventually require them.

We have seen this already in the medicalization of childbirth. Sonograms, amniocentesis, and fetal monitoring during labor are sought by many who view them as the correct choices to ensure the "best" baby. In fact, they have become routine and difficult to avoid, and as the possibility of selecting characteristics improves they may become socially acceptable and eventually socially expected of "sophisticated" or "caring" parents. As Paul Lauritzen inquires, "would a 'good mother' willingly risk a genetic disease for her child by refusing to test for and treat genetic abnormalities?"[51] Thus, the choices opened up by reproductive technologies can become compulsions to choose. A pregnant woman may feel compelled to accept fetal diagnosis and treatment, as others' choices make such procedures commonplace.

Besides undermining "the fragile insistence that each of us has an ontological dignity that we did not create and over which society has no control,"[52] the desire for "quality" pushes toward control of women, at least during pregnancy. For this reason Gena Corea warns that, although NRTs are presented as benevolent expansions of options, they offer a powerful means of social control.[53]

Policy institutionalization may follow. Third-party "stakeholders," such as physicians, insurance companies, and the state, particularly in their roles in managed health care, can become agents of control.[54] Already, when doctors and the state assert the fetus must be protected from damaging maternal behavior, they advance the notion that the best way to help the fetus is to curtail the rights of the pregnant woman.[55] George Schedler articulates this point of view when he argues that "women's reproductive freedom does not extend to giving birth to an infant who will invariably suffer from serious defects for which others must pay a large price."[56] The state may seek to control the quality of children by placing strictures on pregnant or potentially pregnant women.

The Adequacy of Choice as a Framework

Choice has been the watchword for those arguing in favor of women's reproductive rights without state control. However, examining the developments in prenatal interventions and assisted reproduction, and their contributions to the possibility of the custom-made child, raises new cautions about its adequacy as a framework.

Rebecca Albury argues that to define such issues as being about women's "choice" and "rights" is totally inadequate. These concepts derive from liberal philosophy, which presumes no serious difference in power among social groups. Yet in reality we live in a gendered society in which women are subordinate.[57] The focus on individual responsibility and blame rather than social or state obligations in the reproductive arena reflects this. NRTs and the prosecution of women for fetal abuse highlight individual actions. Simultaneously, they divert scrutiny from society's responsibility to provide adequate and universal prenatal care and to remove teratogens from the environment, which also diminish chances for "perfect" babies.

Similarly, the socio-economic system, rather than strictly individual choice, bears on the way the "stock" of babies is to be improved. Higher-income people have easier access to and use of reproductive technologies. In contrast, forcible interventions on behalf of fetuses, such as drug detoxification, primarily target lower-income women and minorities.[58] Both groups of women can invoke choice—higher-income women to take advantage of NRTs and lower-income women to refuse court directives about their behavior. The former group's preferences dovetail neatly with the commercial culture, whereas the latter group runs up against powerful counterpressures embedded in stereotypes about the poor. Thus, choice may work for affluent women but fail women at the lower end of the income scale. Poorer women may be subject to attempts to control their choices, much the same as new welfare policies in several states that prohibit higher payments for additional children.

Issues about choice and control are tangled in other ways as well. Sometimes women want recognition of how their behavior affects fetal development. For example, women have sought and won disability benefits even though they could physically perform work duties, when to do so would increase risks to their fetuses' health.[59] In these instances women requested state action on behalf of "fetal protection." Yet in *UAW v. Johnson Controls, Inc.*, 11 S. Ct. 1196 (1991), women workers challenged the company policy that excluded all fertile women from working in jobs with high exposure to lead. In this case "fetal protection" policies focusing on the relationship between women's behavior and fetal development were at stake.[60] Writing for the majority, Justice Blackmun found that the policy constituted illegal disparate treatment of women. He cast the decision in a way that limited both the state and company role: "Decisions about the welfare of future children must be left to parents who conceive, bear, support, and raise them. ...." *Id.* at 1207.

As we face growing possibilities for influencing the quality of future offspring, the endpoint of which is the tailor-made child, choice may no longer be an adequate basis to ensure women's reproductive rights. As discussed above, choice can be illusory. Policies structure reproductive choices, sometimes explicitly (as with Medicaid coverage of childbirth expenses but not most abortions), and sometimes subtly (as when limitless malpractice settlements impel physicians to use fetal monitors). Moreover, an individual's perception of choice is shaped by what each person learns to want. As Barbara Rothman puts it, the experience of choice is very real for those who want what society wants them to want.[61]

Thus the effects of "chosen" control, or coercive choice, loom ever larger as the medicalization of pregnancy shifts toward the beginning rather than the end of gestation. The combination of people seeking the perfect, tailor-made child and those seeking to prevent imperfect, faulty offspring is a powerful one. In order for women to withstand this juggernaut assailing their autonomy, the mantra of individual choice must be augmented by access to resources and a broadened sense of public responsibility. Policies that provide good nutrition for all and universal health care, including prenatal care, would yield healthier babies and "higher-quality stock" to the benefit of women. Such policies do not pit women's interests against those of the fetus. Similarly, policies that focus on removing or reducing teratogens in the environment assist men as well as women and afford greater reductions of genetic risks to fetuses that result from damaged sperm and eggs.

Yet the difficulty, if not the impossibility, of putting the technological genie back in the bottle—the seemingly inexorable movement of reproductive products and services to the market, exaggerated individualism, and the understandable desire of potential parents to give their offspring the best possible start—all promote the tailor-made child. The implications for the future of humanity, the hubris intrinsic in such a project, and the heeding of the tailor-made child's implications for women are matters of urgent concern.

Notes

1. Murray Edelman, *The Symbolic Uses of Politics* (Urbana: University of Illinois Press, 1964); Marjorie Randon Hershey, "Direct Action and the Abortion Issue: The Political Participation of Single-Issue Groups," in *Interest Group Politics*, 2nd ed., ed. Allan J. Cigler and Burdett A. Loomis (Washington, D.C.: Congressional Quarterly Press, 1986), 27–45.

2. Celeste Michelle Condit, *Decoding Abortion Rhetoric* (Urbana: University of Illinois Press, 1990), 79–91.

3. Dawn E. Johnsen, "The Creation of Fetal Rights: Conflicts with Women's Constitutional Rights to Liberty, Privacy, and Equal Protection," *Yale Law Journal* 95:599 (1986).

4. Alida Brill, "Womb Versus Woman," *Dissent* (Summer 1991):396.

5. Quoted in Janet Gallagher, "Fetus as Patient," in *Reproductive Laws for the 1990s*, ed. Sherrill Cohen and Nadine Taub (Clifton, N.J.: Humana Press, 1989), 198.

6. Michael R. Harrison, Mitchell S. Golbus, and Roy A. Filly, *The Unborn Patient*, 2nd ed. (Philadelphia: W.B. Saunders Co., 1991), 3.

7. See, for example, Jack A. Pritchard, Paul C. MacDonald, and Norman F. Gant, eds., *Williams Obstetrics*, 17th ed. (Norwalk, Conn.: Appleton-Century-Crofts, 1985).

8. Gallagher, "Fetus as Patient," 188.

9. Sally Jane Kenney, *For Whose Protection? Reproductive Hazards and Exclusionary Policies in the United States and Britain* (Ann Arbor: University of Michigan Press, 1992), 1.

10. See Daniel Callahan, "How Technology Is Reframing the Abortion Debate," *Hastings Center Report* 16(1):33 (1986); Don Colburn, "Fetal Surgery to Repair Birth Defects Safe, Study Says," *Washington Post* (Health section), 16 February 1991, 5; Gallagher, "Fetus as Patient"; Steven Greenhouse, "Scientist Says He Transplanted Tissue into Fetus," *New York Times* (national edition), 30 March 1989, 17; Kenney, *For Whose Protection?*; Gina Kolata, "Lifesaving Surgery on a Fetus Works for the First Time," *New York Times* (national edition), 31 May 1990, 1, 8; Gina Kolata, "Surgery on Fetuses Reveals They Heal Without Scars," *New York Times* (national edition), 6 August 1988, 1, 21.

11. Robert L. Anderson and Mitchell S. Golbus. "Social and Environmental Risks of Pregnancy," in *Fetal Diagnosis and Therapy: Science, Ethics and the Law*, ed. Mark I. Evans et al. (Philadelphia: J.B. Lippincott Co., 1989), 114.

12. W. Allen Hogge and Mitchell S. Golbus, "Fetal Therapy," in *Fetal Diagnosis and Therapy: Science, Ethics and the Law*, ed. Mark I. Evans et al. (Philadelphia: J.B. Lippincott Co., 1989), 395.

13. John A. Robertson, "Legal Issues in Fetal Therapy," in *Fetal Diagnosis and Therapy: Science, Ethics and the Law*, ed. Mark I. Evans et al. (Philadelphia: J.B. Lippincott Co., 1989), 435.

14. Lynn D. Fleischer, "What About the Children? The Dilemma of Prematernal Liability," in *Fetal Diagnosis and Therapy: Science, Ethics and the Law*, ed. Mark I. Evans et al. (Philadelphia: J.B. Lippincott Co., 1989), 520–533.

15. Robertson, "Legal Issues in Fetal Therapy," 431–432.

16. Eric P. Finamore, "*Jefferson v. Griffen Spalding County Hospital Authority*: Court-Ordered Surgery to Protect the Life of an Unborn Child," *American Journal of Law and Medicine*, 9:101 (1983).

17. Deborah J. Krauss, "Regulating Women's Bodies: The Adverse Effect of Fetal Rights on Childbirth Decisions and Women of Color," *Harvard Civil Rights-Civil Liberties Law Review* 26:526 (1991).

18. Isabel Wilkerson, "Court Backs Woman in Pregnancy Drugs Case," *New York Times* (national edition), 3 April 1991, A13.

19. Joseph Losco, "Fetal Abuse: An Exploration of Emerging Philosophic, Legal, and Policy Issues," *Western Political Quarterly* 42(2):278–279 (June 1, 1989).

20. Note. "Maternal Rights and Fetal Wrongs: The Case Against the Criminalization of 'Fetal Abuse' " *Harvard Law Review* 101(5):997 (March 1988).

21. Margery Shaw, "Conditional Prospective Rights of the Fetus," *Journal of Legal Medicine* 63:111 (March 1984).

22. The phrase is George Annas's. George Annas, "Women as Fetal Containers," *Hastings Center Report* 16(6):13–14 (December 1986).

23. Robert H. Blank, *Regulating Reproduction* (New York: Columbia University Press, 1990), 6–11.

24. Simon Fishel, "Human In-Vitro Fertilization and the Present State of Research on Pre-embryonic Material," *International Journal on the Unity of the Sciences* (Summer 1988):200–202.

25. Jerry Adler, "Clone Hype," *Newsweek*, November 8, 1993, 60–61.

26. Geoffrey Cowley, "The View from the Womb," *Newsweek*, November 8, 1993, 64.

27. Nora Frankiel, "Planning a Family, Down to Baby's Sex," *New York Times* (national edition), 11 November 1993, B4.

28. Mary Sue Henifen et al., "Prenatal Screening," in *Reproductive Laws for the 1990s*, ed. Sherrill Cohen and Nadine Taub (Clifton, N.J.: Humana Press, 1989), 161–162.

29. Gina Kolata, "Miniature Scope Gives the Earliest Pictures of a Developing Embryo," *New York Times* (national edition), 6 July 1993, B6.

30. Mary E. D'Alton and Alan H. DeCherney, "Prenatal Diagnosis," *New England Journal of Medicine* 328(2):118 (January 14, 1993).

31. Ibid.

32. Eve K. Nichols, *Human Gene Therapy* (Cambridge: Harvard University Press, 1988), 42.

33. Henifen et al., "Prenatal Screening," 175.

34. Tabitha Powledge, "Unnatural Selection: On Choosing Children's Sex," in *The Custom-Made Child: Women-Centered Perspectives*, ed. Helen B. Holmes et al. (Clifton, N.J.: The Humana Press, 1981).

35. Patricia Bayer Richard, "Sex Selection: Implications for Public Policy," paper presented at the Annual Meeting of the American Political Science Association, The Atlanta Hilton and Towers, August 31-September 3, 1989; Betty B. Hoskins and Helen Bequaert Holmes, "Technology and Prenatal Femicide," in *Test-Tube Women: What Future for Motherhood?*, ed. Rita Arditti et al. (London: Pandora Press, 1984); Nancy E. Williamson, "Parental Sex Preferences and Sex Selection," in *Sex Selection of Children*, ed. Neil G. Bennett (New York: Academic Press, 1983); Nancy E. Williamson, *Sons or Daughters: A Cross-Cultural Survey of Parental Preferences* (Newbury Park, Calif.: Sage Publications, 1976).

36. Andrea Bonnicksen, "Genetic Diagnosis of Human Embryos," *Hastings Center Report* 22(4):S7 (July-August, 1992).

37. David L. Wheeler, "Study Suggests X Chromosome Is Linked to Homosexuality," *The Chronicle of Higher Education* (July 21, 1993), A6.

38. Ibid.

39. Natalie Angier, "Research on Sex Orientation Doesn't Neatly Fit the Mold," *New York Times* (national edition), 18 July 1993, 13.

40. Nichols, *Human Gene Therapy*, 58; Michael T. Longaker et al., "Maternal Outcome After Open Fetal Surgery," *Journal of the American Medical Association* (February 13, 1991).

41. Kolata, "Surgery on Fetuses Reveals They Heal Without Scars," 1, 21.

42. Greenhouse, "Scientist Says He Transplanted Tissue into Fetus," 17.

43. Merry-K. Moos, "Preconceptional Health Promotion: A Health Education Opportunity for All Women," *Women and Health* 15(3):56 (1989).

44. Michael D. Bayles, *Reproductive Ethics* (Englewood Cliffs, N.J.: Prentice-Hall, 1984), 1.

45. Blank, *Regulating Reproduction*, 89–90.

46. Christine Overall, *Ethics and Human Reproduction: A Feminist Analysis* (Boston: Allyn and Unwin, 1987), 49.

47. Paul Lauritzen, *Pursuing Parenthood: Ethical Issues in Assisted Reproduction* (Bloomington: Indiana University Press, 1993), 15.

48. See Ruth Hubbard and Elijah Wald, *Exploding the Gene Myth* (Boston: Beacon Press, 1993).

49. Bonnie Steinbock, "The Relevance of Illegality," *Hastings Center Report* 22(1):19 (January-February 1992).

50. President's Commission for the Study of Ethical Problems in Medical and Biomedical and Behavioral Research, *Screening and Counseling for Genetic Conditions: The Ethical and Legal Implications for Genetic Screening, Counseling, and Education Programs* (Washington, D.C.: USGPO, 1983):57–58.

51. Lauritzen, *Pursuing Parenthood*, 16.

52. Jean Bethke Elshtain, "Technology as Destiny," *Progressive* 53(6) (June 1989), 2.

53. Gena Corea, *Man-Made Woman: How New Reproductive Technologies Affect Women* (Bloomington: University of Indiana Press, 1987), 4.

54. Ann Majchrzak, *Methods for Policy Research* (Beverly Hills, Calif.: Sage, 1984).

55. Krauss, "Regulating Women's Bodies," 542.

56. George Schedler, "Does Society Have the Right to Force Pregnant Drug Addicts to Abort Their Fetuses?" *Social Theory and Practice* 17(3):381 (Fall 1991).

57. Rebecca Albury, "Who Owns the Embryo?" In *Test-Tube Women: What Future for Motherhood?*, ed. Rita Arditti et al. (London: Pandora Press, 1984), 55–56.

58. Veronika Kolder et al., "Court-ordered Obstetrical Interventions," *New England Journal of Medicine* 316(19) (1987); and Krauss, "Regulating Women's Bodies."

59. *The Equal Rights Advocate* (San Francisco: Equal Rights Advocates), XII:8 (March 1992).

60. See Kenney, *For Whose Protection?*, 250–277.

61. Barbara Katz Rothman, *The Tentative Pregnancy: Prenatal Diagnosis and the Future of Motherhood* (New York: Viking, 1986), 32.

References

Adler, Jerry. "Clone Hype." *Newsweek*, November 8, 1993, 60–62.

Albury, Rebecca. "Who Owns the Embryo?" In *Test-Tube Women: What Future for Motherhood?*, 54–76. Edited by Rita Arditti et al. London: Pandora Press, 1984.

Anderson, Robert L., and Mitchell S. Golbus. "Social and Environmental Risks of Pregnancy." In *Fetal Diagnosis and Therapy: Science, Ethics and the Law*, 114–139. Edited by Mark I. Evans et al. Philadelphia: J.B. Lippincott Co., 1989.

Angier, Natalie. "Research on Sex Orientation Doesn't Neatly Fit the Mold." *New York Times* (national edition), 18 July 1993, 13.

Annas, George. "Women as Fetal Containers." *Hastings Center Report* 16(6):13–14 (December 1986).

Bayles, Michael D. *Reproductive Ethics*. Englewood Cliffs, N.J.: Prentice-Hall, 1984.

Blank, Robert H. *Regulating Reproduction*. New York: Columbia University Press, 1990.

Bonnicksen, Andrea. "Genetic Diagnosis of Human Embryos." *Hastings Center Report* 22(4):S5–S11 (July-August 1992).

Brill, Alida. "Womb Versus Woman." *Dissent* (Summer 1991):395–399.

Callahan, Daniel. "How Technology Is Reframing the Abortion Debate." *Hastings Center Report* 16(1):33–42 (1986).

Colburn, Don. "Fetal Surgery to Repair Birth Defects Safe, Study Says." *Washington Post* (Health section), 16 February 1991, 5.

Condit, Celeste Michelle. *Decoding Abortion Rhetoric*. Urbana: University of Illinois Press, 1990.

Corea, Gena. *Man-Made Woman: How New Reproductive Technologies Affect Women*. Bloomington: University of Indiana Press, 1987.

Cowley, Geoffrey. "The View from the Womb," *Newsweek*, November 8, 1993, 64.

D'Alton, Mary E., and Alan H. DeCherney. "Prenatal Diagnosis." *New England Journal of Medicine* 328(2):114–120 (January 14, 1993).

Edelman, Murray. *The Symbolic Uses of Politics*. Urbana: University of Illinois Press, 1964.

Elshtain, Jean Bethke. "Technology as Destiny." *Progressive* 53(6):19–23 (June 1989).

The Equal Rights Advocate. San Francisco: Equal Rights Advocates. XII (March 1992), 8.

Finamore, Eric P. "*Jefferson v. Griffen Spalding County Hospital Authority*: Court-Ordered Surgery to Protect the Life of an Unborn Child." *American Journal of Law and Medicine* 9(1):83–101 (1983).

Fishel, Simon. "Human In-Vitro Fertilization and the Present State of Research on Pre-embryonic Material." *International Journal on the Unity of the Sciences* (Summer 1988) 173–214.

Fleischer, Lynn D. "What About the Children? The Dilemma of Prematernal Liability." In *Fetal Diagnosis and Therapy: Science, Ethics and the Law*, 520–533. Edited by Mark I. Evans et al. Philadelphia: J.B. Lippincott Co., 1989.

Frankiel, Nora. "Planning a Family, Down to Baby's Sex." *New York Times* (national edition), 11 November 1993, B1, B4.

Gallagher, Janet. "Fetus as Patient." In *Reproductive Laws for the 1990s*, 185–235. Edited by Sherrill Cohen and Nadine Taub. Clifton, N.J.: Humana Press, 1989.

Greenhouse, Steven. "Scientist Says He Transplanted Tissue into Fetus." *New York Times* (national edition), 30 March 1989, p. 17.

Hanmer, Jalna. "Reproductive Technology: The Future for Women?" In *Machina ex Dea: Feminist Perspectives on Technology*, 183–197. Edited by Joan Rothschild. New York: Pergamon Press, 1983.

Harrison, Michael R. et. al. *The Unborn Patient* (2nd edition). Philadelphia: W.B. Saunders Co., 1991.

Henifen, Mary Sue et. al. "Prenatal Screening." In *Reproductive Laws for the 1990s*, 155–183. Edited by Sherrill Cohen and Nadine Taub. Clifton, N.J.: Humana Press, 1989.

Hershey, Marjorie Randon. "Direct Action and the Abortion Issue: The Political Participation of Single-Issue Groups." In *Interest Group Politics* (2nd edition), 27–45. Edited by Allan J. Cigler and Burdett A. Loomis. Washington, D.C.: Congressional Quarterly Press, 1986.

Hogge, W. Allen, and Mitchell S. Golbus. "Fetal Therapy." In *Fetal Diagnosis and Therapy: Science, Ethics and the Law*, 395–403. Edited by Mark I. Evans et al. Philadelphia: J.B. Lippincott Co., 1989.

Hoskins, Betty B., and Helen Bequaert Holmes. "Technology and Prenatal Femicide." In *Test-Tube Women: What Future for Motherhood?*, 237–255. Edited by Rita Arditti et al. London: Pandora Press, 1984.

Hubbard, Ruth, and Elijah Wald. *Exploding the Gene Myth*. Boston: Beacon Press, 1993.

Johnsen, Dawn E. "The Creation of Fetal Rights: Conflicts with Women's Constitutional Rights to Liberty, Privacy, and Equal Protection." *Yale Law Journal* 95:599–625 (1986).

Kenney, Sally Jane. *For Whose Protection? Reproductive Hazards and Exclusionary Policies in the United States and Britain*. Ann Arbor: University of Michigan Press, 1992.

Kolata, Gina. "Lifesaving Surgery on a Fetus Works for the First Time." *New York Times* (national edition), 31 May 1990, 1, 8.

_____. "Miniature Scope Gives the Earliest Pictures of a Developing Embryo." *New York Times* (national edition), 6 July 1993, B6.

_____. "Surgery on Fetuses Reveals They Heal Without Scars." *New York Times* (national edition), 6 August 1988, 1, 21.

Kolder, Veronika, Janet Gallagher, and Michael T. Parsons. "Court-ordered Obstetrical Interventions." *New England Journal of Medicine* 316(19):1192–1196 (1987).

Krauss, Deborah J. "Regulating Women's Bodies: The Adverse Effect of Fetal Rights on Childbirth Decisions and Women of Color." *Harvard Civil Rights-Civil Liberties Law Review* 26:523–548 (1991).

Lauritzen, Paul. *Pursuing Parenthood: Ethical Issues in Assisted Reproduction.* Bloomington: Indiana University Press, 1993.

Longaker, Michael T. et. al. "Maternal Outcome After Open Fetal Surgery." *Journal of the American Medical Association* 265(6):737–741 (February 13, 1991).

Losco, Joseph. "Fetal Abuse: An Exploration of Emerging Philosophic, Legal, and Policy Issues." *Western Political Quarterly* 42(2):265–286 (June 1, 1989).

Majchrzak, Ann. *Methods for Policy Research.* Beverly Hills, Calif.: Sage, 1984.

Moos, Merry-K. "Preconceptional Health Promotion: A Health Education Opportunity for All Women." *Women and Health* 15(3):55–68, 1989.

Nichols, Eve K. *Human Gene Therapy.* Cambridge: Harvard University Press, 1988.

Note. "Maternal Rights and Fetal Wrongs: The Case Against the Criminalization of 'Fetal Abuse,'" *Harvard Law Review* 101(5):994–1012 (March 1988).

Overall, Christine. *Ethics and Human Reproduction: A Feminist Analysis.* Boston: Allyn and Unwin, 1987.

Powledge, Tabitha. "Unnatural Selection: On Choosing Children's Sex." In *The Custom-Made Child: Women-Centered Perspectives,* 193–199. Edited by Helen B. Holmes et al. Clifton, N.J.: The Humana Press, 1981.

President's Commission for the Study of Ethical Problems in Medical and Biomedical and Behavioral Research. *Screening and Counseling for Genetic Conditions: The Ethical and Legal Implications for Genetic Screening, Counseling, and Education Programs.* Washington, D.C.: USGPO, 1983.

Pritchard, Jack A., Paul C. MacDonald and Norman F. Gant, eds. *Williams Obstetrics.* Norwalk, Conn.: Appleton-Century-Crofts, 1985.

Richard, Patricia Bayer. "Sex Selection: Implications for Public Policy." Paper presented at the Annual Meeting of the American Political Science Association, The Atlanta Hilton and Towers, August 31–September 3, 1989.

Robertson, John A. "Legal Issues in Fetal Therapy." In *Fetal Diagnosis and Therapy: Science, Ethics and the Law,* 431–437. Edited by Mark I. Evans et al. Philadelphia: J.B. Lippincott Co., 1989.

Rothman, Barbara Katz. *The Tentative Pregnancy: Prenatal Diagnosis and the Future of Motherhood.* New York: Viking, 1986.

Schedler, George. "Does Society Have the Right to Force Pregnant Drug Addicts to Abort Their Fetuses?" *Social Theory and Practice* 17(3):369–384 (Fall 1991).

Shaw, Margery. "Conditional Prospective Rights of the Fetus." *Journal of Legal Medicine* 63:63–116 (1984).

Steinbock, Bonnie. "The Relevance of Illegality." *Hastings Center Report* 22(1):19–22 (January–February 1992).

Wheeler, David. L. "Study Suggests X Chromosome Is Linked to Homosexuality." *The Chronicle of Higher Education,* July 21, 1993, A6–A7.

Wilkerson, Isabel. "Court Backs Woman in Pregnancy Drugs Case." *New York Times* (national edition), 3 April 1991, A13.

Williamson, Nancy E. "Parental Sex Preferences and Sex Selection." In *Sex Selection of Children,* 129–145. Edited by Neil G. Bennett. New York: Academic Press, 1983.

———. *Sons or Daughters: A Cross-Cultural Survey of Parental Preferences.* Newbury Park, Calif.: Sage Publications, 1976.

Fetal Personhood: Political Identity Under Construction

DEIRDRE MOIRA CONDIT

VISUALIZE THE FETUS!

—Right to Life bumper sticker

Introducing the Fetal Form

We stand poised at an extraordinary moment in time: As we watch, fetuses are becoming persons within our social, political, and legal culture. For the first time in human history, as if by magic, images of fetal bodies are appearing before our eyes. Fetal images seem to be everywhere: at the doctor's office, on television, at the movies, at the toy store, on political placards displayed on the sidewalks of our streets, and on the billboards that line our highways. Conjured from within the bellies of pregnant women by the sorceries of science, technology, and art, these once hidden and little known fetal bodies are becoming ever more familiar.

In this chapter, I argue that we are increasingly experiencing the fetus as a member of the human community. The fetus now seems more "human," more like a "baby," and more of a "person" than ever before. But visual familiarity alone is not sufficient for us to construct fetuses as persons. The humanity of fetal images is not always self-evident but has to be explained and pointed out by those who ascribe meaning, value, and context to the fetus and help us conceptualize it as a person. This process of anthropomorphizing the fetus is driven by a variety of groups—physicians, pro-life activists, even advertisers and filmmakers—that both fuel and capitalize upon the explosion of fetal imagery in the American visual landscape.

When the fetus is perceived as a tiny human person, the response in a culture founded on an ideology of liberal rights is to afford that new member of the human community its privileges and protections. "Seeing" the fetus in this way, both physically and conceptually, requires that it be perceived separately from the pregnant woman of whom it is a part. This disaggregation of the pregnant body into two separate persons is expressed in and carried out by the development of criminal and civil law aimed at protecting fetal rights and health.

Traditionally, a fetus had no legal standing because it was a part of the pregnant woman. But the cultural creation of fetal personhood and the move toward recognition of fetal rights are driving a legal wedge between the pregnant woman and her fetus. Cases are beginning to emerge in which the rights of the fetus are presented by third-party interests as differing from, competing with, and often threatened by the rights and interests of the pregnant woman. I argue that resolution of such conflicts hinges on the court's perception of the fetus: If the court acknowledges the fetus as a person, fetal interests are usually found to be compelling enough to check the rights of the pregnant woman. If the construction of fetal identity remains uncontested, courts will become even more susceptible to arguments that divide the fetus from the pregnant woman. And as fetuses gain protections and privileges, the bodies and rights of pregnant women will be ever more in jeopardy from the "miracle of life."

The History of Fetal Imagery:
From Nowhere to Everywhere

Widespread visual exposure to the fetal body is a late twentieth-century phenomenon. In earlier times, fetuses were physically and thus conceptually invisible during pregnancy.[1] What we knew about the conceptus was learned either after birth or as a consequence of miscarriage; in either case, it was necessary for the fetus to have separated from the pregnant woman's body to be examined. Thus scientific knowledge about and popular understandings of fetuses were shaped by contact with the fetus outside the woman's body. Upon late-term labor and delivery, the conceptus was a baby; in the event of miscarriage or stillbirth, the form and size of the conceptus varied with the gestational stage of its development. These pre-term fetuses were accorded little value: They were typically disposed of discreetly and were rarely discussed outside medical circles. Until recently, immature or incompletely formed fetal bodies occupied little conceptual space in our epistemology of pregnancy.

Prior to the medicalization of pregnancy, primary data about gestation came from the personal accounts of pregnant women and from the externally observable changes in their bodies, and so pregnancy was predominantly a woman-centered event.[2] As a consequence, our understanding of pregnancy focused on the woman involved and the anticipation of the baby to be produced at birth.[3]

The role of the fetus was relatively unimportant in this earlier conception of pregnancy. The fetus was an unknowable entity, something under construction but without unique value or salience until birth.

Now, of course, physical separation from the pregnant woman is no longer a precondition for "knowing" the fetus. Medical technology gives access to the fetus in utero for a variety of purposes, including visual imaging and fetal treatment. Graphic images of aborted fetal remains are now displayed on placards and in television advertisements by antiabortion political groups. Images of fetuses are even part of the commercial world, used to sell cars, theater tickets, and children's toys.

Fetal Familiarity

Recent technological developments in twentieth-century medicine are dramatically improving our ability to view and learn about the fetus while it is developing inside the woman's body. Ultrasound technology bounces sound waves off the dense areas of the fetal body to outline it in utero.[4] Although the images produced are fairly vague and indistinct to the untrained eye, gross body parts and movements can be discerned, in some cases as early as the eighth week of pregnancy.[5]

The fetoscope permits direct access to the fetus through a miniature camera-equipped device that is surgically inserted through the pregnant woman's abdomen and uterus and into the amniotic sac. Fetoscopy provides clear, color, moving pictures of the fetus and allows the physician to take blood and tissue samples for diagnosis of various diseases.[6]

In addition to visual access, information about the fetus can now be obtained through a number of other technologies. Amniocentesis, chorionic villus sampling (CVS), and sampling of the fetus's blood and skin permit early testing for genetic problems.[7] Internal and external fetal monitoring technology now reveals subtle sounds, motions, and heart rhythms from very early in the pregnancy on through delivery.[8] These technologies have become routine in much prenatal and labor room care, even for normal pregnancies. As a result, doctors can diagnose and treat, and expectant parents can see and hear, the fetus earlier and more fully than ever before.

In addition, "fetal therapies"—surgical and other medical procedures—can now be performed while the fetus is still inside the womb. Christine Overall notes that "[t]here are treatments for fluid build-up in the brain, chest, or abdomen; blocked bladders; fetal hernia; and fetal growth retardation."[9] Recent advances even permit the safe extraction and reimplantation of the fetus in order to perform some surgical procedures.[10] Researchers predict that prenatal fetal surgery is only in its infancy; procedures that reach into the pregnant woman's uterus to extract tissue for genetic analysis and alteration are likely to make intervention and exposure of the fetus during pregnancy more common in the future.[11]

The ability to treat the fetus in these ways elevates it to the full status of patient in the medical community.[12] As the preface to a recent edition of an obstetrical textbook noted: "Quality of life for the mother and her infant is our most
important concern. Happily we live and work in an era in which the fetus is established as our second patient with many rights and privileges comparable to
those previously achieved after birth."[13] Note here that the fetus is a *second* patient and not necessarily a lesser one. For the physician, this conceptual split between pregnant woman and fetus has given rise to a new kind of obstetrical
medicine in which the fetus is a coequal patient with the pregnant woman and,
in some cases, the *primary* patient. New medical subspecialties have developed
in "maternal-fetal" medicine,[14] and "fetal health" is the focus of care at medical
centers like the University of California's San Francisco Fetal Treatment Center.[15]

Doctors are not the only ones using and affected by the technologies that allow access to fetal imagery and the fetal body. Just as sonograms used in prenatal
care make the fetus familiar to physicians and expectant parents, so too casual
public exposure to sonographic and other fetal images is making us all more familiar with what fetal life looks like inside the pregnant belly. Carol Stabile's fas-
cinating look at the history of fetal photography notes that the first widespread
public exposure to pictures of fetal bodies occurred in a 1965 edition of *Life* magazine.[16] In that article, *Life* published a series of photographs of fetuses at various stages of development. The cover photo depicted an 18-week-old fetus en-
cased in its amniotic sac. The fingers and toes of this mid-term fetus are clearly
distinguishable. Back lighting enhances the outline and shape of its body, accen-
tuating how much it looks like a newborn. While the umbilical cord is plainly
evident, it is lit with a softening light that makes it seem more a part of the amniotic sac than the fetus. The picture creates the illusion that the fetus is free-
floating and totally self-contained; there is no evidence of the pregnant body
from which it was extracted.[17] With the exception of one photo taken in utero
using an early version of the fetoscope, all of the pictures were of fetuses that
had been "surgically removed" from the pregnant women who had conceived
them; that fact is obscured by the photos and accompanying text.[18]

Fetuses have appeared on television as well. A 1983 film for the PBS-sponsored
Nova series, entitled "The Miracle of Life," used a camera-equipped fetoscope to
travel into the uterus of a pregnant woman and examine her fetus. This kind of
live action photography gives the viewer a strong sense of the fetus as an autonomous, living entity, though Stabile argues that these images have been constructed through tricks of the camera, accompanying texts, and voice-overs to
make them more familiar and more like "babies."[19]

A 1993 segment of the *Nature of Sex* series on PBS, entitled "A Miracle in the
Making," illustrates her point. This segment featured both sonographic and
fetoscopic fetal imagery. In order to make cognitive sense of these images, the
features most like a human baby were pointed to and explained by an attending
physician in the film. The doctor's explanation is directed at both the pregnant

woman and the audience, represented by the camera. As the narrator's voice-over notes, with the sonogram, "the movement the mother has been feeling can now be given an identity." It "allows parents to begin taking care of their baby before it is born."[20]

Books about pregnancy and childbirth routinely include pictures and drawings of fetuses as well. For example, Lennart Nilsson's pregnancy and childbirth book, *A Child Is Born,* contains numerous fetal pictures and sonographs, including an enhanced picture of a fetus sucking its thumb on the cover. Although much of the language describing the pictures refers to the subject as a fetus, there are many instances when the author employs anthropomorphized language, referring to the first sonogram of a fetus as its "first portrait" and providing the parents their "first sight of the baby."[21] And though this fetal anthropomorphization may not always be ideologically driven, the politics of the antiabortion movement and the development of neonatal medicine have come to depend on the successful equation of fetal images with babies.

The Meaning of Fetal Imagery: The Birth of a Political "Baby"

Many people opposed to legal abortion were stunned at the Supreme Court's 1973 ruling in *Roe v. Wade,* 410 U.S. 113 (1973), which prohibited states from restricting access to abortion during the first three months of pregnancy and allowed increasingly restricted abortions through the final six months.[22] Although the right-to-life movement originated in the Catholic Church during the early 1960s in reaction to efforts to liberalize abortion laws in some states, the *Roe* decision shocked pro-life groups into action. Opponents of abortion have become a serious and well-organized force in U.S. politics. The success of their anti-abortion political strategies is due in large part to their effective use of the fetal images made possible by the new medical technologies.

Americans who had no idea what an early or mid-term fetus looked like before the 1980s are now familiar with fetoscopic photographs and sonographic images of fetuses in utero. As consumers of these images, we incorporate them into our knowledge about pregnancy in such a way that those images now stand for "fetus" in our cultural mind's eye. And yet sonographic images carry no inherent meanings; the pictures created by ultrasound waves are fuzzy and blurred to the untrained eye and the products of conception for early-term abortions are usually an indistinguishable mass of bloody clots and tissue. Had we been bombarded by such indistinct images, we would have had no context in which to place them: They would have been meaningless to us.

A key political objective of the pro-life movement has been to give meaning and context to those vague images for us. Indeed, the vagueness of sonographic imagery has been turned into an advantage for antiabortion rhetoricians. As Cynthia Daniels argues, sonographic imagery is "distinct enough to suggest the similarities between the fetus and the baby (through the shadowy images of head, limbs, even fingers and toes), while it [is] vague enough to mask the dramatic differences between the fetus and the newborn infant (such as immature brain, central nervous system and lungs.)"[23] Several commentators note that antiabortion forces have succeeded in constructing a symbolic meaning for fetuses equivalent to "human baby."[24]

The most recent example of such strategies is an antiabortion television advertisement sponsored by the Arthur S. De Moss Foundation. The 30-second spot features a split screen, with an infant on the left and a sonogram of a fetus labeled "10 weeks conception" on the right. The voice-over directs the viewer's attention and contextualization of the images: "Let's compare these two babies. The baby on the left has a beating heart; so does the baby on the right. The baby on the left has arms, legs, fingers and toes; so does the baby on the right. The baby on the left can turn and jump and kick; so can the baby on the right. The difference is, the baby on the left was just born; and the baby on the right would very much like to be. Life. What a beautiful choice."

Striking here is the attempt to equate the obvious human infant with the obscurely featured fetus. The two images look fundamentally different: The infant is rosy-fleshed with hair, clear-cut features, and is dressed in baby clothing; the fetal image is grey, fuzzy, and full of static. Without direction it would look like a bulbous squirming worm or amoeba. Yet the pictures are matched to give the illusion of identity, and the voice-over denies the visual differences. The narrator describes them as the same; the pictures are the same size, so that the fetus appears to be as big as the infant; and the desires seemingly expressed by the fetus appear to be identical to those of the baby. They are identical, except that one is trapped inside the cave of the pregnant woman surrounding it.

This process of rhetorically constructing the fetus as a baby has been used by pro-life lobbyists to persuade legislators, women entering abortion clinics, and the general public. Activists routinely confront lawmakers with "fetuses" that are made in the shape of baby dolls. The point of course is to make the word "fetus" indistinguishable from the concept of baby in lawmakers' minds, thus making it hard for them to support "murdering babies" through pro-abortion legislation.

Other examples of such tactics are common. Placards displayed outside abortion clinics and the homes of pro-choice legislators by pro-life picketers show graphic photographs of the dismembered bodies of late-term fetuses with captions that read, "Another child killed by abortion." Other placards tell viewers that the fetus is "Alive and growing: heart beats, brainwaves, fingerprints, feels pain."[25] Even the U.S. Supreme Court is bombarded by baby doll–waving protestors who gather outside during oral arguments of key abortion-rights cases. Television commercials by pro-life candidates sometimes employ the same graphic fetal imagery.[26]

Such tactics are remarkably effective: After years of being told that the fuzzy, grey-and-red blob we once thought of as fetal tissue (if we thought of it at all) is *really* a tiny human, we now *see* something that, as the male narrator in *Silent*

Scream says, "Sure *looks like* a baby!"[27] The association is not a difficult one to make in an environment where there is virtually no countervailing discourse about the fetal images bombarding the average American. Pro-choice political strategies have focused primarily on the harms women experience when forced to resort to illegal abortions, but they have virtually ignored the rhetorical and visual campaigns about fetal personhood employed by their pro-life opponents. America's sidewalks are not lined with pro-choice activists carrying placards with pictures of bloody, lumpy early-term abortions or unenhanced early-term sonograms. Consequently, pro-life rhetoric is gaining the upper hand.

The success of that strategy can be measured in part by its spread to the less political realm of U.S. popular culture. Evidence of this gestalt-like switch from not thinking about fetuses to thinking of them as babies can increasingly be found in purely commercial settings. Commercial media interests are eager to exploit anything that can be used to sell and entertain. Whereas cultural taboos and the simple invisibility of the fetus before the 1960s would have assured that fetal images would not be used in advertising campaigns or commercial films, the modern fetus-as-baby is a star.

For example, in a recent Volvo advertisement, a fetal sonogram that appears to have been doctored to increase clarity and detail is displayed over a Volvo station wagon.[28] Identifying details—the outline of the head, eye, nose, chin, lips, ear, toes, and musculature in the legs—are perfently evident. The fetus's arm is outstretched as though it is waving and each of its fingers is completely distinguishable. The caption asks the reader, "Is something inside telling you to buy a Volvo?" The advertisement works because the fetal image in the sonogram *looks* like a baby; the fetus has been endowed with a distinct and valuable identity within the family unit.

Filmmakers have also spied the potential profit in exploiting fetal imagery. The plots of two recent movies, *Look Who's Talking* and *My Life,* revolve around fetal imagery and fetal personification. In the first, a fetus in utero is given an adult, male voice. The "fetus" talks to itself and "thinks" about what's going on in the world around it (outside of the uterus). The film *Look Who's Talking* works because we find humor in ascribing adult qualities to babies, which we willingly extend to the fetus as a baby in utero. If we thought of the fetus as a talking, bloody, fatty blob of tissue or an internal organ (particularly a reproductive organ in a female body), we would be more horrified than amused. As with the photographs and rhetoric of the antiabortion groups, this comic portrayal of the fetus as baby makes it "real" in a new sense. In *My Life,* a dying father tries to communicate with the fetus his wife is carrying.[29] The film makes no distinction between the fetus in progress and the son the father will never know. That is how he can talk to the fetal image in the same way he does once the fetus is physically transformed into a baby by birth.

Fetal imagery is also used occasionally in some commercial medical endeavors. For example, a billboard for a New Jersey infertility clinic featured the image of a fetus over the caption, "Miracles Can Happen." Here the fetus stands for three things: the fetus *as an end in itself,* the pregnancy, and the end-product baby. The billboard thus plays upon the desire to become pregnant and ultimately have a baby and presents those desires as culminating in the fetus.

Commercialized fetal images are now aimed at children as well as adults. A 1993 Tyco doll, called "Mommy's Having a Baby," allows children to "feel the baby in Mommy's tummy" and help "deliver" it.[30] The doll comes with a "baby scope" that allows the child to "see baby move" while it is in utero. The toy ultrasound uses a holograph-like image that changes when tilted—the image shifts from lying on its back to sucking its thumb and kicking its feet. The "sonograph" pictures a well-defined baby, not a fetus, and the image floats in a waving sea of fluid with no evidence of the pregnant "Mommy's" body in sight. The "baby," which is proportionally sized and developmentally constructed to more closely resemble a toddler than an infant, can be put back in the mother's "womb," thus eliding the difference for the young consumer between being born and not being born. The word "fetus" never appears in any of the literature accompanying the toy; it refers to the fetus exclusively as a "baby." In the minds of the children who learn about pregnancy from this doll, there will be no fetuses; there will be only babies.

These rhetorical translations of fetal images into babies have a cumulative effect: We perceive these fetuses as babies because we've been exposed to them as such previously. We walk away from each encounter having incorporated those images in a way that shapes our next exposure to a fetal image. Gradually, the symbolic meaning of "fetus" is being radically transformed. Where the abstract idea of fetus once signified an invisible, unknowable potential, it is coming to designate an extant, corporeal entity with a knowable autonomous identity as a baby.

This autonomous status is possible only through a sort of mental separation and distinction of the fetus from the body of the woman of whom it is a part. The perceptual shift suggests that although the two may be connected by shared tissue—uterus, amniotic fluid, the umbilical cord, the same space—they are, as some physicians now describe them, "separate *individuals.*"[31] Such language suggests that the fetus has been elevated to a position of equality with the pregnant woman in the medicine of pregnancy. But others believe we have moved past equality to a reversal in value between the pregnant woman and the fetus. On this argument, seeing the fetus, both physically and conceptually, depends on the erasure of the pregnant woman.[32] The sonogram, for example, erases the external belly of the pregnant woman to allow access to the fetus inside. The *Life* cover shows a fetus encapsulated, not by a pregnant woman's uterus and body, but rather by an amniotic sac that appears to be a part of it. These pictorial presentations of the fetus, unobscured by the visible presences of the woman and womb of which it is a part, create the sense that the fetus is, as Rosalind

Petchesky puts it, an "autonomous, atomized mini–space hero" floating independently in a sort of capsule.[33] In this construction, the woman's body has become the unknowable void of outer space.

This dramatic shift in the status and relationship between the pregnant woman and her fetus means that the paramount importance of the woman's self-report about her body and the externally visible cues about change are rendered increasingly irrelevant. The sonogram and CVS reveal more about the fetus than the woman. As a result, pregnancy is becoming increasingly fetus-centered in modern culture.

The reorientation of the fetus—from the invisible "bulge" beneath the maternity smock of a pregnant woman to an identifiable, individuated and autonomous "baby person"—has implications far beyond medicine. Exposure to fetal imagery, framed by a rhetorical campaign equating fetuses and babies, fosters the idea that fetuses are baby persons in the general culture. This reconstruction of the symbolic meaning of pregnancy is vital to the success of the antiabortion and fetal rights movements. As more people experience the fetus as a baby, they find themselves compelled to offer the same legal and medical protections to fetal persons as afforded all other persons in modern U.S. society.[34]

The Legal Construction of Fetal Identity: "Baby Persons" Before the Law

This powerful change in our cultural perception of the fetus is strongly reflected in the changing status of the fetus under law. The U.S. Supreme Court's pronouncement in *Roe v. Wade* that fetuses have never been considered "persons" under the Fourteenth Amendment notwithstanding, some courts and legislative bodies are increasingly recognizing fetuses as just that and thus in need of legal respect and protection by the state.

Fetal Identity Grows in the Courts

In *Roe v. Wade* the Supreme Court found that the fetus has never been considered a person under the Fourteenth Amendment and thus had no standing to challenge a woman's right to an abortion. However, the Court also found that the state does have an interest in the potential life of the fetus that increases as pregnancy progresses toward birth. Therefore a woman's right to privacy and thus to terminate her pregnancy is not absolute, but circumscribed by state interests that increase over the course of the pregnancy. The Court deliberately refused to decide when life begins, arguing that the judiciary is "not in a position to speculate as to the answer." 410 U.S. at 159. However, it hinted that if the fetus was a person the relationship between the pregnant woman and the fetus would be profoundly affected. As the fetus metamorphizes toward cultural personhood, the final step is legal independence, which requires the conceptual separation of the fetus from the pregnant body of which it is a part. As this process unfolds, the Court's words are proving to be strikingly prescient.

Despite its past invisibility, the fetus has been noted in various bodies of law for thousands of years. Early criminal and property laws acknowledged the possibility of harm to the fetuses of pregnant women. In the Bible, the Book of Exodus prescribes the appropriate punishment for injuring a pregnant woman or causing a miscarriage.[35] Similar prohibitions on abortion and criminal sanctions for injury to a pregnant woman resulting in miscarriage have traditionally afforded recognition of fetal existence under law. But the notion of harm generally applied only to the property interests of a third party, like the father, or to the actual physical damage done to the pregnant woman, fetal interest was not at issue. However, as the personhood of the fetus gains cultural recognition, the traditional approach to recognizing fetal harm is giving way to one that recognizes independent status.

Tort Law

The fetus first emerged as the subject of legal redress in property disputes over inheritance. As early as 1887 a child, born alive, was able to inherit from the estate of someone who died while he or she was still in utero.[36] The point was to protect the property interests of fathers and testators after death, without acknowledging the fetus as having independent standing. Live birth was also a requirement in order to sue for injuries suffered in utero. A Massachusetts court held in *Dietrich v. Northampton,* 138 Mass. 14 (1884) that prenatal injuries were not recoverable, because no duty was owed to a person who did not exist. In this case the pregnancy miscarried in the fourth or fifth month following an accident in which the pregnant woman tripped on a flaw in the road; the fetus lived only a few minutes after birth. Justice Holmes reasoned that the fetus and the pregnant woman constitute one person; though a duty could be owed to her, no separate duty could be owed to the fetus. 138 Mass. at 15.

Courts continued to deny tortious claims arising during pregnancy until 1946. In *Bonbrest v. Kotz,* 65 F. Supp 138 (1946) a cause of action for a fetus was recognized if the injury occurred after the point of viability and the fetus was later born alive. In 1960, a New Jersey court sustained the live birth requirement, arguing as earlier decisions had that otherwise injuries sustained in utero were not recoverable because the fetus was a part of the mother and thus had no independent status. See *Smith v. Brennan,* 157 A.2d 497 (1960).[37] The same court required that the defendant be a third party to avoid actions by minor children against their parents, supporting the notion of parent-child immunity.[38]

Today, all states recognize standing for those injured in utero so long as the case meets the live birth and viability standards.[39] But some states are beginning to abandon the viability standard. For example, a Georgia court ruled in 1956 that the developmental stage of the fetus at the time of injury was not important if the pregnancy resulted in a live birth. *Hornbuckle v. Plantation Pipe Line,* 212 Ga. 504 (1956). And in 1971 a Michigan court recognized the right of a person to sue for injuries sustained in a car accident as a four-month-old fetus. *Womack v. Buchhorn,* 187 N.W.2d 218, 219–223 (1971). Challenges to the viability standard are ongoing in many states because a number of courts have reasoned that since it is difficult to determine the exact point of viability the standard itself is not sufficiently exact.[40]

Furthermore, a growing number of states now reject the requirement that the defendant must be a third party in order to ensure parent-child immunity.[41] In the first case of this type, a woman was sued in 1980 by her child for having used the antibiotic tetracycline during pregnancy, which allegedly caused the child to have poor tooth enamel. The court ruled that the child had standing to sue based on a neglect and abuse ruling that argued for a "reasonable pregnant woman" standard.[42] And in 1987, an Illinois appellate court recognized the claims of an infant born alive to sue its mother for injuries suffered in an automobile accident when the child was a five-and-a-half-month-old fetus.[43] Reaching a similar result, a New Hampshire court allowed a child born alive to sue its mother for injuries caused by negligence that occurred to the child while in utero. See *Andre Bonte f/n/f Stephanie Bonte v. Sharon Bonte,* No. 9–461 (H.C.S.C., N.H. 1992).[44] In this case, the woman was struck by a car during the seventh month of pregnancy. Her fetus, born by emergency cesarean section, suffered severe brain damage from the accident. The *Bonte* court relied on a 1958 case that held "a fetus becomes a *separate* organism from the time of conception"[45] (emphasis added) and that the pregnant woman "is required to act with the appropriate duty of care, as we have consistently held other persons are required to act, with respect to the fetus."[46]

The erosion of the parent-child immunity standard marks a fundamental change in courts' perceptions of the relationship between the pregnant woman and the fetus. Decisions like those in *Bonte* and the tetracycline case dramatically change the perceived responsibilities of the pregnant woman to the fetus. Even though laws are inconsistent, confused, and often contradictory across and sometimes within states,[47] fetuses appear to be gaining autonomous standing in tort law and more protections from state courts. The unfolding story of the status of the fetus in criminal law is much the same.

Criminal Law

The question most commonly posed under criminal law has been, Is the killing of a fetus homicide? Here too the live birth standard has been controlling. Unless the fetus is born alive, courts have held that most homicide statutes do not apply to the death of a fetus, reasoning that unborn fetuses are not "persons" and thus not entitled to state protection. This standard remains intact in many jurisdictions,[48] but recently there has been encroachment on the live birth standard even in criminal law.[49] For example, a Massachusetts court found in 1989 that a viable fetus is in fact a human being for the purpose of common law murder.[50] And in 1990, a Minnesota court found that the state's homicide statutes do not require that the living organism in the womb (whether an embryo or a fetus) be considered a person or human being and that the statute does not require the state to prove it to have been a "person" at the time of death.[51]

The primary difficulty for criminal law has been to determine exactly what constitutes a "live birth."[52] Increasingly, judges find that the question of when a fetal birth is a live one becomes complicated by medical technologies that smudge the lines between born and uterine life.[53]

In an attempt to clarify this question, some states have amended their statutes to specifically include fetuses within homicide and other laws in order to preclude the need for determining whether or not the fetus was alive at the time of injury.[54] The California Penal Code, for example, defines murder as "the unlawful killing of a human being, or a fetus with malice aforethought."[55] At least twenty-one other states now impose some kind of criminal penalties for killing a fetus.[56]

Laws like the amended California Penal Code allow for prosecution in cases where fetal death occurs, without applying the words "person" or "personhood" to fetuses. This linguistic contortion is necessary to circumvent *Roe v. Wade*, which held that a fetus is not a "person" under the Constitution.[57] Courts and legislatures are often sympathetic to claims brought for fetal harm or death, interpreting and writing laws in such a way that courts can treat the fetus like a person without having to label it as such. In fetal personhood cases, some courts rely on legislative intent to determine whether fetuses should be included under homicide and manslaughter statutes.[58] Where intent is unclear, many courts have invited the legislature to address the issue for subsequent cases.[59] As one commentator observed, "Courts are loath to answer such questions" as when life begins.[60]

The status of fetuses under criminal law is inconsistent, often contradictory, and changing daily across jurisdictions.[61] Thus some legal scholars, right-to-life activists, and fetal rights advocates have joined with the judiciary in calling for legislatures to standardize the status of fetal personhood under law.[62] Like the California legislature, many legislative and political bodies throughout the country are responding.

Legislating Fetal Identity

Although many judges point to *Roe* as the controlling precedent on fetal personhood, others are more interested in the Supreme Court's later decision to let stand—virtually without comment—the preamble to the Missouri antiabortion law contested in *Webster v. Reproductive Health Services*, 492 U.S. 490 (1989), which declared that "the life of each human being begins at conception." *Id.* at 506–507. Legal scholars may argue that documents like preambles and the Declaration of Independence have no power to set precedent, but also acknowledge that they have strong symbolic influence on the public consciousness. The fact that Missouri legislators declared that fetuses are persons with the Supreme Court's imprimatur marks an important political shift.

Since the decision in *Webster,* antiabortion groups have been active at the state level, lobbying for so-called "human life amendments" and other legislation that officially recognizes the fetus in some capacity. Many states have passed or considered legislation that either defines the fetus as a person directly or indirectly through restrictions on access to abortion. For example, Illinois, Kentucky, Massachusetts, Oklahoma, and Missouri have defined the fetus as an "unborn child" upon either fertilization or conception.[63] Other states, including Minnesota, New York, Ohio, and Wyoming, require burial of fetal remains in ways required for other persons under the law.[64] At the federal level, pro-life forces have pushed for a national law defining fetuses as persons under the U.S. Constitution.[65]

Legal Separation for the Fetus: Guardians Ad Litem

Over the last several years, both judge-made and legislated laws concerning fetal rights have moved toward showing that the fetus qualifies as a person for purposes of showing harm. As the images, assumptions, and standards that keep the fetus conceptually embedded within pregnancy disappear, it gains cultural and legal legitimacy. This new vision culminates in the appointment of third parties as guardians ad litem to represent fetuses and embryos.[66] Hospitals, physicians, and state social service agencies have been authorized as fetal guardians.[67]

This legal gambit completely abrogates the reasoning behind the live birth and parent-child immunity standards that recognize the fetus as a dependent part of the pregnant woman until birth. Simultaneously, it allows the fetus to "appear" at court proceedings, not within the body and person of the pregnant woman, but in the form of the guardian who speaks and acts for it. Much like the sorceries of ultrasound, guardians ad litem abstract the fetus by erasing the connection between the pregnant woman and the fetus inside her. Through a bizarre linguistic and mental stratagem, courts have even gone so far as to award custody of the fetus in utero to third parties.[68] Some states even support such maneuvers with legislation. The Texas Family Code, for example, allows suits to terminate the parent-child relationship to be filed before the child is born,[69] clearing the way for a third party to be appointed as guardian ad litem to represent fetal interests independently of the pregnant woman.

The appointment of a guardian ad litem is based on the presumption that the interests of the fetus have diverged from those of the pregnant woman. It both assumes and creates a kind of incommensurable conflict between the pregnant woman and the fetus that the courts then must resolve. Resolution of these conflicts can only be realized in this adversarial model when the freedom of one gives way to the freedom of the other. In many cases, it is the rights of the pregnant woman that are surrendered to those of her developing fetus. This is the growing reality in cases of "nonconsensual" obstetrical and fetal intervention and official efforts to dictate the lifestyle choices of pregnant women.

The Incommensurability Problem: The Divergence of Fetal Interests and Pregnant Women's Rights

Under the older paradigm of pregnancy—where women were the authorities on fetal development—neither woman nor law distinguished between the demands and needs of mother and fetus. But constructing the fetus as an independent person means recognizing the same distinct interests that all people have. In this framework, the needs and demands of the pregnant woman and her fetus may conflict. The most obvious example of this is abortion: A woman's right to terminate a pregnancy is irreconcilable with the rights of a fetus to exist if the fetus is recognized as having such rights. When third parties—such as doctors, hospital administrators, lawyers, police officers, the fetus' father, or the state—intervene in the pregnancy, the interests they define for the fetus are often in direct conflict with the interests the woman defines for herself. In recognizing the argument for fetal rights, courts have often chosen to subordinate the rights of the pregnant woman.

Forced Medical Treatment

As noted earlier, the explosion in new medical technologies that has brought us visually closer to the fetus has also brought new medical therapies and treatments to improve fetal life. Doctors today are able to provide amazing remedies to aid the health and quality of life of the developing fetus.[70] Driven to do what they can to preserve life[71] and pushed by the fear of malpractice suits, doctors often translate their *ability* to treat a problem into an *imperative* to do so.[72] When a pregnant woman refuses treatment for her fetus, some doctors have turned to the courts for the power to make her comply.[73]

Court-ordered medical treatments for pregnant women have been occuring for about three decades. Courts first ordered pregnant women to undergo blood transfusions in two separate cases in 1964; both women had declined the transfusions on religious grounds.[74] The courts reasoned that compelling the women to undergo blood transfusions would allow them to meet their duty to care for their fetuses without having to make the decision to violate their religious practices.[75] Since then the list of court-ordered medical procedures has grown to include cerclage (requested by the father of the fetus),[76] transfer from one hospital to another,[77] hospital detention,[78] fetal blood transfusions,[79] and cesarean sections.[80]

Researchers found that over a five-year period representatives of hospitals specializing in maternal-fetal care in twenty-four states and the District of Columbia sought legal recourse forty-two times to overrule pregnant women's refusals of treatment.[81] The interventions pursued included cesarean sections, blood transfusions to either the fetus or the pregnant woman, and hospital detention of the pregnant woman. At least seventeen of these cases resulted in enforcement of court-ordered treatment.[82] Of the women targeted for such legal actions 81 percent were women of color and 24 percent did not speak English as their primary language.[83]

Court-ordered medical intervention can be delivered only upon the woman's submission to the court's demands or through the violation of her body. Janet Gallagher recounts the painful experience of one woman forced to undergo a cesarean section:

> In 1984, in Chicago, a Nigerian woman expecting triplets was hospitalized for the final period of her pregnancy. The woman and her husband steadfastly reiterated their unwillingness to consent to the Caesarian section that doctors regarded as necessary for a safe multiple birth. As the woman's due date approached, doctors and hospital legal counsel obtained a court order granting the hospital administrator temporary custody of the triplets and authorizing a C section as soon as the woman went into labor. ...
>
> Eventually, in the face of the C section, the husband was forcibly removed from the hospital, the woman was strapped down, anaesthetized and a C section was performed on her body.[84]

In the face of court orders to comply, most women either submit or fail to return for treatment;[85] few have appealed their cases. In the few cases to reach the appellate level, the courts' responses have been mixed. In 1981, the Georgia Supreme Court upheld a decision that gave custody of a fetus in utero to state human resource officials and ordered a cesarean section against the wishes of the pregnant woman.[86] And in an unreported order, the District of Columbia Superior Court in 1986 affirmed a decision empowering a hospital to perform a forced cesarean section.[87] The only other case to reach the appellate level to date resulted in a 1990 decision by the District of Columbia Court of Appeals to overturn the mandated cesarean section of Angela Carder.[88] Three years earlier, a court-ordered cesarean section was performed on Carder, who was terminally ill, in an attempt to save the life of her fetus. Both mother and fetus died shortly after the procedure; her family appealed the case on her behalf that became known as *In re A.C.*

Many feminist legal scholars take heart at this appellate decision, believing that the judicial system has finally drawn a line at this kind of forced treatment.[89] The majority opinion stressed that "the patient's wishes, once they are ascertained, must be followed in virtually all cases, unless there are truly extraordinary or compelling reasons to override them."[90] The court based its opinion on the woman's rights to bodily integrity, to accept or forgo medical treatment, and on the determination that her wishes have been fully recognized.[91] However, the split decision by the District of Columbia's Court of Appeals is cold comfort to those concerned with forced treatment of pregnant women. The majority opinion specifically declined to overturn the lower court's finding that the state interest in Carder's fetus was compelling and therefore merited the forced medical procedure[92] and was in fact more concerned with issues of competency and substituted judgment than with the maternal-fetal conflict. Furthermore, language about "truly extraordinary or compelling [state] reasons to override" the wishes of the pregnant woman is an open invitation for future challenges, as intimated by the majority[93] and the dissenting judge.[94]

Celebrating the majority decision in *In re A.C.* grossly underestimates the cumulative power of cultural exposure to fetal imagery and the political discourse of fetal personhood. For example, Judge Belson grounds his dissent on the personhood of the fetus. Arguing that the "unborn child's and the state's interests are entitled to substantial weight" when balancing the interests of the pregnant woman and the fetus, Belson makes clear that he perceives the fetus as a "child" with numerous and compelling rights.[95] Belson even goes so far as to describe the fetus as a "captive" within the pregnant body and to argue that the pregnant woman's rights can be compromised because she elected to carry the pregnancy.[96]

Most cases of forced treatment are instigated by physicians, hospitals, or family members, generally arise from emergencies threatening the life and well-being of the fetus, and are decided by local judges in hurried hearings.[97] As therapies like fetal surgery become more routine, one can only wonder at the future pressures on women to comply with even more invasive medical procedures. Some physicians indicate that despite the ruling in *In re A.C.*, liability issues and concern for their "second patient" may oblige them to *increase* their demands for court-ordered therapies.[98] One fetal-maternal specialist sums up his thinking about forced care: "If medical probability indicates that the fetus will die or become permanently brain damaged because of the maternal refusal of treatment, the state's interests in the integrity of the medical profession, the preservation of life and the protection of innocent third parties are sufficiently compelling to remove the maternal abdominal wall as a barrier to fetal health care."[99]

As the fetus gains identity and personhood culturally and legally, non-medical third parties encroach on the bodies of pregnant women as well. As noted earlier, in *Taft v. Taft*, the biological father of an early-term fetus was granted a court order forcing his wife to undergo "purse string" surgery to sustain her pregnancy.[100] Noting that the Supreme Judicial Court of Massachusetts ultimately overturned that decision, one commentator argues strongly that legal recognition of fetal rights provides a rationale for court-ordered medical interventions to ensure the biological father's interests in the fetus.[101] But concerns about fetal health care and fetal rights that demand the abrogation of the rights and interests of pregnant women are by no means limited only to doctors and family members. The fetal abuse debate has led to broader public demands for legal action against pregnant women who inflict such "abuse."

The Social Construction of "Fetal Abuse": Drugs, Alcohol, and Lifestyle Choices

In the eyes of those who perceive the fetus as a tiny person, a pregnant woman who engages in activities that can endanger fetal development, such as using legal and illegal drugs, smoking, drinking, or engaging in immoderate exercise or sexual activity, is committing "fetal abuse" or "child abuse." Increasingly, courts and legislatures are recognizing the fetus as person enough to offer legal protection.

There are compelling reasons for wanting to dissuade pregnant women from harmful activities. Babies born to drug-using women can suffer from withdrawal and devastating physical and mental maladies; as many as 11 percent of U.S. babies are now born to women who used drugs while pregnant.[102] Fetal alcohol syndrome (FAS), affecting babies born to women who drank heavily while pregnant, is well documented. FAS "is the third leading cause of mental retardation following Down's syndrome and spina bifida"; FAS children often suffer from low birth weight and poor intellectual development.[103] Babies born to smokers are also much more likely to suffer low birth weight and other physical and developmental problems. As the fetus comes to be perceived as a person deserving of the state's protection, pregnant women are being prosecuted and sued for engaging in these behaviors.[104]

The earliest cases of prosecution for fetal abuse and neglect stem from illegal drug use. These early cases were dismissed by judges who rejected the argument that the fetuses were "children," making charges of child abuse and neglect inapplicable. In an attempt to circumvent defendant-biased statutory wording, law enforcement agencies have sought to expand their charges. The courts have also begun to change their understanding of what constitutes a "child," and as we have seen some legislatures have specifically amended the language of the law to include the fetus in statutes prohibiting abuse. As a consequence, women are now being convicted of abusing their own fetuses.[105] Pregnant women prosecuted for drug use have faced a host of criminal charges, including criminal neglect,[106] felony use of a controlled substance, and misdemeanor child abuse.[107] Many have been incarcerated,[108] lost custody of other children,[109] and lost custody of newborns.[110] Between 1987 and 1991, nineteen states and the District of Columbia brought more than fifty charges against women suspected of illegal drug use during pregnancy.[111]

Courts have also prosecuted pregnant women for consuming legal drugs such as alcohol and antibiotics. For example, a Wyoming woman was charged with child abuse for drinking when four months pregnant.[112] The charges were ultimately dropped because the prosecutor could not prove injury to the fetus, which "was unavailable for examination."[113] In another case, a woman was prosecuted for child neglect for drinking while pregnant, and the child was removed from her custody after birth.[114] And a Michigan woman was charged with child abuse and temporarily lost custody of her infant because she had taken Valium while pregnant to relieve pain from injuries she suffered in a car accident.[115]

Women have been charged or sued for a growing list of legal behaviors that others allege could prove harmful to their fetuses, including taking a prescription drug, smoking cigarettes, having sexual intercourse, drinking alcohol, failing to follow doctors' orders, and not eating properly while pregnant.[116] However, it is a fact of daily life that pregnant women engage in all sorts of behaviors that could potentially damage their fetuses, from walking, to flying, to changing their cat boxes,[117] to cleaning house,[118] to failing to undergo genetic testing.[119] Some commentators suggest that with the rise of fetal rights and consequent erosion of the parent-child immunity standard the list of potential tort and criminal statutes enacted to protect the fetus will balloon. Dawn Johnsen suggests that in the future, "A woman could be held civilly or criminally liable for fetal injuries caused by accidents resulting from maternal negligence, such as automobile or household accidents. She could also be held liable for any behavior during her pregnancy having potentially adverse affects on her fetus, including failing to eat properly, using prescription, nonprescription and illegal drugs, smoking, drinking alcohol, exposing herself to infectious disease or to workplace hazards, engaging in immoderate exercise or sexual intercourse, residing at high altitudes for prolonged periods, or using a general anesthetic or drugs to induce rapid labor during delivery."[120]

Many seem to support making pregnant women liable for behavior that endangers their fetuses. For example, a recent argument by Dr. Margery Shaw takes the fetal protection argument to the extreme. She advocates "giving the courts the power to require women to undergo genetic counseling before conception, to follow medically recommended regimens during pregnancy, to undergo fetal therapy to benefit 'the would-be child' and even to abort a fetus diagnosed as having a serious, non-correctable defect."[121]

Shaw's remarks reflect a growing public sentiment that views the fetus as worthy of protection and the pregnant woman as its potential abuser. Recently concern for fetal health has spawned a growing distrust of pregnant women's competence to gestate their fetuses, as suggested by the national controversy that erupted when a Seattle bar refused to serve a hugely pregnant patron. The bartenders said they feared potential liability suits.[122] When women can't be trusted to care for the fetuses they are creating, the state is called upon to ensure fetal health. One commentator notes, "Her unborn child's health and safety remain almost exclusively within her control if state legislatures fail to pass laws that effectively protect the fetus. ... Legislative and judicial bodies cannot afford to appear impotent when *one member of society harms another.*"[123] A few fetal rights advocates even argue for the use of forced cesarean sections "as an intervention for the protection of children facing the effects of the mother's drug abuse," a procedure that "will become a more probable one as [it] becomes safer and the problem of gestational substance abuse grows worse."[124]

In general, there seems to be substantial public support for such draconian approaches to "fetal abuse." According to a 1988 Gallup poll, 48 percent of the respondents thought that a woman who smokes or drinks while pregnant should be held liable for potential damages.[125] Support for legal interventions and control over the behavior of pregnant women is also fueled by the opinions expressed in public forums by well known and authoritative figures like Harvard Law Professor Alan Dershowitz, who openly advocates such police state actions.[126]

Conclusions

As I suggested at the outset, seeing the fetus physically has rendered the pregnant body invisible. To the extent that one sees the fetus as an "individual" and a "member of society," one must construct pregnancy as an inherently adversarial encounter between the pregnant woman and the fetus—rather than as a symbiotic creation.[127] Supporting the "rights" of the fetus requires that we conceptually reduce pregnant women to nothing more than their wombs. According to Mary Kennedy, "Because of the integral role a mother's care of her body during pregnancy plays in fetal development, a woman's right to control her body ought to be restricted for the welfare of her child once the decision has been made not to abort."[128] In Kennedy's view, the duty to care begins as soon as the pregnant woman knows she's pregnant and decides not to terminate it.[129]

The model of pregnancy that views pregnant women as mere containers for little fetal people necessarily pits the pregnant woman against the fetus. In Overall's words, "[T]he female body is seen as dangerous even to the embryo/fetus because the pregnant woman cannot be trusted not to abuse it, pass on defective genes to it, or even kill it, let alone to protect it from environmental harm and give birth to it safely."[130] But every person ever to live in this world was born to a woman who nurtured it with her body and who was also a person in her own right. This is what those who "see" the fetus as a person must exclude from their vision of pregnancy.

Petchesky and other feminist theorists argue that if we are to check the erosion of pregnant women's rights and the ascension of fetal personhood, we must conceptually re-locate the fetus and again see it as part of the pregnant woman. To stop the ascension of fetal personhood we must metaphorically avoid looking at the sonogram. One wonders if that is possible rhetorically or, perhaps more important, whether it is likely politically. The persuasive power of medical images, antiabortion campaigns, and commercial interests will have an increasingly powerful influence on a culture as visually dependent as ours. Those fetal images will not be easily willed back into the bodies of pregnant women. Nor should they, because in fact fetuses do have value and material reality.

The problem lies not in the existence of the fetus but rather in how we look at pregnancy and in the meanings we construct for what we see. Pregnant bodies have been in our view since the dawn of history but we have not "seen" women (pregnant or not) as citizens and persons with equal rights until very recently. When courts compel pregnant women to undergo medical procedures or stop behaviors that may endanger their fetuses, they subordinate women's rights to control their bodies and pregnancies and treat them as nothing more than fetal containers. This once again subordinates the social, political, and legal identity of women to their physical bodies. Except in this instance the pregnant woman is considered illegitimate even as a physical identity for she is a threat to her own fetus's survival and health.

This chapter has argued that the construction of fetal identity is "a contingent matter, rationally undecidable and rhetorically constructed, rather than a basic fact of nature"[131] and that construction of the fetus as a separate person depends upon the physical and legal erasure of pregnant women. That is not to suggest it is impossible to value both the fetus and the pregnant woman to the benefit of both. We can "*choose* how to count the fetus"[132] and we can *choose* how to count the pregnant woman. Medical, antiabortion, and commercial forces are currently making those choices for us. Their version of the fetus as a person can be had *only* through a construction of separation from the pregnant woman. Their understanding of the pregnant woman is of an "irrational" woman[133] who is expressing her "latent antagonism"[134] to her fetus. Women's concerns for their religious beliefs, their fears of surgery, and the facts of their personal lives that drive them toward drug use during pregnancy are discounted as irrelevant.[135]

But fetuses do not exist without pregnant women. The solution is not to stop looking, but rather to look more closely. Whereas fetal rights have many advocates who are pushing judicially and legislatively to expand and formalize fetal rights even more, there is little public advocacy for an expansion of "pregnancy rights."[136] Petchesky is right that we need to re-embed the fetus in the pregnant form. But that can only be done by "seeing" the pregnant woman as prominently in culture and in law as we now see the fetus inside. To do so is to legitimize, honor, and facilitate a woman's decision to be pregnant. If we do that, perhaps we can begin to ascribe a value to the fetus that allows us to act on our protective impulses without impairing the rights of the pregnant woman.

Notes

An earlier version of this essay was presented at the 1991 Annual Meeting of the Midwest Political Science Association, Palmer House, Chicago, Illinois, April 18–20, 1991. I would like to thank Mary Segers, Linda Zerelli, Susan Lawrence, Cliff Fox, Milton Heumann, and Pat Boling for their insightful comments.

1. Jeffrey P. Phelan, "The Maternal Abdominal Wall: A Fortress Against Fetal Health Care?" *Southern California Law Review* 65:463 (1991).

2. Rosalind Pollack Petchesky, *Abortion and Woman's Choice: The State Sexuality and Reproductive Freedom* (revised edition) (Boston: Northeastern University Press, 1990).

3. In many cultures, it was not until the moment of "quickening" (the first fetal movement felt by the pregnant woman) that pregnancy was thought to have occurred. As late as the nineteenth century, a woman's decision to abort a fetus was thought of as restoring menses and making her body "regular" again rather than as the elimination of a pregnancy (Petchesky, *Abortion and Women's Choice*, 53).

4. Arlene Eisenberg, Heidi E. Murkoff, and Sandee H. Hathaway, *What to Expect When You're Expecting* (New York: Workman Publishing, 1991), 45.

5. Phelan, "Maternal Abdominal Wall," 463 at n. 18.

6. Eisenberg, Murkoff, and Hathaway, *What to Expect When You're Expecting*, 47.

7. Ibid., 51; Harriet L. Hornick, "Mama vs. Fetus," *Medical Trial Technique Quarterly*, 1993 Annual:565.

8. Eisenberg, Murkoff, and Hathaway, *What to Expect When You're Expecting*, 280.

9. Christine Overall, *Ethics and Human Reproduction: A Feminist Analysis* (Boston: Allen & Unwin, 1987), 43.

10. The first successful operation of this kind was performed in 1986 on a twenty-three-week-old fetus to correct a blocked urethra. In 1993, fetal surgery successfully corrected the diaphragmatic hernia of a twenty-four-week-old fetus. "Saving Lives Not Yet Begun," *People Weekly*, June 18, 1990, 40.

11. Val Cardinale, "New Technologies to Revolutionize the Health-Care Field," *Drug Topics*, January 11, 1993, 47.

12. Phelan, "The Maternal Abdominal Wall," 462.

13. As cited in Hornick, "Mama vs. Fetus," 537.

14. Phelan, "Maternal Abdominal Wall," 463.

15. N. Scott Adzick, Michael R. Harrison, Alan W. Flake, Lori J. Howell, Mitchell S. Golbus, Roy A. Filly, and The UCSF Fetal Treatment Center. "Fetal Surgery for Cystic Adenomatoid Malformation in the Lung." *Journal of Pediatric Surgery* 28(6), (1993).

16. The magazine cover featured an allegedly eighteen-week-old fetus, seemingly floating independently in an amniotic sac. *Life* published these same photographs again in 1972, captioned on the cover, "The First Pictures Ever of How Life Begins." Carole Stabile, "Shooting the Mother: Fetal Photography and the Politics of Disappearance," *Camera Obscura* 28:182 (1992). See Stabile's analysis of the text changes for an interesting discussion of the influence of the abortion debate on the rhetorical construction of these photographs.

17. Stabile, "Shooting the Mother," 179.

18. Ibid., 185.

19. Ibid., 182.

20. *The Nature of Sex*, "A Miracle in the Making," Genesis Films, 1993.

21. Lennart Nilsson, *A Child Is Born* (New York: Dell Publishing, 1990), 59, 104.

22. Marian Faux, *Roe v. Wade* (Ontario: Mercer Books, 1988).

23. Cynthia R. Daniels, *At Women's Expense: State Power and the Politics of Fetal Rights* (Cambridge, Mass.: Harvard University Press, 1993), 16.

24. Rosalind Pollack Petchesky, "Fetal Images: The Power of Visual Culture in the Politics of Reproduction." *Feminist Studies* 13:2 (1987), 264. Celeste Michelle Condit, *Decoding Abortion Rhetoric, Communicating Social Change* (Urbana: University of Illinois, 1990). For example, Celeste Condit shows that pro-life activists have succeeded in translating terms

like "fetus," "unborn," "blastocyst," and "embryo" into the single, empathy-inducing signifier "baby" through a careful rhetorical strategy of metonymy and effective use of the 1980s "cult of appearances." (*Decoding Abortion Rhetoric,* 82).

25. Conversation with Kansas State Legislator Nancy Brown, 1991.

26. "Fetuses Shown in Campaign Commercial," *Facts on File,* 52:2686 (May 14, 1992), 353.

27. Petchesky, "Fetal Images," 264.

28. *Time Magazine,* October 29, 1990, 117.

29. In a peculiar paradox, the future son is equated throughout with the fetus that resides within; thus while actor Michael Keaton is talking to his son in the future he is also talking to his son in utero. The plot begins with a fetal sonogram filling the big screen. Much of the film is shot as though the camera eye occupies the perspective of the fetus. Thus, the audience is exposed to images of the fetus and virtually becomes one with the fetus as the dying father points a camera at himself and addresses both simultaneously.

30. This is from the literature that accompanies the doll.

31. Phelan, "Maternal Abdominal Wall," 462.

32. Petchesky, "Fetal Images"; Stabile, "Shooting the Mother," 187.

33. Petchesky, "Fetal Images," 277. It is interesting to note that the "belly" of the pregnant mommy doll in the Tyco toy "Mommy's Having a Baby" is actually part of a maternity dress that can be removed so that the Mommy figure can be pregnancy-free. Thus the woman's belly has become detached even from her: a disposable ectogenic womb. What is more, the shape of this pregnancy device strongly resembles a capsule in shape and form.

34. See, for example, Beth Driscoll Osowski, "The Need for Logic and Consistency in Fetal Rights," *North Dakota Law Review* 68 (1992); Richard A. Erb and Alan W. Mortensen, "Wyoming Fetal Rights—Why the Abortion 'Albatross' Is a Bird of a Different Color: The Case for Fetal-Federalism." *Land and Water Law Review* 28(2) (1993); Alan M. Dershowitz, *Contrary to Popular Opinion* (New York: Pharos Books, 1992).

35. For example, see the Book of Exodus, 22:21, 22–25.

36. See *Cowles v. Cowles* 56 Conn. 240, 13 A. 414 (1887).

37. See Osowski, "The Need for Logic," 173.

38. Ibid., 173 & n. 20.

39. Ibid., 174.

40. See, for example, *Smith v. Mercy Hospital and Medical Center,* 148 Ill. Dec. 567, 560 N.E.2d 1164 (1990), where the court found, "Although parents of stillborn child alleged in their complaint in wrongful death action against hospital that mother was being treated for full-term pregnancy when negligent act occurred they were not obligated to establish viability at trial." Also see *Fryover v. Forbes,* 439 N.W.2d 284 (1989) in which the court found, "Nonviable fetus not born alive is 'person' within meaning of Wrongful Death Act, so that wrongful death action can be maintained on behalf of fetus." Cf. *Humes v. Clinton,* 792 P.2d 1032 (1990) where court found, "Unborn, nonviable fetus is not 'person' within definition of wrongful death statute and is incapable of bringing action on its own behalf; viability is appropriate condition precedent to liability in wrongful death action." Cited in 17 10th D. Pt 1-297.

41. Mary K. Kennedy, "Maternal Liability for Prenatal Injury Arising From Substance Abuse During Pregnancy: The Possibility of Cause of Action in Pennsylvania," *Duquesne Law Review* 29(1):554 (1991).

42. *Grodin v. Grodin,* 102 Mich. App. 396, 301 N.W.2d 869 (1980). Ms. Grodin had been told by her physician that it was impossible for her to get pregnant so she continued taking the drug. When she learned she was pregnant in her third trimester, she stopped taking the antibiotic.

43. *Stallman v. Youngquist,* 153 Ill. App. 3d 683, appealed, 115 Ill. 2d 551 (1987), cited in Hornick, "Mama vs. Fetus," at n. 20.

44. See *Andre Bonte f/n/f Stephanie Bonte v. Sharon Bonte,* No. 91-461 (H.C.S.C., N.H. October 30, 1992), cited in John P. Griffith, Helen G. Honorow, and Gary F. Karnedy, "After Bonte: What Is Reasonable?" *New Hampshire Bar Journal* (March 1993), at n. 1.

45. *Bennet v. Hymers,* 101 N.H. 486, 147 A.2d 109 (1958).

46. No. 91-461 (H.C.S.C., N.H. October 30, 1992) at 2, cited in Griffith et al., "After Bonte: What Is Reasonable?" 47.

47. S. Jeffrey Gately, "Texas Fetal Rights: Is There a Future for the Rights of Future Texans?" *St. Mary's Law Journal* 23:309 & n. 33 (1991).

49. See for example, *U.S. v. Spencer,* 839 F.2d 1341 (9th Cir. 1988), in which court found that infliction of injuries on a fetus who was born alive but later died as a result of the injuries was murder under federal statutes; also see *State v. Horne* 282 S.C. 444 (1987) in which court argued that unborn viable fetus was not a "person" and therefore the reckless killing of the fetus was not manslaughter under the state statutes.

49. Phelan, "Maternal Abdominal Wall," 479 & n. 129.

50. *Commonwealth v. Lawrence* 536 N.E.2d 571, 404 Mass. 378 (1989).

51. *State v. Merrill* 450 N.W.2d 318 (1990).

52. Leonard Glantz, "Is the Fetus a Person? A Lawyer's View." In *Abortion, Medicine, and the Law* (4th edition), ed. J. Douglas Butler and David F. Walbert (New York: Facts on File, 1992), 109.

53. Glantz, "Is a Fetus a Person?" 110–111.

54. Hornick, "Mama vs. Fetus," 539.

55. See California Penal Code, Section 187 (West 1983), as cited in Hornick, "Mama vs. Fetus," 539.

56. Those states are: Arizona, Florida, Georgia, Illinois, Indiana, Iowa, Louisiana, Michigan, Mississippi, Montana, New Hampshire, Nevada, New York, Rhode Island, South Dakota, Tennessee, Utah, Washington, and Wisconsin, as cited in Robin M. Trindel, "Fetal Interests vs. Maternal Rights: Is the State Going Too Far?" *Akron Law Review* 24(3 & 4): n.11 & 12 (1991).

57. Erb and Mortensen, "Wyoming Fetal Rights," 2.

58. See *Witty v. American General Capital Distributors, Inc.,* 727 S.W.2d 503 (Tex. 1987), in which the court ruled that the legislature did not intend the words "individual" or "person" to include fetus.

59. See *Hudak v. Georgy,* 567 A.2d 1095 (Penn. 1989), in which the court argued that creation of a cause of action for a nonviable fetus would be the function of the legislature, not the judiciary.

60. Gately, "Texas Fetal Rights," 312. The amendment to the California Penal Code was the result of judicial disinclination to decide, expressed as a challenge to the legislative branches to pick up the gauntlet. The court found itself unhappily bound by legislative language that precluded a cause of action for a stillborn, five-pound, late-third-trimester fetus. The fetus' death was caused by a fractured skull, suffered when the father kicked the pregnant woman repeatedly in the abdomen. The court's hands were tied in the prosecution because the statute did not specifically include fetuses as possible victims. *Keeler v. Superior Court,* 87 Cal. Rpt. 481, 470 P. 2d 617 (1970). Glantz, "Is a Fetus a Person?" 110–111.

61. Gately, "Texas Fetal Rights"; Erb and Mortensen, "Wyoming Fetal Rights."

62. Gately, "Texas Fetal Rights"; Osowski, "The Need for Logic"; Erb and Mortensen, "Wyoming Fetal Rights."

63. B.J. George, Jr., "State Legislatures Versus the Supreme Court: Abortion Legislation in the 1990's," in *Abortion, Medicine, and the Law* (4th edition), ed. J. Douglas Butler and David F. Walbert (New York: Facts on File, 1992), 25.

64. George, "State Legislatures vs. the Supreme Court," 54.

65. For example, S. 158, 97th Cong., 1st Session, 127 Cong. notes: "Section 1 (a) Congress finds that the life of each human being begins at conception. (b) Congress further finds that the fourteenth amendment to the Constitution of the United States protects all human beings."

The Republican Party is a long-time supporter of fetal personhood legislation. The 1988 Republican platform supported the Human Life Amendment, setting the model for the states and attempting to grant national legitimacy to the idea that fetuses are persons under the Constitution. Some 1988 Republican presidential candidates, conservative evangelist Pat Robertson in particular, based a significant portion of their campaigns on support for the Human Life Amendment. Four years later, the 1992 Republican National Convention featured presidential candidate Pat Buchanan recalling the need for legislation protecting fetal life.

66. Susan Goldberg, "Of Gametes and Guardians: The Impropriety of Appointing Guardians Ad Litem for Fetuses and Embryos," *Washington Law Review* 66:413 (1991).

67. Ibid., 523–524; Janet Gallagher, "Prenatal Invasions and Interventions: What's Wrong With Fetal Rights?" *Harvard Women's Law Journal* 10(9): 9 (Spring 1987); Lawrence J. Nelson, Brian P. Buggy, and Carol J. Weil, "Forced Medical Treatment of Pregnant Women: 'Compelling Each to Live as Seems Good to the Rest,'" *The Hastings Law Journal* 37:727 (May 1986).

68. Ibid., 727 at n.86 & 87. Complying with this court order of course requires that the guardian ad litem also take possession of the pregnant woman as well.

69. Tex. Fam. Code Ann. sec. 15.021(a) (Vernon supp. 1991).

70. Michael T. Flannery, "Court-Ordered Prenatal Intervention: A Final Means to the End of Gestational Substance Abuse," *Journal of Family Law* 30(3):579–584 (1991–1992).

71. Rennee I. Solomon, "Future Fear: Prenatal Duties Imposed by Private Parties," *American Journal of Law and Medicine* 17(4):427 (1991).

72. Phelan, "Maternal Abdominal Wall," 471–472; Veronika Kolder, Janet Gallagher, and Michael T. Parsons, "Court-ordered Obstetrical Interventions," *The New England Journal of Medicine* 316(19):1194–1195 (1987); Nelson, Buggy, and Weil, "Forced Medical Treatment," 713.

73. Phelan, "Maternal Abdominal Wall," 473–474; Kolder, Gallagher, and Parsons, "Court-Ordered Obstetrical Interventions," 1193.

74. *Raleigh Fitkin-Paul Morgan Memorial Hospital v. Anderson*, 42 N.J. 421, 201 A.2d 537, *cert. denied*, 377 U.S. 985 (1964); and *Application of the President and Directors of Georgetown College Hospital*, 331 F.2d 1000 (1964), cited in Kolder, Gallagher, and Parsons, "Court-Ordered Obstetrical Interventions," 1194–1195.

75. Kolder, Gallagher, and Parsons, "Court-Ordered Obstetrical Interventions," 1195.

76. Cerclage is a procedure to suture the cervix to enable the pregnant woman to retain a pregnancy. *Taft v. Taft*, 388 Mass. 331, 446 N.E.2d 395 (1983). The trial court judge granted the order, which was later overturned by the Supreme Judicial Court of Massachusetts on the grounds that in this case the state did not have interests compelling enough to "justify curtailing the wife's constitutional rights." 446 N.E.2d at 397. Some commentators note that the judge left the door open for future cases in which the state's interest could be construed as compelling enough. What is more, the court declined to comment on the validity of the father's actions. (See Solomon, "Future Fear," 423 & n.76–79.)

77. Petition For Emergency Protective Services at 2, *In re Walters & Unborn Fetus*, No. 52658 (Md. Cir. Ct. Jan. 12, 1990). Woman was in premature labor and did not want to be transferred to a hospital a great distance from her home and family. Cited in Goldberg, "Of Gametes and Guardians," n. 156.

78. See *In Re Steven S.*, 126 Cal App. 3d 23, 178 Cal Rptr. 525 (1981), in which a woman was held in a psychiatric hospital until she gave birth. See also Kolder, Gallagher, and Parsons,

"Court-Ordered Obstetrical Interventions," where they describe a young Wisconsin girl who was held against her will because she "tended to be on the run" and lacked "motivation or ability to seek prenatal care." Court-imposed cesarean sections may also require physical restraints.

79. See, e.g., *In re Jamaica Hosp.,* 128 Misc. 2d 1006, 491 N.Y.S.2d 989, 899 (Sup. Ct. 1985). Court-ordered blood transfusion for woman eighteen weeks pregnant. See also Nancy K. Rhoden, "The Judge in the Delivery Room: The Emergence of Court-Ordered Caesareans," *California Law Review* 74:1951 (1986).

80. Kolder, Gallagher, and Parsons, "Court-Ordered Obstetrical Interventions," 1987.

81. Ibid., 1192. In addition to these cases, Kolder et al. note that a number of other documented cases of forced cesarean sections were not reached by their research design. See for example, *Taft v. Taft,* 388 Mass. 331, 446 N.E.2d 395 (1983).

82. It is unclear how many total procedures were ordered and enforced, because Kolder et al. excluded a number of cases that involved either maternal blood transfusions or treatment given after delivery. Additionally, it is not clear whether they include six cases of enforced court orders that were reported to them second-hand from other facilities. Kolder, Gallager, and Parsons, "Court-Ordered Obstetrical Interventions," 1193–1194.

83. Ibid., 1193.

84. Gallagher, "Prenatal Invasions and Interventions," 10; See also Kolder, Gallagher, and Parsons, "Court-Ordered Obstetrical Interventions," 1193.

85. Kolder, Gallagher, and Parsons, "Court-Ordered Obstetrical Interventions," 1193.

86. *Jefferson v. Griffin Spalding County Hospital Authority,* 247 Ga. 86, 274 S.E.2d 457 (1981), as cited in *In Re A.C.,* 573 A.2d 1235 (D.C.App. 1990) at 1243. The woman left the hospital before the court directive could be carried out and subsequently delivered a healthy baby at home, despite earlier medical warnings that her condition of placenta previa (where the placenta prematurely pulls away from the uterus) was life-threatening to both her and her fetus. Flannery, "Court-Ordered Prenatal Intervention," 593.

87. *In Re Madyun,* 114 Daily Wash L Rptr 2233 (DC Sup Ct July 26, 1986).

88. That same court had refused the opportunity to stay the order mandating the cesarean section while Ms. Carder was still alive. *In Re A.C.,* 573 A.2d 1235 at 1237 (D.C. App. 1990).

89. See, for example, Daniels, *At Women's Expense.*

90. *In Re A.C.,* 573 A.2d 1235 at 1249, 1247.

91. Ibid., 1247.

92. Ibid., 1252.

93. Ibid., 1235 at n23.

94. Ibid., 1256–1257, Belson dissenting.

95. Ibid., 1254, 1255, 1254–1258, Belson dissenting.

96. Ibid., 1256, Belson dissenting.

97. Kolder, Gallagher, and Parsons, "Court-Ordered Obstetrical Interventions," 1193.

98. Phelan, "Maternal Abdominal Wall," 485–488. Kolder et al.'s recent survey of physicians at maternal-fetal care centers found that 46 percent of the doctors questioned "thought that mothers who refused medical advice and thereby endangered the life of the fetus should be detained in hospitals or other facilities so that compliance could be ensured." And 47 percent said that the "precedent set by the courts in cases requiring emergency cesarean sections for the sake of the fetus should be extended to include other procedures that are potentially lifesaving for the fetus, such as intrauterine transfusion, as these procedures come to represent the standard of care." In perhaps the most shocking finding, 26 percent "advocated state surveillance of women in the third trimester who stay outside the hospital system." Kolder, Gallagher, and Parsons, "Court-Ordered Obstetrical Interventions," 1193–1194.

99. Phelan, "Maternal Abdominal Wall," 490.

100. Discussed earlier at note 76.

101. Says Kevin Apollo ominously: "In the context of forced medical treatment, the biological father's interest in post viable fetal life should subordinate a woman's constitutional right to privacy. The biological father could require a pregnant woman to bear an increased health risk, through forced medical treatment, until the point when abortion becomes necessary to preserve the life or health of the mother. ... The father ... could force a pregnant woman to submit to nonconsensual medical procedures designed to sustain fetal life before the point of viability so long as the mother's fundamental right to abortion is not endangered." Kevin M. Apollo, "The Biological Father's Right to Require a Pregnant Woman to Undergo Medical Treatment Necessary to Sustain Fetal Life," *Dickinson Law Review* 94(1):219 (Fall 1989).

102. Shona B. Glick, "The Prosecution of Maternal Fetal Abuse: Is This the Answer?" *University of Illinois Law Review* 1991(2):533 (1991); Jerelyn Weiss and Mary Jo Hansell, "Substance Abuse During Pregnancy," *Nursing and Health Care* 13(9):472–473 (November 1992); Tiffany M. Romney, "Prosecuting Mothers of Drug-Exposed Babies: The State's Interest in Protecting the Rights of a Fetus Versus the Mother's Constitutional Rights to Due Process, Privacy and Equal Protection," *Journal of Contemporary Law* 17:328 (1991).

103. Mary K. Kennedy, "Maternal Liability for Prenatal Injury Arising From Substance Abuse During Pregnancy: The Possibility of Cause of Action in Pennsylvania," *Duquesne Law Review* 29(1):557–558 (1991).

104. Romney, "Prosecuting Mothers," 326; Glick, "Prosecution of Maternal Fetal Abuse," 538.

105. An early case was that of Jennifer Johnson, who was convicted in 1988 of delivering cocaine to her twins through the umbilical cord. The court gave her a fifteen-year sentence, including one year of supervised custody and fourteen years of probation. She is required to go to a drug rehabilitation program, do community service, obtain her high school equivalency certificate, abstain from all controlled substances and alcohol, and stay out of bars unless given permission by her probation officer; should she become pregnant again she must enter an approved prenatal program. Kary Moss, "Substance Abuse During Pregnancy," *Harvard Women's Law Journal* 13:280–281 (1990).

106. *People v. K.H.,* No. 89-2931-FY (Mich. Dist. Ct., Muskegon County arraignment on Nov. 12, 1989), cited in Moss, "Substance Abuse During Pregnancy," 284 and n. 37.

107. Moss, "Substance Abuse During Pregnancy," 285 at n. 43.

108. Ibid., 285.

109. Romney, "Prosecuting Mothers," 325–326.

110. Wendy Chavkin, Machelle Harris Allen, and Michelle Oberman, "Drug Abuse and Pregnancy: Some Questions on Public Policy, Clinical Management, and Maternal and Fetal Rights," *Birth* 18(2):110 (June 1991).

111. Romney, "Prosecuting Mothers," 326.

112. *New York Times,* 22 January 1990, B8, Col.6.

113. Solomon, "Future Fear," 416.

114. *In re Danielle Smith,* 128 Misc.2d 979 (N.Y. Fam Ct., 1985), cited in Gallagher, "Prenatal Invasions and Interventions," n. 164.

115. *In Re Jeffrey,* No. 99851 (Mich. Ct. App. filed Apr. 9, 1987), cited in Dawn E. Johnsen, "The Creation of Fetal Rights and Conflicts with Women's Constitutional Rights to Liberty, Privacy and Equal Protection," *Yale Law Journal* 95(3):599–625 (January 1986) 261.

116. Johnsen, "Creation of Fetal Rights," 267. In the "improper eating" case, the fact that the woman "paid no attention to the nutritional value of the food she ate during her pregnancy—she simply picked the foods that tasted good to her without considering whether they were good for her unborn child" was used as evidence in a custody battle over her newborn. She lost custody of the child by court order. Johnsen, 261.

117. Weiss and Hansell, "Substance Abuse During Pregnancy," 475.

118. Ann Oakley, "Commentary: Whose Work Is It, Then?" *Birth,* 20(2):93 (1993); Jeanne F. DeJoseph, "Redefining Women's Work During Pregnancy: Toward a More Comprehensive Approach," *Birth* 20(2):87–89 (1993).

119. Janet L. Tucker, "Wrongful Life: A New Generation," *Journal of Family* 27(3):675 (1988–1989).

120. Johnsen, "Creation of Fetal Rights," 604.

121. Quoted in Kenneth Jost, "Mother Versus Child," *ABA Journal,* April 1989, 87.

122. Susan Bordo, *Unbearable Weight: Feminism, Western Culture, and the Body* (Berkeley: University of California Press, 1993), 82; Gallagher, "Prenatal Invasions and Interventions," n. 177.

123. Kristen Barrett, "Prosecuting Pregnant Addicts for Dealing to the Unborn," *Arizona Law Review* 33(1):230 (1991), emphasis added.

124. Flannery, "Court-Ordered Prenatal Intervention," 597.

125. Barbara Kantrowitz and Vicki Quade, "The Pregnancy Police," *Newsweek,* April 29, 1991, 52.

126. Alan M. Dershowitz, *Contrary to Popular Opinion* (New York: Pharos Books, 1992), 210. Dershowitz also subscribes to compelling women to undergo medical interventions against their will for the sake of the fetus.

127. Apollo, "The Biological Father's Right," 201.

128. Kennedy, "Maternal Liability," 573.

129. Ibid., 571.

130. Overall, *Ethics and Human Reproduction,* 55.

131. C. Condit, *Decoding Abortion Rhetoric,* 206.

132. Ibid., 206.

133. Phelan, "Maternal Abdominal Wall," 461.

134. Apollo, "Biological Father's Right," 201.

135. Rhoden, "The Judge in the Delivery Room," 1959.

136. Osowski, "Need for Logic and Consistency"; Gately, "Texas Fetal Rights"; and Erb and Mortensen, "Wyoming Fetal Rights."

References

Abortion Report [database online]. Falls Church, Va.: American Political Network [cited 8 March 1991]. INTERNET.

Adzick, N. Scott, Michael R. Harrison, Alan W. Flake, Lori J. Howell, Mitchell S. Golbus, Roy A. Filly, and The UCSF Fetal Treatment Center. "Fetal Surgery for Cystic Adenomatoid Malformation in the Lung." *Journal of Pediatric Surgery* 28(6) (1993).

Apollo, Kevin M. "The Biological Father's Right to Require a Pregnant Woman to Undergo Medical Treatment Necessary to Sustain Fetal Life." *Dickinson Law Review* 94(1) (Fall 1989).

Barrett, Kristen. "Prosecuting Pregnant Addicts for Dealing to the Unborn." *Arizona Law Review* 33(1):221–237 (1991).

Bordo, Susan. *Unbearable Weight: Feminism, Western Culture, and the Body.* Berkeley: University of California Press, 1993.

Cardinale, Val. "New Technologies to Revolutionize the Health-Care Field." *Drug Topics,* January 11, 1993.

Chavkin, Wendy, Machelle Harris Allen, and Michelle Oberman. "Drug Abuse and Pregnancy: Some Questions on Public Policy, Clinical Management, and Maternal and Fetal Rights." *Birth* 18:2 (June 1991).

Cohen, Marshall. *Ronald Dworkin and Contemporary Jurisprudence.* Totowa, N.J.: Rowman and Allenheld, 1983.

Condit, Celeste Michelle. *Decoding Abortion Rhetoric, Communicating Social Change.* Urbana: University of Illinois, 1990.

_____. "Within the Confines of the Law: Abortion and a Substantive Rhetoric of Liberty." *Buffalo Law Review* 38(3) (1990).

Condit, Deirdre. "Tugging at Pregnant Consumers: Competing Messages About Cigarette Smoking in the Media." In *Women's Health Care Campaigns: The Rhetoric of Reproduction.* Edited by Roxanne Parrott and Celeste Condit. Urbana: University of Illinois Press, forthcoming (1994).

Crimes Against the Foetus. Ottawa: Law Reform Commission of Canada, 1989.

Danet, Brenda. "Baby or Fetus? Language and the Construction of Reality in a Manslaughter Trial." *Semiotica* 32:4 (1980).

Daniels, Cynthia R. *At Women's Expense: State Power and the Politics of Fetal Rights.* Cambridge, Mass.: Harvard University Press, 1993.

DeJoseph, Jeanne F. "Redefining Women's Work During Pregnancy: Toward a More Comprehensive Approach." *Birth* 20:2 (1993).

Dershowitz, Alan M. *Contrary to Popular Opinion.* New York: Pharos Books, 1992.

Eisenberg, Arlene, Heidi E. Murkoff, and Sandee H. Hathaway. *What to Expect When You're Expecting.* New York: Workman Publishing, 1991.

Erb, Richard A., and Alan W. Mortensen. "Wyoming Fetal Rights—Why the Abortion 'Albatross' is a Bird of a Different Color: The Case for Fetal-Federalism." *Land and Water Law Review* 28(2) (1993).

Facts on File. "Fetuses Shown in Campaign Commercial." 52:2686 (May 14, 1992).

Faux, Marian. *Roe v. Wade.* Ontario: Mercer Books, 1988.

Flannery, Michael T. "Court-Ordered Prenatal Intervention: A Final Means to the End of Gestational Substance Abuse." *Journal of Family Law* 30(3) (1991–1992).

Gallagher, Janet. "Prenatal Invasions and Interventions: What's Wrong With Fetal Rights?" *Harvard Women's Law Journal* 10(9):9–58 (Spring 1987).

Gately, S. Jeffrey. "Texas Fetal Rights: Is There a Future for the Rights of Future Texans?" *St. Mary's Law Journal* 23:305 (1991).

George, B.J. Jr. "State Legislatures Versus the Supreme Court: Abortion Legislation in the 1990's." In *Abortion, Medicine, and the Law* (4th ed). Edited by J. Douglas Butler and David F. Walbert. New York: Facts on File, 1992.

Glantz, Leonard. "Is the Fetus a Person? A Lawyer's View." In *Abortion, Medicine, and the Law* (4th ed). Edited by J. Douglas Butler and David F. Walbert. New York: Facts on File, 1992.

Glick, Shona B. "The Prosecution of Maternal Fetal Abuse: Is This the Answer?" *University of Illinois Law Review* 1991(2) (1991).

Goldberg, Susan. "Of Gametes and Guardians: The Impropriety of Appointing Guardians Ad Litem for Fetuses and Embryos." *Washington Law Review* 66:413 (1991).

Griffith, John P., Helen G. Honorow, and Gary F. Karnedy. "After Bonte: What Is Reasonable?" *New Hampshire Bar Journal* (March 1993).

Hornick, Harriet L. "Mama vs. Fetus." *Medical Trial Technique Quarterly,* 1993 Annual.

Johnsen, Dawn E. "The Creation of Fetal Rights and Conflicts with Women's Constitutional Rights to Liberty, Privacy and Equal Protection." *Yale Law Journal* 95(3):599–625 (January 1986).

Jost, Kenneth. "Mother Versus Child." *ABA Journal* (April 1989).

Kantrowitz, Barbara and Vicki Quade. "The Pregnancy Police." *Newsweek,* April 29, 1991.

Kelly, James R. "A Political Challenge to the Prolife Movement and Towards a Post-*Webster* Agenda." *Commonweal,* November 23, 1990.

Kennedy, Mary K. "Maternal Liability for Prenatal Injury Arising From Substance Abuse During Pregnancy: The Possibility of Cause of Action in Pennsylvania." *Duquesne Law Review* 29(1) (1991).

Knopoff, Katherine A. "Can a Pregnant Woman Morally Refuse Fetal Surgery?" *California Law Review* 79:499 (1991).

Kolder, Veronika E.B., Janet Gallagher, and Michael T. Parsons. "Court-ordered Obstetrical Interventions." *The New England Journal of Medicine* 316(19):1192–1196 (1987).

Luker, Kristin. *Abortion and the Politics of Motherhood.* Berkeley: University of California Press, 1984.

Moss, Kary. "Substance Abuse During Pregnancy." *Harvard Women's Law Journal* 13:278 (Spring 1990).

The Nature of Sex, "A Miracle in the Making," Genesis Films, 1993.

Nelson, Lawrence J., Brian P. Buggy, and Carol J. Weil. "Forced Medical Treatment of Pregnant Women: 'Compelling Each to Live as Seems Good to the Rest.'" *The Hastings Law Journal* 37(5):703–763 (May 1986).

New York Times. 22 January 1990, B8, Col.6.

Nilsson, Lennart. *A Child Is Born.* New York: Dell Publishing, 1990.

Note. "Torts, Wrongful Death and Unborn Child." *Michigan Law Review* 70(4) (1972).

Oakley, Ann. "Commentary: Whose Work Is It, Then?" *Birth,* 20(2) (1993).

Olsen, Frances. "Comment: Unraveling Compromise," *Harvard Law Review* 103:43 (1989).

Okin, Susan Moller. *Women in Western Political Thought.* Princeton, N.J.: Princeton University Press, 1979.

Osowski, Beth Driscoll. "The Need for Logic and Consistency in Fetal Rights." *North Dakota Law Review* 68:171 (1992).

Overall, Christine. *Ethics and Human Reproduction: A Feminist Analysis.* Boston: Allen & Unwin, 1987.

Packwood, Robert. "The Rise and Fall of the Right-to-Life Movement in Congress: Response to the *Roe* Decision, 1973–1983." In *Abortion, Medicine and the Law* (4th ed). Edited by J. Douglas Butler and David F. Walbert. New York: Facts on File, 1992.

Petchesky, Rosalind Pollack. "Fetal Images: The Power of Visual Culture in the Politics of Reproduction." *Feminist Studies* 13(2) (1987).

_____. *Abortion and Woman's Choice: The State Sexuality and Reproductive Freedom* (revised edition). Boston: Northeastern University Press, 1990.

Phelan, Jeffrey P. "The Maternal Abdominal Wall: A Fortress Against Fetal Health Care?" *Southern California Law Review* 65:46 (1991).

Pollitt, Katha. "Fetal Rights: A New Assault on Feminism." *The Nation,* March 26, 1990.

Rhoden, Nancy K. "The Judge in the Delivery Room: The Emergence of Court-Ordered Caesareans." *California Law Review* 74:1951 (1986).

Rodgers, Sanda. "Fetal Rights and Maternal Rights: Is There a Conflict?" *Canadian Journal of Women and the Law* 1(2) (1986).

Romney, Tiffany M. "Prosecuting Mothers of Drug-Exposed Babies: The State's Interest in Protecting the Rights of a Fetus Versus the Mother's Constitutional Rights to Due Process, Privacy and Equal Protection." *Journal of Contemporary Law* 17(2):325–344 (1991).

Sartorius, Rolf. "Dworkin on Rights and Utilitarianism." In *Ronald Dworkin and Contemporary Jurisprudence.* Edited by Marshall Cohen. Totowa, N.J.: Rowman and Allenheld, 1984.

"Saving Lives Not Yet Begun." *People Weekly,* June 18, 1990, 40.

Solomon, Rennee I. "Future Fear: Prenatal Duties Imposed by Private Parties." *American Journal of Law and Medicine* 17:4 (1991).

Stabile, Carol. "Shooting the Mother: Fetal Photography and the Politics of Disappearance." *Camera Obscura* 28:179 (January 1, 1992).

Tribe, Lawrence H. *Abortion: the Clash of Absolutes*. New York: W. W. Norton, 1990.

Trindel, Robin M. "Fetal Interests vs. Maternal Rights: Is the State Going Too Far?" *Akron Law Review* 24(3 & 4):743–762 (1991).

Tucker, Janet L. "Wrongful Life: A New Generation." *Journal of Family* 27(3):673–696 (1989).

Volpe, F. Peter. *Patient in the Womb*. Macon, Ga.: Mercer University Press, 1984.

Weiss, Jerelyn and Mary Jo Hansell. "Substance Abuse During Pregnancy." *Nursing and Health Care* 13:9 (November 1992).

White, James Boyd. "Thinking About Our Language." *The Yale Law Journal* 96:1960 (1987).

Wilkin, Robert N. *Origins of the Natural Rights Tradition*. Port Washington, N.Y.: Kennikat Press, 1954.

Fetal Endangerment Versus
Fetal Welfare: Discretion
of Prosecutors in
Determining Criminal Liability

RUTH ANN STRICKLAND &
MARCIA LYNN WHICKER

WE SURVEYED THE FIFTY STATE ATTORNEYS GENERAL in the United States and asked them what criminal charges might be applicable to pregnant women who expose fetuses to "prenatal hazards." As of July 1992, no state had a law on the books that made it a crime for a pregnant woman to expose her child to any potentially damaging drug, substance, or prenatal hazard. Yet we found a wide array of policies toward substance abuse during pregnancy, including local prosecutors who utilize a number of existing child welfare statutes to charge pregnant substance abusers.

We ascertained the treatment for pregnant defendants that sixteen attorneys general recommended to state prosecutors or district attorneys in this rapidly developing legal area. Numerous offices were quite helpful; some had no authority to provide guidance to state prosecutors; others stated reluctance to participate in this survey because policy in their state was not fully formulated. In some instances, attorneys general did not complete the survey because fetal endangerment is a political hot potato and generally difficult to address. In order to broaden our information base, we also contacted and requested information from various interest groups and government agencies.[1]

Substance Abuse, Prenatal Hazards, and Fetal Endangerment

Substance Abuse and Pregnancy: According to a 1988 survey of thirty-six hospitals conducted by the National Association for Perinatal Addiction Research and Education (NAPARE), approximately 375,000 newborns may be affected by substance abuse in the United States every year. In the hospitals surveyed, the drug exposure rate varied from less than 1 percent to a high of 26 percent. Another 1988 survey of eighteen hospitals (fourteen public and four private) in fifteen large urban centers conducted by the U.S. House of Representatives Select Committee on Children, Youth, and Families found a substantial rise since 1985 in the number of infants exposed prenatally to crack and other illegal drugs. In urban areas, one out of every ten babies may have been exposed to cocaine in the womb. Another study estimates that a child is born every ninety seconds in the United States who has been exposed to alcohol or a drug.[2] A study released by the National Institutes of Health in 1989 found that one of the fastest growing groups of new drug users is women aged eighteen to thirty-four, who are in their prime childbearing years.[3]

Prenatal Hazards: Prenatal risks or hazards encompass a complex set of environmental and genetic influences, ranging from crack cocaine, to alcohol, to cigarettes (see Table 4.1). Despite today's heated debate concerning prenatal hazards, many other risk factors receive little attention, including malnutrition, exposure to poverty, lack of prenatal medical care, lack of prenatal education, and battering of pregnant women and their fetuses.[4] Maternal substance abuse and prenatal hazards are not new issues, but the recent dramatic rise in the number of infants exposed to drugs and the concomitant burden placed on child welfare agencies has drawn attention to the issue of fetal abuse or fetal endangerment.[5]

Although there are numerous prenatal hazards that might lead to charges of fetal endangerment, the most widely discussed are cocaine and alcohol. A new term has been coined for children born to mothers who abuse drugs or alcohol—the "bio-underclass." Cocaine exposure may cause the mother's uterus to contract spasmodically, resulting in premature birth. It may also block the flow of nutrients and oxygen to the developing fetal body and brain—in effect strangling and starving the fetus. NAPARE claims that a mother's cocaine use places infants at ten times higher risk of crib death. Cocaine use while pregnant may also contribute to low birth weight, fetal strokes, brain damage, withdrawal convulsions, physical malformations, respiratory disorders, and other long-term health problems for the surviving infant.[6]

Fetal alcohol syndrome, induced by heavy drinking during pregnancy, can also lead to fetal disorders, including nervous system dysfunction, mental retardation, learning disabilities, delirium tremors, hyperactivity, and antisocial be-

TABLE 4.1   Prenatal Hazards: Estimates of Exposure and Adverse Effects

Types of Hazards/Risks	Estimates of Exposure/Adverse Effects
Crack/cocaine	Ten thousand to 100,000 infants per year are affected by exposure to crack/cocaine.
	Harmful Effects: premature birth, low birth weight, tremors, genital-urinary tract disorders, irritability, and fetal tachycardia
Other illicit drugs (i.e., marijuana, amphetamines, opiates, PCP)	Approximately 350,000 to 375,000 infants may be exposed to some illicit substance.
	Harmful Effects: lethargy, premature birth, low birth weight, skull malformations, neurological disorders, developmental problems, tremors, wakefulness, and heightened risk of sudden infant death syndrome
Tobacco	Approximately 750,000 infants are exposed to cigarette smoke and by-products each year.
	Harmful Effects: spontaneous abortion, decreased birth weight, increased likelihood of sudden infant death syndrome, tremors, and abnormal responses to sound
Carbon monoxide	No estimates exist of fetal exposure to carbon monoxide concentrations in major urban areas or of those living near industrial plans.
	Harmful Effects: same as exposure to one pack of cigarettes a day
Lead	Over 40,000 prenatal exposures occur annually. In the United States, the average woman is not exposed in high risk employment industries but rather the exposure comes from lead-based paints and leaded gasolines.
	Harmful Effects: post-birth delay in cognitive development, neurobehavioral problems, and impaired hearing
Alcohol	As many as 6,000 to 8,000 infants per year are born with fetal alcohol syndrome.
	Harmful Effects: irritability, lowering of IQs, mental retardation, hyperactivity, facial abnormalities such as malformed lips or misaligned teeth, impulsiveness, lack of concentration, and social withdrawal
Genetic conditions	An estimated 30,000 infants per year are born with a major genetic condition.
	Harmful Effects: vary according to the condition
Infectious diseases	It is expected that 4,000 to 5,000 infants will contract HIV from their mother during pregnancy.
	Harmful Effects: neurological problems, frequent illnesses, stunted physical growth, and death

SOURCES: Kathleen Nolan, "Protecting Fetuses from Prenatal Hazards: Whose Crime? What Punishment?" *Criminal Justice Ethics* 9:14–15 (Winter-Spring 1990); B. Bower, "Alcohol's Fetal Harm Lasts a Lifetime." *Science News* 139:244 (20 April 1991); Ariel Ahart, Carolyn Rutsch, and Cynthia Holmes, Macro Systems, Inc. *Programs Serving Drug-Exposed Children and Their Families*. Vol. 1. Contract No. HHS-100-87-0039. Submitted to Assistant Secretary for Planning and Evaluation, U.S. Department of Health and Human Services, 1991; Helen M. Barr, Ann Pytkowicz Streissguth, Betty L. Darby, and Paul D. Sampson, "Prenatal Exposure to Alcohol, Caffeine, Tobacco and Aspirin: Fine and Gross Motor Performance in 4-Year-Old Chidren," *Developmental Psychology* 26:339–348 (1990).

havior. The heightened public awareness of fetal alcohol syndrome has led some concerned citizens to intrude on the privacy of some pregnant women. For example, in Seattle, Washington, bartenders refused to serve an expectant mother a strawberry daiquiri; they were fired for rudeness but became local heroes for adhering to their principles. In New York City, a pregnant woman in a restaurant asked her waiter for a glass of wine with her meal. A stranger came over to admonish her, angrily asking, "Don't you know you're poisoning your baby?" He pointed to a sign, mandated by local ordinance, that explained that drinking during pregnancy is a prenatal hazard, possibly causing birth defects.[7] Since the mid-1980s, the behavior of pregnant women has also been increasingly monitored by the state and has resulted increasingly in criminal charges and prosecutions.

A Sample of Fetal Abuse Cases: Criminal Charges and Prosecutions

An examination of thirteen instances where women were either charged criminally or coerced into treatment for fetal endangerment illustrates the complexity of this policy problem. Because many states do not consider a fetus to be a "person" until after birth, many of these cases are quite complex. Prosecutors have typically relied on the charge of delivering drugs to a minor, which they arrived at by reasoning that drugs may have been delivered to the infant via the umbilical cord in the moments immediately following birth. As one prosecutor put it, "Our theory is that once the child has passed through the birth canal and showed signs of life, but prior to the time the umbilical cord was detached, that the delivery of the crack cocaine occurred during that time period."[8]

1. *Pamela Ray Stewart Monson:* In 1986, Pamela Ray Stewart Monson's failure to follow her doctor's instructions—to avoid illegal drug use, abstain from sexual intercourse in the final months of pregnancy, stay off her feet, and seek immediate medical attention should she start hemorrhaging—generated the first case to reach the courts on grounds of fetal endangerment. Criminal charges were levied against her, and though the judge threw her case out of court, her conduct focused attention on the problem of infants born with severe physical and psychological abnormalities. Since Monson's debut in court, women in over twenty states and the District of Columbia have been charged with or prosecuted for testing positive for illegal substances during their pregnancies.[9]

2. *Lynn Bremer:* In Muskegon County, Michigan, Lynn Bremer, an attorney, gave birth to a child in 1991 who tested positive for the presence of drugs. Although Bremer had a good job, she was unable to shake her cocaine addiction after she became pregnant. After her daughter tested positive, health officials placed the child into temporary custody. Subsequently, Bremer was charged with felonious delivery of drugs to a newborn via her umbilical cord. To regain

custody of her child, Bremer had to undergo drug rehabilitation. The prosecutor claimed that the only way to bring pregnant addicts to treatment was the threat of a prison term. On appeal, the case against Bremer was thrown out.[10]

3. *Doris Coney:* In Cordele, Georgia, Doris Coney became the first woman in state history to be convicted of delivering drugs to an unborn child. Her daughter tested positive for cocaine and showed cocaine withdrawal symptoms in 1989. Coney pleaded guilty to one count of cocaine distribution. As a mother of three, Coney appeared to care for her children and was allowed to keep them prior to sentencing while under intensive supervision by the Department of Family and Children Services. The prosecutor planned to recommend probation rather than a prison sentence that would range from five to thirty years.[11]

4. *Latrena Grayson:* In Sedgwick County, Kansas, Latrena Grayson informed physicians that she had smoked marijuana laced with cocaine before arriving at the hospital to give birth to daughter Kalina in 1991. After the child was born the doctor advised Grayson not to breast-feed because she still had cocaine in her body and might pass the drug on to the baby. Despite this warning, Grayson was found breast-feeding Kalina three times by a social worker. After the third encounter, the child was placed into the custody of the Department of Social and Rehabilitation Services and Grayson was charged with child endangerment.[12]

5. *Toni Suzette Hudson:* In Altamonte Springs, Florida, Toni Hudson gave birth to a baby boy on November 13, 1988. At the time of birth, she passed on syphilis and an addiction to cocaine. Hudson confessed to a social worker that she smoked crack cocaine nearly every day during her pregnancy and was subsequently charged with delivering cocaine to a minor. These charges were eventually dropped when Hudson pleaded guilty to drug possession, accepted probation, sought treatment, and offered up her son for adoption.[13]

6. *Teresa Boster:* In Alaska, Teresa Boster gave birth in 1988 to a baby who was eight weeks premature. It was born trembling, indicating the presence of drugs. Doctors administered urine tests and discovered that both mother and infant had drugs in their bodies. The child's father, Charles Boster, provided a written statement alleging that his wife had used cocaine before the birth. Teresa Boster was charged with reckless endangerment of the infant rather than assault because the baby appeared to be unharmed.[14]

7. *Laura Moute:* In Orange County, California, Laura Moute, a pregnant prostitute who was also a routine cocaine user, snorted three to five lines of cocaine one day in November 1988 and went into labor the next. She failed to go to the hospital in the first twenty-four hours after contractions began. When she did arrive at the hospital and the doctors detected a fetal heartbeat, she tried to leave the emergency room, claiming that she would prefer that the fetus died. She stayed only because of the baby's breech position and hospital warnings that if she left without a cesarean section she too would die. Moute's newborn daughter had underdeveloped lungs and required six weeks of hospitalization. Moute was never charged with a crime, although the district attorney wanted to

charge her with attempted homicide. At that time, California's child abuse laws made no provision for fetal abuse.[15]

8. *Connie Sue O'Neal:* In 1990, Connie Sue O'Neal, a drug addict, exhibited needle marks from head to toe and even on her breasts—evidence of fifteen years of drug addiction. She injected oxycodone, a painkiller, into her neck just days before giving birth to her son, Steven. Steven suffered tremors, vomiting, sleeplessness, and could have died or been permanently impaired. O'Neal became the first woman in Kentucky to be convicted of second degree criminal abuse of a child by taking drugs during pregnancy. She was also convicted on possession of narcotics and possessing the paraphernalia to inject them.[16]

9. *Beverly Amos (aka Traci Jackson):* While visiting some friends and smoking crack cocaine, Amos went to the bathroom for a half-hour. A stillborn boy was later found wrapped in a shirt inside the bathroom closet. Known as a Houston prostitute, Amos was charged with possession of cocaine after traces of the drug were found in the stillborn's body and a grand jury indicted her for ingesting a "deadly weapon." Jackson was sentenced to twelve years in prison for drug abuse during pregnancy. The American Civil Liberties Union (ACLU) took the case and plans to claim sex discrimination in its defense of Amos. The ACLU's strategy on appeal will be to claim unequal application of a law, invasion of privacy, and unreasonable search and seizure.[17]

10. *Louise Whitfield:* In 1991, Louise Whitfield, a crack cocaine addict in Tallahassee, Florida, gave birth to her third child in three years. In 1989, her first child was taken away because cocaine was found in his bloodstream. In 1990, her second child was made a ward of the state because she tested positive for cocaine. The child born in 1991 was taken away because she too had cocaine in her system. After being released from the hospital, Whitfield was taken to jail and charged with delivering cocaine to a child. The police investigator claimed that Whitfield's sister had also been arrested on a similar charge and that between the two sisters there were five crack babies.[18]

11. *Carol W.:* In Butte County, California, heroin addict Carol W. was pregnant. Her county was putting together a treatment program for methamphetamine addiction, not geared to her addiction. She commuted 140 miles daily to Sacramento to reach the nearest methadone clinic. After several months of commuting, her car broke down and the money she needed for the $200-per-month methadone treatment ran out. Carol W. could have gone cold turkey, but experts agreed that this strategy could traumatize and even kill the fetus. So Carol rekindled her heroin addiction. At the hospital to deliver the child, Carol W. admitted to a heroin problem and was identified for possible prosecution. As a result of statements made by the Butte County District Attorney and a petition from Butte County Child Protective Services, Carol W.'s child, Stephen W., was made a dependent of juvenile court and placed in the custody of his grandparents. Carol W. fought for her son's custody but has so far been denied.[19]

12. *Diane Pfannenstiel:* Cal Rerucha, the county prosecutor of Albany County, Wyoming, filed criminal child abuse charges against Diane Pfannenstiel in 1989, alleging that she had endangered her as-yet-unborn infant by consuming an excessive amount of alcohol. Pfannenstiel had participated in an Antabuse program as directed by the Department of Social Services but stopped a short time before she discovered her pregnancy. In his presentation against her, the prosecutor cited her failure to continue receiving treatment. Expert witnesses, who were scheduled to be called if the case had gone to trial, claimed that the Antabuse drug has fetal risks that outweigh exposure to alcohol. The judge dismissed the charges on the grounds that proving what caused the injury, if indeed harm had occurred, could not be easily established since either alcohol or the treatment for alcohol abuse, Antabuse, might be the source.[20]

13. *Barbara Myles:* In Long Beach, California, Barbara Myles gave birth to Kristopher. The Harbor-UCLA Medical Center staff conducted a urine test and "found" cocaine; shortly thereafter in 1986 the baby was taken away. Myles demanded a retest, claiming that she didn't use drugs. The second test revealed no traces of cocaine and Kristopher was returned to his mother. Seven months after the event, Myles claimed that she had been emotionally damaged by the forced separation from her son and her attorney filed a $10 million medical malpractice lawsuit against the Torrance hospital and Los Angeles County.[21]

*   *   *

As these stories of women's encounters with the criminal justice system suggest, pregnant substance abusers are beginning to be treated as criminals because of the harm they do their babies in utero.

Reasons for Prosecutions

Several states are considering statutes that would specifically criminalize the use of drugs during pregnancy, and other states are using a variety of already existing criminal statutes to prosecute substance-abusing mothers.[22] To date, South Carolina, where thirty women were indicted by 1992 for criminal negligence of a child, drug possession, or distributing drugs to a minor, is the most aggressive state. A number of reasons to justify criminal prosecutions of maternal drug use and fetal endangerment have been put forward by prosecutors, judges, and public health officials. These arguments are based on several assumptions, claims, and positions. Among the most prominent are the following:

1. *A Woman Has a Moral Duty to Her Offspring:* Despite fetal endangerment prosecutions, most states grant women the right to abortion through the ninth month of pregnancy. Still, many argue that the unborn have rights as well. They contend that once a woman has decided to carry the fetus to full term, she takes on a moral obligation to her offspring. Thus, those in favor of criminalizing fetal

abuse argue that the maternal rights of privacy and bodily integrity must be balanced against the well-being of the fetus.[23]

Under this view, children have a right to be born drug-free and parents have a responsibility to bear healthy children. In justifying a ruling against a substance-abusing mother, Family Court Judge Frederica S. Brenneman argued there is no difference between taking out a needle and injecting cocaine into oneself hours before delivering a child and taking out a needle and injecting cocaine into the baby's body after it has been delivered.[24] And in an interview with the *Boston Globe,* Harvard Law School Professor Alan Dershowitz expressed reservations about a pregnant woman's unregulated privacy rights by stating that he thought it immoral for a pregnant woman to drink or smoke, although he did not know whether he would make it a crime.[25] Indeed, many believe that society has an obligation to protect the unborn from intentional harm. Many courts have held that mothers must exercise a reasonable standard of care.

2. Roe v. Wade *Gives the State an Interest in Fetal Protection:* In *Roe v. Wade* (1973), the U.S. Supreme Court recognized that viability of the fetus imposes some obligations on the state. Blackmun wrote that the state had a "compelling" interest in protecting potential life once the fetus could survive outside the mother's womb. In *Webster v. Reproductive Health Services* (1989) and more recently in *Planned Parenthood v. Casey* (1992), the Supreme Court expanded the state's ability to regulate abortion. Some see the *Webster* decision, which upheld requiring viability testing for twentieth-week and later pregnancies, as lending support both to fetal rights and to legislation regulating fetal harm.[26]

3. *Fetuses Have Rights:* There is controversy surrounding whether the fetus has the same rights as a person and, if so, the point at which such rights accrue. Some right-to-life advocates and prosecutors claim that if the fetus could survive outside of the mother's womb it should be protected to the same degree as a newborn. After viability, which is still roughly considered twenty-four weeks, some argue that the substance-abusing mother can be prosecuted for delivering drugs to a minor. In South Carolina, some prosecutors argue that case law supports the notion that the fetus is a person if it is viable and can survive without the aid of medical machinery.[27]

4. *Prosecution Will Enhance Treatment:* In Charleston, South Carolina pregnant women who are identified as substance abusers are told that if they attend free classes on substance addiction they will not be prosecuted. But the threat of prosecution is always there.[28] Many prosecutors do not wish to go to trial or punish substance-abusing mothers and instead use deferred prosecution, drug education, and treatment combined with urinalysis as a condition of probation.[29] Offering only the choice between a drug rehabilitation program and jail, prosecutors believe most women will seek treatment. In their view, the leverage created by the threat of incarceration is the only way to force abusers into treatment since most believe that pregnant women who use drugs will not voluntarily seek help.[30]

5. *Prosecution May Deter Future Drug Abuse:* A number of prosecutors claim that if substance-abusing mothers are threatened with a jail term, probation, or some other penalty, all pregnant women will be deterred from drug abuse. For example, after Connie O'Neal's conviction, Boyd County, Kentucky's prosecutor D. David Hagerman stated that he believed his success in this case would have a "chilling effect" on other addicts in Kentucky.[31]

6. *Physiological Costs of Drug-Exposed Infants, Especially Prematurity and Low Birth Weight, Are Great:* In 1980 alone, low birth weight among newborns accounted for 60 percent of all infant deaths (the data do not indicate how many of these newborns were drug-exposed). Low birth weight infants are also more prone to suffer from cerebral palsy, epilepsy, mental retardation, breathing problems, blindness, and delayed speech. An estimated 30 percent of drug-exposed infants are born prematurely; most are underweight. Furthermore, drugs such as heroin, cocaine, and methadone induce fetal addiction during pregnancy, causing newborns exposed to these drugs to experience withdrawal symptoms. The development of drug-exposed infants may vary from the norm—many are supersensitive babies who early on avoid eye contact, have a high-pitched cry, and are hard to console when upset. Some cocaine-exposed infants may experience motor development problems, such as differences in reflex reactions and tremors in the arms and hands. Studies show that although drug use may adversely affect the fetus at any point during pregnancy, women who cease using drugs early during pregnancy have healthier babies than those who use drugs consistently throughout the pregnancy.[32] (Table 4.1 summarizes information on possible physiological effects of drugs on the fetus.)

7. *Societal Costs of Drug-Addicted Infants Are Great:* Hospitals, insurance plans, and Medicaid plans are forced to expend scarce resources when crack mothers deliver babies with substantial health problems. For example, in 1986, there were 915 prenatal substance abuse cases; those newborns incurred $32 million in hospital care costs—$34,970 per newborn. Furthermore, many drug-exposed babies remain in hospitals even though they no longer require medical care, because of parental abandonment, backlogged child welfare authorities, and lack of foster homes. In June 1989, a survey of five major U.S. cities found that there were 304 "boarder" babies, most of whom were victims of their mother's drug abuse.[33] The costs of hospital care for drug-exposed infants run to tens of thousands of dollars per baby, and the need to deter mothers from substance abuse is underlined by the increasing numbers of infants who require sophisticated neonatal care[34] and by the overwhelmed child welfare systems.[35]

Fetal Endangerment and Criminal Prosecution: A Pregnancy Police State?

Some people view prosecutions for fetal endangerment as an ill-advised response to our nation's drug problem, arguing that such prosecutions are much more likely to be brought against poor and nonwhite women and are unlikely to be effective. These critics argue that drug abuse during pregnancy should be viewed as a public health problem and not a criminal justice problem. Reasons for stopping criminal prosecutions for fetal endangerment are as follows:

1. *Prosecution May Deter Women from Seeking Medical Care or Treatment:* Representatives from the ACLU have claimed that aggressive prosecution for substance abuse will drive pregnant women underground. Fear of prosecution will deter substance-abusing mothers from seeking prenatal services. For example, Candace Woolery of Greenville, South Carolina was charged with criminal neglect for giving birth to a baby with heroin in her bloodstream. Woolery stated that she did not believe in abortion so she carried the child to term and also stated that she did not seek prenatal care for fear of losing custody of her children. Woolery, who was unemployed and did not complete a high school education, had no money for treatment; although she tried to find an in-patient hospital to kick the heroin addiction, no hospital would take her.[36]

A 1990 General Accounting Office report suggests, more women choose to have babies at home rather than risk drug prosecution from the state or possible separation from their children. If true, then the health of children will be further endangered. Waiting lists for treatment programs indicate that pregnant substance abusers are indeed interested in voluntary treatment.[37] Others claim that when uniformed police officers arrive at hospitals to investigate a mother's possible drug abuse, patient-doctor trust is undermined. If drug-abusing mothers don't trust their physicians, infants may be denied crucial prenatal and neonatal care.[38]

2. *Fetal Endangerment Is a Health Care Problem, Not a Criminal Problem:* Some claim that prosecuting substance-abusing mothers is blaming the victim. Many of the women who abuse drugs while pregnant have endured sexual or physical abuse for which the perpetrators were not arrested or prosecuted. Yet when they turn to drugs as a means of coping, they are arrested and prosecuted. Further, putting pregnant substance abusers in jail will not necessarily end their drug habit, since drugs flow freely in jail cells.[39] As a consequence, it is no surprise that at least thirty-six national interest groups and organizations oppose criminal prosecution for maternal substance abuse (see Table 4.2).

3. *Fetal Abuse Prosecutions Weaken the Family Structure:* If a mother is jailed for drug abuse and separated from her child, the baby may either be placed in foster care or with a close relative. In either scenario the child loses, especially if drug treatment might have kept the family unit together. Children who are placed in foster homes are often shifted from home to home, which can exacerbate the problems associated with prenatal substance abuse. Furthermore, many babies of substance-abusing mothers are never adopted and never experience parental stability.[40]

4. *A Woman's Bodily Integrity and Privacy Must Be Maintained:* If the decision to have a child and not abort means that one has waived the constitutional right

TABLE 4.2   Organizations Opposing Criminal Prosecution of Maternal Substance Abuse

American Academy of Pediatrics
American Association for Counseling and Development
Americal Civil Liberties Union
American College of Nurse Mid-Wives
American College of Obstetricians and Gynecologists
American Medical Association
American Medical Students Association
American Nurses Association
American Public Health Association
American Society of Addiction Medicine
Association of Marriage and Family Therapists
Association of Maternal and Child Health Programs
Association of Maternal and Child Health Therapists
Center for Child Protection and Family Support
Center for Law and Social Policy
Center for Reproductive Law and Policy
Center for Science in the Public Interest
Child Welfare League of America
Children of Alcoholics Association
Criminal Justice Policy Association
Legal Action Center
March of Dimes
National Abortion Rights Action League
National Association for Children of Alcoholics
National Association of Alcoholism and Drug Abuse Counselors
National Association of Perinatal Addiction Research and Education
National Association of Public Child Welfare Administrators
National Council of Jewish Women
National Council on Alcohol and Drug Dependence
National Family Planning and Reproductive Health Association
National Women's Health Network
National Women's Law Center
NOW Legal Defense and Education Fund
Southern Regional Project on Infant Mortality
Women's Legal Defense Fund

SOURCE: Janet Dinsmore, "Pregnant Drug Users: The Debate over Prosecution." [monograph] American Prosecutors Research Institute: National Center for Prosecution of Child Abuse, Appendix A (March 1992). Used by permission.

to privacy, then the state has created a serious penalty for becoming pregnant.[41] Many fear that women's rights to bodily integrity will be sacrificed because of the irresponsibility of a few: Women who abuse drugs and alcohol or engage in other harmful behaviors while pregnant make it more likely that others will question the judgment of any pregnant woman who chooses to have a social drink or to engage in some other "high risk" activity.[42]

5. *The Fetus Is Not an Independent Person:* Using laws to prosecute women for fetal abuse appears to grant the fetus personhood. To the extent that prosecu-

tions recognize the harm that drugs can have on the fetus, they could severely restrict or even end a woman's access to abortion. Should a woman's right to choose abortion be threatened? Should a woman be put in an adversarial position against her baby?[43] Since the fetus has not been traditionally recognized as an independent and separate person, the new adversarial stance taken toward women by prosecutors in prenatal substance abuse cases deviates dramatically from precedent.[44]

6. *Criminal Prosecutions May Encourage Abortion:* On the one hand, right-to-life activists want rights for the unborn; on the other hand, criminal prosecution or threat of legal intervention may drive drug-abusing mothers underground as they choose abortion over a jail term.[45] As Robert E. Griesemer, executive director of the Schenectady County Right to Life Committee, stated: "I might get in trouble for injuring my unborn baby, so I'll kill it."[46]

7. *Criminal Prosecutions Are Discriminatory:* Although drug use is as prevalent among the middle class as among the poor, women who are prosecuted tend to be poor and minorities. Studies show that black and white women are equally predisposed to drug use during pregnancy, yet a disproportionate share of black infants are reported as drug addicted.[47] In an ACLU study of fifty substance abuse cases where women were arrested, 80 percent of those charges were brought against "women of color, poor women and battered women."[48]

Some argue that this pattern in reporting and charging is caused by the greater likelihood of black and poor women to use publicly funded programs when delivering a baby (where they are under greater government supervision by welfare agencies or probation officers), whereas a greater share of white women can rely on private physicians who are less likely to report infant drug addiction. The case of Lynn Bremer, the Michigan attorney charged with fetal abuse, is the exception rather than the rule. Most of the women who are tested are uninsured or underinsured. More affluent mothers are less likely to be declared unfit mothers or to have their children taken away.[49]

Furthermore, men somehow escape scrutiny even though recent research suggests that excessive alcohol consumption, cocaine abuse, and exposure to other chemicals by a father can affect his sperm and cause harm to his offspring.[50] Why aren't the authorities as diligent in monitoring fathers?

8. *Criminal Intent Cannot Easily Be Established:* So far illicit drugs are the focus of criminal prosecutions, but how do we keep the net of social control from widening? Any act that causes harm to the fetus—whether it is smoking, drinking coffee, driving a car, or even jogging—might be interpreted as intentional, knowing, reckless, or negligent.[51] Recall the case of Dianne Pfannenstiel, the Wyoming woman charged with child abuse for drinking alcohol during pregnancy. The question of intent was unclear. Absent proof to the contrary, how could she have known that she may have been inflicting harm on the fetus?

9. *Available Treatment Is Woefully Inadequate:* Nationwide, the number of available drug treatment facilities for pregnant women is very low; there are only

ten to twenty programs set up specifically to treat pregnant women.[52] Often substance-abusing mothers want treatment but help is not available or easily accessible, as in the case of Carol W. Substance-abusing pregnant women are confronted with long commutes, costly payments for treatment, and long waiting lists to get into drug treatment programs. A survey of New York City found that of seventy-eight day treatment centers, over half did not accept pregnant women and 87 percent would not treat poor women on Medicaid who were addicted to crack. Only 2 percent of the programs provided day care services.[53]

One reason that clinics are reluctant to accept pregnant addicts is they are often relatively expensive clients to treat. Thus, at the Berkeley Addiction Treatment Clinic where Carol W. sought treatment for heroin addiction, the state only reimburses the clinic at $10 per patient, no matter what complications or risks are associated with treatment. Similarly, some hospitals will accept pregnant women for drug treatment within the first six months of pregnancy but turn them away during the last trimester. Because such late-term pregnancies are usually high risk, many hospitals simply refuse to treat them.[54]

10. *Fetal Abuse Prosecutions Should Be Voided for Vagueness Because They Violate Due Process:* If prosecutors seek to define a list of "prenatal hazards" that goes beyond illicit drugs to include tobacco, exposure to carbon monoxide, aspirin, lead found in lead-based paint, alcohol, and infectious diseases such as AIDs,[55] charging women with fetal endangerment under child welfare statutes is likely to result in those statutes being voided for vagueness. It is difficult to craft a criminal statute narrowly enough to avoid impinging on a woman's privacy rights and bodily integrity; obviously, no woman can provide the "perfect womb."[56] Prosecuting pregnant women under broadly phrased child welfare laws, which may not give proper notice that use of drugs is illegal, violates women's due process rights.[57]

The degree of flexibility accorded to prosecutors as they implement such statutes, along with existing sanctions for negligence, child abuse, and "distributing drugs to a minor," violates pregnant women's due process rights and relegates them to second-class citizenship. How much bodily integrity and self-determination will be taken away by state paternalism and fetal rights lobbyists? How much discretion should prosecutors have in determining criminal liability in so-called "fetal abuse" cases?

Civil libertarians, child health professionals, and women's groups question the wisdom and constitutionality of applying existing statutes on child endangerment, delivering drugs to a minor, child abuse, and assault with a deadly weapon to substance-abusing mothers. Such an approach is problematic on a number of grounds: It fails to give pregnant women adequate warning what behaviors are illegal; it treats fetuses as though they were already persons under the law; it pits women's rights against the rights of their fetuses; and it encourages prosecutors to overreach the proper bounds of their authority and discretion.

Survey of Attorneys General Offices

Because we found these arguments interesting and important, we decided to survey offices of state attorneys general. We surveyed all fifty attorneys general in the United States to gauge their reactions to fetal abuse prosecutions and to ascertain their views on how fetal abuse cases should be handled. Our findings follow.

In our survey, sixteen offices provided responses to the survey questions and four other offices provided reasons for not responding at this time. (See Appendix I for survey instrument.) Eight of the sixteen offices noted that no criminal prosecutions had occurred in their states. Eight states utilized existing statutes to prosecute maternal substance abuse and charged women with assault, criminal abuse, criminal feticide, motor vehicle homicide, delivering drugs to a minor, reckless endangerment, and child abuse and neglect. The most popular sanction among the respondents was drug rehabilitation and education. This was followed by jail time, periodic urinalysis, fines, removing the child from the custody of the mother, and contraceptive implants. (For a summary of their responses, see Table 4.3.)

State Laws and Criminal Charging Practices

Although no state currently has a law on the books that specifies fetal abuse as a crime, local prosecutors in several states have charged women with fetal abuse by employing existing statutes on child abuse, child neglect, contributing to the delinquency of a minor, causing the dependency of a child, child endangerment, delivering drugs to a minor, assault with a deadly weapon, voluntary or involuntary manslaughter, and homicide. There are also a number of states that have passed child welfare laws addressing the problem of prenatal substance abuse by defining substance-exposed infants as abused, neglected, or harmed, by requiring drug testing of infants that are suspected of having been exposed to prenatal substance abuse and by requiring that reports be filed with child welfare agencies.[58]

As of May 1992, twelve states have implemented child welfare laws that specifically refer to prenatal substance abuse.[59] Seven of these statutes define substance-abused infants as abused, neglected, harmed, or in need of treatment.[60] Three states (Minnesota, Wisconsin, and Iowa) have hospital testing requirements. Minnesota's law, for example, requires physicians to test a suspected maternal drug user. If the test is positive, the results must be reported to a child welfare agency; if negative, a report must still be filed if drug use is suspected. In Wisconsin, a drug test may be performed with the consent of a parent or guardian; if the test is positive a report must be filed. Iowa's law leaves testing judgment in the hands of the physician; if a physician decides to test for drugs, positive findings should be reported to a child welfare agency. Five other states' statutes (California, Florida, Illinois, Massachusetts, and Utah) do not require testing but do require reports on prenatal substance exposure.

From 1989 through 1992, eight states and the U.S. Congress have considered fetal endangerment laws aimed at substance-abusing mothers. In July 1989, then-Senator Pete Wilson (R.—Calif.) introduced a bill entitled "Child Abuse During Pregnancy Act of 1989." Its purpose was to encourage state governments to criminalize substance abuse during pregnancy and to impose a penalty of three years' incarceration in a rehabilitation center. The Wilson bill included in its definition of substance abuse not only ingestion of illegal substances but ingestion of any substance that would prove injurious to the fetus when consumed in excess, including alcohol.[61]

At least six states have bills pending that would mandate criminal penalties related to maternal drug abuse.[62] Bills pending in Ohio and Rhode Island would allow child abuse and neglect definitions to expand to include prenatal drug abuse. In June 1989, twenty bills were pending in California's legislature related to substance-abusing mothers, ranging from proposals to create new treatment programs to proposals for new criminal penalties. In Illinois, pending bills seek to establish drug treatment programs for substance-abusing mothers, require drug screening of newborns, and mandate that results of such drug screenings be reported to the state child abuse agency. Even though states have not enacted criminal legislation, at least one (Minnesota) allows for involuntary civil commitment of pregnant women who are known to be "chemically dependent." All fifty states recognize prenatal injury as a legitimate civil cause of action under tort law.[63]

As of 1992, twenty-six states have prosecuted women for prenatal substance abuse, using criminal charges usually aimed at other types of behavior.[64] Two states, Florida and South Carolina, account for the largest number of prosecutions; almost all are based in the counties that encompass Miami and Greenville.[65] States have been criminally prosecuting women whether they have child welfare laws addressing prenatal exposure or not.[66] This suggests the discretion prosecutors have at their disposal, since some prosecutors have been more zealous in this area of the law than others.

Despite the growing popularity of charging pregnant drug users, child health professionals view the practice with disfavor. In a survey of 229 child welfare administrators and staff, hospital staff, social services staff, and attorneys from twelve states, most deemed prosecution of maternal substance abuse ineffective, unfair, or inappropriate. Of the 165 respondents out of 222 who expressed an opinion, 43 out of 55 child welfare administrators, 49 out of 58 child welfare staff, 38 out of 55 legal professionals, and 35 out of 54 hospital staff were strongly opposed to prosecution.[67]

By July 1992, some 167 women in 26 states had been arrested and charged criminally because of their use of drugs during pregnancy or because of some other prenatal risk, such as excessive alcohol consumption or failure to follow a

TABLE 4.3 Survey of Attorneys General on Fetal Abuse

State	Respondent	Criminal Prosecutions (and no.)	Types of Charges Utilized	Form of Charge Deemed Appropriate	Punishment/Treatment Recommended
Alaska	Asst. AG	yes (1–4 times)	assault	do not encourage fetal abuse prosecutions	drug rehab. & education
Delaware	Attorney General	no	none	none	drug rehab. & education; remove child from mother's custody
Georgia	Staff Atty.	yes (1–4 times)	distributing drugs	none; fetus is not a person under Georgia law	a matter for General Assembly to decide
Iowa	Deputy AG	no	none	child abuse/neglect via juvenile court	drug rehab. & education; remove child from mother's custody
Hawaii	Deputy AG—Criminal Justice Div.	no	none	none	none
Kentucky	Asst. AG	yes (1–4 times)	criminal abuse	no reply	no reply
Louisiana	Director, Criminal Justice Div.	yes (unknown)	criminal feticide	criminal feticide	jail time or fines by statute
Massachusetts	Director, Policy & Training; Asst. AG	yes (1–4 times)	motor vehicle homicide; delivering drugs to a minor	depends on facts of case	drug rehab. & education; depends on facts of case
Montana	Executive Asst.	no	none	no opinion	no opinion
North Dakota	Chief Deputy AG	yes (1–4 times)	reckless endangerment	combination	jail time; probation; drug rehab. & education; periodic urinalysis, all depends on circumstances

(continues)

TABLE 4.3 Survey of Attorneys General on Fetal Abuse *(continued)*

State	Respondent	Criminal Prosecutions (and no.)	Types of Charges Utilized	Form of Charge Deemed Appropriate	Punishment/Treatment Recommended
Ohio	Sr. Policy Analyst	yes (1–4 times)	child endangerment	child neglect statute pending	statute would levy fines, possible jail time; contraceptive implants; drug rehab.
Oregon	Attorney General	no	none	none	none
Pennsylvania	Executive Dir., Pa. D.A. Assn.	no	none	none	none
Rhode Island	Asst. AG	no	none	delivering drugs to a minor; possession of narcotics	drug rehab. & education; periodic urinalysis
Wisconsin	Asst. AG	no	child protection laws after birth	no statutes to address issue	drug rehab. & treatment; periodic urinalysis
Wyoming	Deputy AG	yes (one case)	child abuse or neglect	combination	no reply

NOTE: The Attorney's General office in New Jersey was unable to supply answers to the survey questions at this time; policy toward fetal abuse is still being formulated. Florida's Attorney General has no jurisdiction in this matter. Virginia's Assistant Attorney General stated that her office does not respond to questionnaires and deemed response to this questionnaire inappropriate. South Carolina's Executive Assistant for the Attorney General was unable to respond due to limited staff. Ohio's office responded via a memorandum that discussed legislation pending before the Ohio General Assembly and rulings in the Ohio Supreme Court that negated the ability of state to regulate the conduct of a pregnant woman for the purpose of protecting an unborn child.

TABLE 4.4   Court Decisions on Maternal Drug Abuse Cases

Case	Holding
State Supreme Court Cases	
State of Wyoming v. Osmus, 276 P.2d 359 (1954)	Struck down manslaughter and criminal neglect convictions of a mother whose baby was found dead a few days after birth; concluded that the criminal neglect statute was not applicable to the woman's prenatal conduct
Ohio v. Gray, 62 Ohio St.3d 514, 584 N.E.2d 170 (1992)	Held that a child is not a child until born; noted pending Ohio statutes that make prenatal substance abuse a crime and therefore asserted judicial restraint, refusing to offer an interpretation of an action that the legislature is addressing
Appellate Court Cases	
Reyes v. Superior Court, 75 Cal. App. 3rd 214 (1977)	Unanimously held that California's felony child endangerment statute did not cover a woman's prenatal conduct
People v. Hardy, 188 Mich. App. 305, 469 N.W.2d 50 (1991)	Unanimously struck down criminal prosecution of delivery of cocaine to a baby via the umbilical cord and insisted that the state statute on child abuse be interpreted strictly
Johnson v. State, 578 So.2d 419 (Fla. Fifth Dist. Ct. App. 1991)	A majority of a divided panel upheld application of Florida's statute prohibiting delivery of drugs to a minor to transferrence of cocaine after birth but before the umbilical cord was severed; accepted for review by Florida's supreme court
State v. Gathers, 585 So.2d 1140 (Fla. Fourth Dist. Ct. App. 1991)	Dismissed a criminal prosecution of maternal drug use under Florida's child abuse statute claiming that such prosecutions would harm family preservation by separating mother and child and would also deter pregnant drug abusers from seeking prenatal and postnatal care
Welch v. Commonwealth, No. 90-CA-1189-MR (Ky. Ct. App. 1992)	Struck down a child abuse conviction based on maternal drug use by arguing that the child abuse statute did not refer to the fetus or unborn child as a protected class
Trial Court Cases	
People v. Stewart, No. M508197 (San Diego Min. Ct. 1987)	Struck down use of a criminal child support statute as a means of imposing criminal liability on maternal drug abuse
United States v. Vaughan, No. F-2172-88B (Sup. Ct. of D.C. 1988)	Defendant pleaded guilty to second-degree theft and when the judge found that she was pregnant he mandated a drug test; when she tested positive he penalized her by sentencing her to jail long enough to cover the pregnancy even though she was never found guilty of illegal drug use; judge stated that he acted to protect the fetus
State v. Andrews, No. JU 68459 (Ohio C.P. 1989)	Held that only post-natal living children who were placed at risk could be covered by Ohio's child endangerment statute

(continues)

TABLE 4.4 Court Decisions on Maternal Drug Abuse Cases (*continued*)

Case	Holding
State v. Yurchak, No. 64D01-8901-CF-181B (Porter County Sup. Ct., Indiana, filed 1989)	Mother was charged with possession of cocaine when child was born addicted to drugs; case dismissed when prosecutor dropped charges at oral argument
Commonwealth v. Pellegrini, No. 87970, slip op. (Mass. Sup. Ct. 1990)	Struck down application of Massachusetts's drug delivery statute to maternal drug abuse due to right to privacy, due process, separation of powers, and statutory interpretation principles
State v. Carter, No. 89-6274, slip op. (Fl. Cir. Ct., Escambia Co., 1990)	Dismissed charge of delivery of drugs to a minor because defendant lacked intent at the time she ingested cocaine; child abuse and possession charges were not dismissed
State v. Black, No. 89-5325 (Fl. Cir. Ct., Escambia Co., 1990)	Defendant was sentenced to an eighteen-month prison term and three years probation for delivering drugs to her infant via the umbilical cord
People v. Cox, No. 90-53454 FH slip op. (Mi. Cir. Ct., Jackson Co., 1990)	Held that Michigan's drug delivery law did not apply to prenatal conduct
State v. Bremer, No. 90-32227-FH (Mi. Cir. Ct., Muskegon Co., 1991)	Dismissed charge of delivery of drugs to an infant on the grounds that such charges constituted a radical departure from existing law
State v. Inzar, No. 90CRS6960, 90CRS6961 (Gen. Ct. of Justice, Super. Ct. Div., Robeson Co., N.C., 1991)	Dismissed charges of assault with a deadly weapon and delivery of drugs to a minor by a pregnant woman because a fetus is not a person
Commonwealth v. Smith, No. CR-91-05-4381, slip op. (Va. Cir. Ct., Franklin Co., 1991)	Dismissed finding that Virginia's child abuse statute was not intended to cover fetuses or prenatal conduct; no appeal
Commonwealth v. Turner, No. 91-054382, slip op. (Va. Cir. Ct., Franklin Co., 1991)	Granted motion to dismiss finding that Virginia's child abuse statute was not intended to cover fetuses or prenatal conduct; no appeal
Commonwealth v. Wilcox, No. A-44116-01 (Va. Norfolk Jur. & Dom. Rel. Dist. Ct. 1991)	Dismissed child abuse charges against a mother accused of using cocaine while pregnant; application of the child abuse law was beyond the intent of the statute enacted by the General Assembly
State v. Luster, No. 91-2626 (Super. Ct. Ga. 1991)	Dismissed charges against a pregnant woman of distributing a controlled substance, holding that the fetus is not a "legal entity" and that extending the statute to cover prenatal conduct deprived the defendant of due process notice
People v. Morabito, (N.Y. Mun. Ct. 1992)	Dismissed child endangerment charge against a woman accused of using cocaine while pregnant; held that unborn children were not covered by the child welfare statute and that to interpret "child" to include the fetus was a denial of due process

SOURCES: The Center for Reproductive Law and Policy; National Center for Prosecution of Child Abuse.

doctor's instructions. In most of these prosecutions, women were encouraged to plead guilty or plea bargain. Many pregnant drug users have been convicted. (See Table 4.4.) So far, judges have ruled in 19 cases that the prosecutions were illegal, unconstitutional, or both. Only one prosecution has been upheld thus far, and it was thrown out on appeal to the Florida Supreme Court.[68]

Conclusions

What emerges from our findings is a mixed picture. There is a wide degree of prosecutorial discretion with regard to charging pregnant substance abusers, reflected in divergent and localized patterns of charging women with harming their fetuses and babies. Yet even though our research findings are far from complete, they suggest that the zeal to prosecute pregnant substance abusers is tempered by an appreciation that treatment and education are better solutions than incarceration. A recent letter from the National District Attorneys Association to a newsletter published by the National Center for Prosecution of Child Abuse reflects these tensions. The letter recommended that prosecutors exercise discretion by dealing with maternal drug use during pregnancy in the following ways:

1. Expand drug rehabilitation, health care, and education services;

2. focus on deferred prosecution, diversion programs, and make drug and alcohol treatment a condition of probation;

3. seek stiffer penalties for those who sell drugs to child caretakers and pregnant women; and

4. use the criminal justice system to encourage treatment and recognize that the ability to do this will depend on the existence of statutes and case law that facilitate the filing of criminal charges for child abuse or neglect or possession or delivery of illegal drugs.

Indeed, there are many tensions and contradictions that beset attempts to address the problem of maternal substance abuse by prosecuting women for fetal abuse. A woman's moral obligation to protect her unborn child from potential harm and the state's interest in protecting a viable fetus conflict with a woman's right to privacy and bodily integrity. Those who view maternal substance abuse as a health care problem rather than a criminal justice problem often claim that prosecutions of fetal abuse are a form of blaming the victim: The real solution lies in expanding treatment centers set up to meet the special needs of pregnant drug abusers. The belief that prosecution will enhance treatment is at odds with the belief that prosecutions will drive substance-abusing mothers away from hospitals and treatment centers for fear of being detected by the criminal justice system. Jailing pregnant women to punish them and possibly treat them does not square with the conventional wisdom that imprisonment rarely rehabilitates and that drugs flow freely in prisons. The notion that fetal abuse laws could be constructed narrowly clashes with the idea that such statutes would only result in widening the net of social control and would continue to be enforced in a discriminatory way against the poor and women of color. Advocates of fetal abuse prosecution argue that substance-abusing mothers are unfit parents who must be forced into treatment if they wish to keep their children, whereas opponents of fetal abuse prosecution argue that such prosecutions weaken the family structure and force children into foster care, causing displacement and possibly exacerbating problems associated with prenatal substance abuse.

In our view, at this point the dangers of abuse outweigh the efficacy of using criminal prosecutions to force pregnant women to stop engaging in practices that endanger their fetuses. Allowing prosecutors wide latitude in charging women suspected of fetal abuse may drive pregnant addicts underground due to fear of losing their parental rights, ultimately making the cure worse than the disease.

Notes

1. These interest groups and agencies included the Alcohol and Drug Problems Association of North America, the American Medical Association, the American Civil Liberties Union, the Center for Reproductive Policy and Law, the Center for Women Policy Studies, the Children's Defense Fund, Children's Healthcare Is A Legal Duty, the Child Welfare League of America, the Eagle Forum, Families USA Foundation, the National Abortion Rights Action League, the National Center for the Prosecution of Child Abuse, the National Clearinghouse on Child Neglect and Abuse, the National Organization of Women, the National Right to Life Committee, Inc., the Planned Parenthood Federation, the U.S. Department of Health and Human Services, and the Women's Legal Defense Fund.

We owe special thanks to Lynn Paltrow and her Administrative Assistant, Kathryn McGowan, of the Center for Reproductive Law and Policy for the information they so generously shared. We would also like to thank the American Prosecutors Research Institute and Eva J. Klain, Staff Attorney for the National Center for Prosecution of Child Abuse, for the data they so graciously supplied. We additionally thank Regina Weiss, a paralegal for Planned Parenthood, for the articles and information she supplied.

2. Josephine Gittler and Merle McPherson, "Prenatal Substance Abuse," *Children Today,* 19:3–7 (July-August 1990).

3. Jo Ann Moslock, "Prosecutors Beginning to Hear Drug Babies' Cries," *Asbury Park (N.J.) Press,* 22 October 1989.

4. See Chapter 5 in this volume by Jean Schroedel and Paul Peretz, dealing with fetal abuse, for a discussion of the reasons why battering is not treated as a factor in fetal abuse.

5. Richard P. Kusserow, "Prenatal Substance Exposure: State Child Welfare Laws and Procedures," U.S. Department of Health and Human Services: Office of the Inspector General, May 1992; Gittler and McPherson, "Prenatal Substance Abuse."

6. Bruce Henderson, "Mothers of Infant Addicts: Does Prosecution Help?" *Charlotte Observer,* 26 August 1989; Paul Marcotte, "Crime and Pregnancy: Prosecutors, New Drugs, Torts Pit Mom Against Baby," *American Bar Association Journal* 75:14–16 (August 1989); Andrew C. Revkin, "Crack in the Cradle," *Discover* 10:63–69 (September 1989).

7. Barbara Kantrowitz, Vicki Quade, Bennie Fisher, James Hill, and Lucille Beachy, "The Pregnancy Police," *Newsweek,* April 29, 1991, 52–53; Katha Pollitt, "Fetal Rights: A New Assault on Feminism," *The Nation,* March 26, 1990, 409ff.

8. Jacquelynn Boyle, "ACLU to Back Mom on Charge of Delivering Crack-Addict Baby," *Detroit Free Press*, 28 October 1989.

9. Susan LaCroix, "Birth of a Bad Idea: Jailing Mothers for Drug Abuse," *The Nation*, May 1, 1989, 585–586, 588; Joseph Losco, "Fetal Abuse: An Exploration of Emerging Philosophic, Legal and Policy Issues," *Western Political Quarterly* 42:265–286 (June 1989); John Kleinig, "Editor's Introduction: Criminal Liability for Fetal Endangerment," *Criminal Justice Ethics* 9:11–13 (Winter-Spring 1990); Olivia Winslow, "Search for Answers in Care, Not Courts, Many Experts Agree," *Richmond Times-Dispatch*, 15 September 1991.

10. Richard Lacayo, "Do the Unborn Have Rights?" *Time*, 136(19):22–23 (Fall 1990); Michael G. Walsh, "Court Dumps 'Coke Mom Case'" *Muskegon Chronicle*, 2 April 1991.

11. David Goldberg, "Mother Guilty of Giving Fetus Drugs," *Providence Journal* ,21 November 1989.

12. Stan Finger, "Legal Quandary Awaits Mothers Who Expose Babies to Drugs," *Wichita Eagle*, 21 July 1991.

13. Amy Linn, "The Corruption of Motherhood," *Philadelphia Inquirer*, 17 September 1989.

14. Charles P. Wohlforth, "Mother Indicted for Endangering Baby By Drug Use," *Anchorage Daily News*, 17 December 1988.

15. Jean Davidson, "Drug Babies Push Issue of Fetal Rights," *Los Angeles Times*, 25 April 1989.

16. Todd Pack, "Woman Guilty of Abusing Unborn by Taking Drugs During Pregnancy," *Lexington Herald-Leader*, 23 May 1990; Andrew Wolfson, "Treatment, Not Jail, Urged for Pregnant Drug Addicts," *Louisville Courier-Journal*, 10 June 1990.

17. John Makeig, "ACLU Plans to Use a Sex-Bias Defense in Unique Drug Trial," *Houston Chronicle*, 23 June 1990; Lori Montgomery, "Mom Jailed for Cocaine in Baby," *Dallas Times Herald*, 2 July 1991.

18. Barrington Salmon, "Are Crack Mothers a Law-Enforcement or Public Health Dilemma?" *Tallahassee Democrat*, 11 January 1992.

19. Claire Cooper, "Drug Mothers on a Legal Cliff," *Sacramento Bee*, 5 July 1990.

20. Charles Pelkey and Emily Quarterman, "Attorneys in Pfannenstiel Case Say Ruling Win for Privacy Rights Advocates," *Caspar-Star Tribune*, 4 February 1990.

21. Susan Pack, "Even Babies Tested for Drugs," *Long Beach (Calif.) Press Telegram*, 16 September 1986.

22. Janet Gallagher, "Prenatal Invasions and Interventions: What's Wrong with Fetal Rights?" *Harvard Women's Law Journal* 10:9–58 (Spring 1987); Paul A. Logli, "Drugs in the Womb: The Newest Battlefield in the War on Drugs," *Criminal Justice Ethics* 9:23–29 (Winter-Spring 1990); Wendy K. Mariner, Leonard H. Glantz, and George J. Annas, "Pregnancy, Drugs, and the Perils of Prosecution," *Criminal Justice Ethics* 9:30–41 (Winter-Spring 1990); Lynn Paltrow, "When Becoming Pregnant Is a Crime," *Criminal Justice Ethics* 9:41–47 (Winter-Spring 1990).

23. John Robertson, "Fetal Abuse: Should We Recognize It as a Crime? Yes," *American Bar Association Journal* 75:38 (August 1989).

24. Suzanne Sataline, "State Tackles Issue of Pre-Natal Child Abuse," *Hartford Courant*, 20 October 1991.

25. John H. Kennedy, "Cloudy Future After Infant-Cocaine Case," *Boston Globe*, 23 August 1989.

26. Further, the *Webster* decision also described abortion as a "liberty interest" rather than a fundamental right, which has led some prosecutors to believe that the Court would support laws criminalizing conduct by pregnant women that harmed their fetuses in cases where women carried their pregnancies to term rather than aborting them. Logli, "Drugs in the Womb."

27. Andy Brack, "Laws Protect Babies Born to Drug Users," *Charleston (S.C.) News and Courier,* 29 October 1989. Jed Rebenfeld has also argued that the Court must provide better arguments for making viability the threshold for a recognized state interest in potential life, unless it wants to repudiate the right to privacy altogether. Jed Rubenfeld, "On the Legal Status of the Proposition That 'Life Begins at Conception,'" *Stanford Law Review* 43:634 (February 1991).

28. Moslock, "Prosecutors Beginning to Hear Babies' Cries."

29. Henderson, "Mothers of Infant Addicts"; Goldberg, "Mother Guilty of Giving Fetus Drugs."

30. LaCroix, "Birth of a Bad Idea: Jailing Mothers for Drug Abuse"; Stephen Goldsmith, "Prosecution to Enhance Treatment," *Children Today* 19:13–16, 36 (July-August 1990). Reasons why pregnant substance abusers fail to seek treatment are not addressed by these sources. As Iris Young suggests in Chapter 6 in this volume, failure to seek treatment may have to do with mandatory reporting laws and lack of drug treatment facilities that accept pregnant addicts.

31. Similarly, in Greenville, South Carolina, where numerous women have been charged, Solicitor Joseph Watson argued that he used criminal prosecution to "get the mother's attention." Greenville drug counselor Paula Keller also believes the threat of prosecution is working. She claims that one of her clients who was fearful of arrest stopped drug use during pregnancy and that others have also stayed clean. Further, she stated that all the women she has worked with to date had told her that they would not have stopped using drugs had they not been arrested. Wolfson, "Treatment, Not Jail, Urged for Pregnant Drug Addicts."

32. Laura Feig, "Drug Exposed Infants and Children: Service Needs and Policy Questions," Washington, D.C.: Office of Human Services Policy, U.S. Department of Health and Human Services, 1990.

33. Gittler and McPherson, "Prenatal Substance Abuse"; Salmon, "Are Crack Mothers a Law-Enforcement or Public Health Dilemma?"

34. Goldsmith, "Prosecution to Enhance Treatment."

35. For discussions of these increases, see Douglas J. Besharov, "Crack Children in Foster Care," *Children Today,* 19:21–25, 35 (July-August 1990); Celia W. Dugger, "HRS Moves to Ease Drug-Baby Jam," *Miami Herald,* 24 November 1988; Davidson, "Drug Babies Push Issue of Fetal Rights"; Gittler and McPherson, "Prenatal Substance Abuse."

36. Henderson, "Mothers of Infant Addicts: Does Prosecution Help?"; Beryl Lieff Benderly, "Saving the Children," *Health,* 21:74–75 (December 1989).

37. Personal letter from Kathryn McGowan, The Center for Reproductive Law and Policy; Shoop, "States Cannot Punish Pregnant Women for 'Fetal Abuse.'"

38. Wolfson, "Treatment, Not Jail, Urged For Pregnant Drug Addicts."

39. Linn, "The Corruption of Motherhood."

40. Kathleen B. DeBettencourt, "The Wisdom of Solomon: Cutting the Cord That Harms," *Children Today* 19:17–20 (July-August 1990); D. Mathieu, "Respecting Liberty and Preventing Harm: Limits of State Intervention in Prenatal Choice," *Harvard Journal of Law and Politics* 8:19–55 (1985).

41. Helene M. Cole, "Legal Interventions During Pregnancy: Court-Ordered Medical Treatments and Legal Penalties for Potentially Harmful Behavior by Pregnant Women," *Journal of the American Medical Association* 264:2663–2670 (November 28, 1990).

42. Leslie Goldberg, "Just Whose Baby Is It, Anyway?" *San Francisco Examiner,* 18 February 1992.

43. Selwyn Crawford, "Legal System Grapples with Newborn Addicts," *Dallas Morning News,* 29 July 1989; Lynn M. Paltrow, "Fetal Abuse: Should We Recognize It as a Crime? No," *American Bar Association Journal,* 75:39 (August 1989).

44. Kary Moss, "Substance Abuse During Pregnancy," *Harvard Women's Law Journal* 13:278–299 (May 1990); Dawn Johnsen, "Shared Interests: Promoting Healthy Births Without Sacrificing Women's Liberty," *Hastings Law Journal* 43:569–614 (March 1992).

45. Eileen McNamara, "Fetal Endangerment Cases on the Rise," *Boston Globe*, 3 October 1989.

46. John Caher, "Mothers Held Liable for Behavior While Pregnant," *Albany Times Union*, 1 April 1990.

47. A study in Pinnellas County, Florida, found that black women were approximately ten times more likely to be reported for child abuse than white women. In addition, a disproportionate number of black mothers lost custody of their children. Moss, "Substance Abuse During Pregnancy."

48. Janet Dinsmore, "Pregnant Drug Users: The Debate over Prosecution," American Prosecutors Research Institute: National Center for Prosecution of Child Abuse, March 1992.

49. Linn, "The Corruption of Motherhood"; Dianna Hunt, "Jail Worsens 'Cocaine Baby' Problem, Doctor Says," *Houston Chronicle*, 20 May 1990; William Cooper, Jr., "Twice As Many Blacks Cited for Using Drugs During Pregnancy," *Palm Beach Post*, 20 November 1989; Dorothy E. Roberts, "Punishing Drug Addicts Who Have Babies: Women of Color, Equality, and the Right to Privacy," *Harvard Law Review* 104:1419 (May 1991), 1419–1482.

50. Goldberg, "Just Whose Baby Is It Anyway?"; Dinsmore, "Pregnant Drug Users: The Debate over Prosecution."

51. Mariner et al., "Pregnancy, Drugs, and the Perils of Prosecution," note that it is difficult to separate intent and motive.

52. Brack, "Laws Protect Babies Born to Drug Users."

53. McNamara, "Fetal Endangerment Cases on the Rise"; Dinsmore, "Pregnant Drug Users: The Debate over Prosecution"; Shoop, "States Cannot Punish Pregnant Women for 'Fetal Abuse.'"

54. Brack, "Laws Protect Babies Born to Drug Users." For other discussions of inadequate drug treatment facilities for pregnant women, see Salmon, "Are Crack Mothers a Law-Enforcement or Public Health Dilemma?"; Dinsmore, "Pregnant Drug Users: The Debate over Prosecution"; McGowan, letter; Shoop, "States Cannot Punish Pregnant Women for 'Fetal Abuse.'"

55. Kathleen Nolan, "Protecting Fetuses from Prenatal Hazards: Whose Crimes? What Punishment?" *Criminal Justice Ethics* 9:13–23 (Winter-Spring 1990); Carol Tavris, "The Politics of Pregnancy," *Vogue*, September 1989, 572ff.

56. Paltrow, "Fetal Abuse: Should We Recognize It as a Crime?" 39.

57. Moss, "Substance Abuse During Pregnancy."

58. Shoop, "States Cannot Punish Pregnant Women for 'Fetal Abuse' Cases"; Kusserow, "Prenatal Substance Exposure: State Child Welfare Laws and Procedures"; Dawn Johnsen, "From Driving to Drugs: Governmental Regulation of Pregnant Women's Lives After *Webster*," *University of Pennsylvania Law Review* 138:179–215 (1989).

59. These states are California, Florida, Illinois, Indiana, Iowa, Massachusetts, Minnesota, Missouri, Nevada, Oklahoma, Utah, and Wisconsin.

60. Florida, Illinois, Indiana, Minnesota, Missouri, Nevada, and Oklahoma.

61. Johnsen, "From Driving to Drugs."

62. California, Hawaii, Kansas, Nevada, Ohio, and South Carolina.

63. Shoop, "States Cannot Punish Pregnant Women for 'Fetal Abuse' Cases"; Marcotte, "Crime and Pregnancy: Prosecutors, New Drugs, Torts Pit Mom Against Baby"; National Association of Perinatal Addiction Research and Education, "1991 State Legislation Regarding Prenatal Drug Abuse." (1991).

64. The states are Alaska, California, Connecticut, Florida, Georgia, Idaho, Illinois, Indiana, Kentucky, Massachusetts, Michigan, Mississippi, Missouri, Nebraska, Nevada, New York, North Carolina, North Dakota, Ohio, Oklahoma, South Carolina, South Dakota, Texas, Virginia, Washington, and Wyoming.

65. McGowan, letter.

66. Kusserow, "Prenatal Substance Exposure: State Child Welfare Laws and Procedures."

67. Ibid., 11–12.

68. McGowan, letter.

References

Ahart, Ariel, Carolyn Rutsch, and Cynthia Holmes. Macro Systems, Inc. *Programs Serving Drug-Exposed Children and Their Families.* Vol. 1. Contract No. HHS-100-87-0039. Submitted to Assistant Secretary for Planning and Evaluation, U.S. Department of Health and Human Services. 1991.

Barr, Helen M., Ann Pytkowicz Streissguth, Betty L. Darby, and Paul D. Sampson. "Prenatal Exposure to Alcohol, Caffeine, Tobacco and Aspirin: Fine and Gross Motor Performance in 4-Year-Old Children." *Developmental Psychology* 26:339–348. 1990.

Benderly, Beryl Lieff. "Saving the Children." *Health* 21:74–75. 1989.

Besharov, Douglas J. "Crack Children in Foster Care." *Children Today* 19:21–25, 35. 1990.

Bower, B. "Alcohol's Fetal Harm Lasts a Lifetime." *Science News* 139:244. 1991.

Boyle, Jacquelynn. "ACLU to Back Mom on Charge of Delivering Crack-Addict Baby." *Detroit Free Press,* 28 October 1989.

Brack, Andy. "Laws Protect Babies Born to Drug Users." *Charleston (S.C.) News and Courier,* 29 October 1989.

Burek, Deborah M. *Encyclopedia of Associations.* Vol. 1, Part 2. Detroit: Gale Research, Inc., 1991.

Caher, John. "Mothers Held Liable for Behavior While Pregnant." *Albany Times Union,* 1 April 1990.

Cole, Helene M. "Legal Interventions During Pregnancy: Court-Ordered Medical Treatments and Legal Penalties for Potentially Harmful Behavior By Pregnant Women." *Journal of the American Medical Association* 264:2663–2670 (28 November 1990).

Cooper, Claire. "Drug Mothers on a Legal Cliff." *Sacramento Bee,* 5 July 1990.

Cooper Jr., William. "Twice as Many Blacks Cited for Using Drugs During Pregnancy." *Palm Beach Post,* 20 November 1989.

Crawford, Selwyn. "Legal System Grapples with Newborn Addicts." *Dallas Morning News,* 29 July 1989.

Davidson, Jean. "Drug Babies Push Issue of Fetal Rights." *Los Angeles Times,* 25 April 1989.

DeBettencourt, Kathleen B. "The Wisdom of Solomon: Cutting the Cord That Harms." *Children Today* 19:17–20 (July-August 1990).

Dinsmore, Janet. "Pregnant Drug Users: The Debate over Prosecution." [monograph] American Prosecutors Research Institute: National Center for Prosecution of Child Abuse. March 1992.

Dugger, Celia W. "HRS Moves to Ease Drug-Baby Jam." *Miami Herald,* 24 November 1988.

Farkas, Karen. "Flaws Found in the Armor of Drug Law." *Cleveland Plain Dealer,* 18 November 1990.

Feig, Laura. "Drug Exposed Infants and Children: Service Needs and Policy Questions." Washington, D.C: Office of Human Services Policy, U.S. Department of Health and Human Services. 1990.

Finger, Stan. "Legal Quandary Awaits Mothers Who Expose Babies to Drugs." *Wichita Eagle,* 21 July 1991.

Gallagher, Janet. "Prenatal Invasions and Interventions: What's Wrong with Fetal Rights?" *Harvard Women's Law Journal* 10:9–58 (Spring 1987).

Gittler, Josephine, and Merle McPherson. "Prenatal Substance Abuse." *Children Today* 19:3–7 (July-August 1990.)

Goldberg, David. "Mother Guilty of Giving Fetus Drugs." *Providence Journal,* 21 November 1989.

Goldberg, Leslie. "Just Whose Baby Is It, Anyway?" *San Francisco Examiner,* 18 February 1992.

Goldsmith, Stephen. "Prosecution to Enhance Treatment." *Children Today* 19:13–16, 36 (July–August 1990).

Henderson, Bruce. "Mothers of Infant Addicts: Does Prosecution Help?" *Charlotte Observer,* 26 August 1989.

Horowitz, Robert. "A Coordinated Public Health and Child Welfare Response to Perinatal Substance Abuse." *Children Today* 19:8–12 (July-August 1990).

Hunt, Dianna. "Jail Worsens 'Cocaine Baby' Problem, Doctor Says." *Houston Chronicle,* 20 May 1990.

Johnsen, Dawn. "From Driving to Drugs: Governmental Regulation of Pregnant Women's Lives After *Webster."* *University of Pennsylvania Law Review* 138:179–215 (1989).

_____. "Shared Interests: Promoting Healthy Births Without Sacrificing Women's Liberty." *Hastings Law Journal* 43:569–614 (March 1992).

Jost, Kenneth. "Do Pregnant Women Lose Legal Rights?" *Editorial Research Reports* 2:414–427 (28 July 1989).

Kantrowitz, Barbara, Vicki Quade, Binnie Fisher, James Hill, and Lucille Beachy. "The Pregnancy Police." *Newsweek,* April 29, 1991. 52–53.

Kennedy, John H. "Cloudy Future After Infant-Cocaine Case." *Boston Globe,* 23 August 1989.

Kleinig, John. "Editor's Introduction: Criminal Liability for Fetal Endangerment." *Criminal Justice Ethics* 9:11–13 (Winter-Spring 1990).

Kusserow, Richard P. "Prenatal Substance Exposure: State Child Welfare Laws and Procedures." Department of Health and Human Services: Office of the Inspector General. May 1992.

Lacayo, Richard. "Do the Unborn Have Rights?" *Time* 136(19):22–23 (Fall 1990).

LaCroix, Susan. "Birth of a Bad Idea: Jailing Mothers for Drug Abuse." *The Nation,* May 1, 1989;585–586, 588.

Linn, Amy. "The Corruption of Motherhood." *Philadelphia Inquirer,* 17 September 1989.

Logli, Paul A. "Drugs in the Womb: The Newest Battlefield in the War on Drugs." *Criminal Justice Ethics* 9:23–29 (Winter-Spring 1990).

Losco, Joseph. "Fetal Abuse: An Exploration of Emerging Philosophic, Legal and Policy Issues." *Western Political Quarterly* 42:265–286 (June 1989).

Makeig, John. "ACLU Plans to Use a Sex-Bias Defense in Unique Drug Trial." *Houston Chronicle,* 23 June 1990.

Marcotte, Paul. "Crime and Pregnancy: Prosecutors, New Drugs, Torts Pit Mom Against Baby." *American Bar Association Journal* 75:14, 16 (August 1989).

Mariner, Wendy K., Leonard H. Glantz, and George J. Annas. "Pregnancy, Drugs, and the Perils of Prosecution." *Criminal Justice Ethics* 9:30–41 (Winter-Spring 1990).

Mathieu, D. "Respecting Liberty and Preventing Harm: Limits of State Intervention in Prenatal Choice." *Harvard Journal of Law and Politics* 8:19–55 (1985).

McGowan, Kathryn. Personal letter. New York, New York: The Center for Reproductive Law and Policy (16 July 1992).

McNamara, Eileen. "Fetal Endangerment Cases on the Rise." *Boston Globe,* 3 October 1989.

Montgomery, Lori. "Mom Jailed for Cocaine in Baby." *Dallas Times Herald,* 2 July 1991.

Moslock, Jo Ann. "Prosecutors Beginning to Hear Drug Babies' Cries." *Asbury Park (N.J.) Press,* 22 October 1989.

Moss, Kary. "Substance Abuse During Pregnancy." *Harvard Women's Law Journal* 13:278–299 (May 1990).

National Association of Perinatal Addiction Research and Education. 1991 State Legislation Regarding Prenatal Drug Abuse. 1991.

National Center for Prosecution of Drug Abuse. "NDAA Approves Policy Statement on Drug-Affected Infants and Children." 5, no. 2 (February 1992).

Nolan, Kathleen. "Protecting Fetuses from Prenatal Hazards: Whose Crimes? What Punishment?" *Criminal Justice Ethics* 9:13–23 (Winter-Spring, 1990).

O'Neal, Donna. "Court Hears Coke-Babies Case." *Orlando Sentinel,* 7 March 1992.

Pack, Susan. "Even Babies Tested for Drugs." *Long Beach (Calif.) Press Telegram,* 16 September 1986.

Pack, Todd. "Woman Guilty of Abusing Unborn Child by Taking Drugs During Pregnancy." *Lexington Herald-Leader,* 23 May 1990.

Paltrow, Lynn M. "Fetal Abuse: Should We Recognize It as a Crime? No." *American Bar Association Journal* 75:39 (August 1989).

———. "When Becoming Pregnant Is a Crime." *Criminal Justice Ethics* 9:41–47 (Winter-Spring 1990).

Pelkey, Charles, and Emily Quarterman. "Attorneys in Pfannenstiel Case Say Ruling Win for Privacy Rights Advocates." *Caspar Star-Tribune,* 4 February 1990.

Pollitt, Katha. "Fetal Rights: A New Assault on Feminism." *The Nation,* March 26, 1990. 409–410, 414–416, 418.

Revkin, Andrew C. "Crack in the Cradle." *Discover* 10:63–69 (September 1989).

Roberts, Dorothy E. "Punishing Drug Addicts Who Have Babies: Women of Color, Equality, and the Right to Privacy." *Harvard Law Review* 104(7):1419–1482 (1991).

Robertson, John A. "Procreative Liberty and the Control of Conception, Pregnancy and Childbirth." *Virginia Law Review* 69(3):405–464 (April 1983).

Robertson, John. "Fetal Abuse: Should We Recognize It as a Crime? Yes." *American Bar Association Journal* 75:38 (August 1989).

Robin-Vergeer, Bonnie I. "The Problem of the Drug-Exposed Newborn: A Return to Principled Intervention." *Stanford Law Review* 42:745–809 (February 1990).

Roe v. Wade, 410 U.S. 113 (1973).

Ruane, Rosalie, ed. *State Executive Directory.* Washington, D.C.: Carroll Publishing Company. November 1990–February 1991.

Rubenfeld, Jed. "On the Legal Status of the Proposition That 'Life Begins at Conception.'" *Stanford Law Review* 43:599–635 (1991).

Salamone, Debbie. "Mom Was Pusher, State Says." *Orlando Sentinel,* 13 July 1989.

Salmon, Barrington. "Are Crack Mothers a Law-Enforcement or Public Health Dilemma?" *Tallahassee Democrat,* 11 January 1992.

Sataline, Suzanne. "State Tackles Issue of Pre-Natal Child Abuse." *Hartford Courant,* 20 October 1991.

Shaw, Margery W. "Conditional Prospective Rights of the Fetus." *Journal of Legal Medicine,* March 1984. 63–116.

Shoop, Julie Gannon. "States Cannot Punish Pregnant Women for 'Fetal Abuse' Cases, Court Says." *Trial,* May 1992. 11–12, 14.

Tavris, Carol. "The Politics of Pregnancy." *Vogue,* September 1989. 572–573, 576, 578.

Taylor, Frances Grandy. "The Endangered Unborn." *Hartford Courant,* 31 March 1989.

Walsh, Michael G. "Court Dumps 'Coke Mom Case'." *Musekgon Chronicle*, 2 April 1991.

Webster v. Reproductive Health Services, 109 S.Ct. 3040 (1989).

Wehrwein, Peter. "Fetal Cops: Shielding Unborn Thorny Rights Issue." *Albany Times Union*, 2 June 1991.

Weiss, Regina. Planned Parenthood Federation of America. Personal communication. July 29, 1992.

Winslow, Olivia. "Search for Answers in Care, Not Courts, Many Experts Agree." *Richmond Times-Dispatch*, 15 September 1991.

Wohlforth, Charles P. "Mother Indicted for Endangering Baby by Drug Use." *Anchorage Daily News*, 17 December 1988.

Wolfson, Andrew. "Treatment, Not Jail, Urged for Pregnant Drug Addicts." *Louisville Courier-Journal*, 10 June 1990.

SURVEY OF STATE ATTORNEYS GENERAL: FETAL ENDANGERMENT STATUTES

We are surveying all the Attorneys General in the United States. We would
like to ascertain the treatment that these offices generally recommend to
state prosecutors/district attorneys vis-a-vis the issue of fetal abuse or
endangerment.

This questionnaire will be used for academic purposes only. If you have any
questions about the survey, please feel free to contact: Dr. Ruth Ann
Strickland at (704) 262-6169 or 262-3085. A self-addressed, stamped envelope
is enclosed to make your response more convenient. We greatly appreciate your
willingness to participate in this survey.

(1)   NAME:_____

       POSITION/TITLE:_____

       STATE: _____

(2)   Does your state: (A) employ a fetal abuse/fetal endangerment statute;
       (B) is passage of such a statute pending; or (C) is your state not
       concerned with fetal abuse at this time?

(3)   If your state does not have a fetal abuse/fetal endangerment statute,
       have prosecutors/district attorneys in your state prosecuted women for
       fetal abuse by using other charge mechanisms (i.e. assault, involuntary
       manslaughter, delivery of drugs to a minor or child abuse/neglect)?
       (A)   Yes   (B) No

       If yes, please circle the charges that have been utilized:
       (A)   assault   (D) involuntary manslaughter
       (B)   delivering drugs to a minor (E) voluntary manslaughter
       (C)   child abuse/neglect   (F) other (specify)_____

(4)   What forms of charge would you deem appropriate to use in a case of
       fetal abuse (in other words, if a state prosecutor or district attorney
       sought advice from your office, which approach to fetal abuse cases
       would you advise from the following options?)
(1)   employ the charge of delivering drugs to a minor
(2)   employ the child abuse/neglect charge
(3)   employ an involuntary manslaugher charge if the fetus dies
(4)   employ a voluntary manslaughter charge if the fetus dies
(5)   employ an assault charge
(6)   some combination of the above depending on the severity of the abuse
(7)   other (specify) _____
(8)   none of the above; our office would not encourage fetal abuse
       prosecutions

Comments:

(5) What forms of treatment/punishment would you advocate for fetal abuse?
(1) jail time
(2) probation
(3) drug rehabilitation and education
(4) periodic urinalysis as a condition of probation
(5) involuntary use of a contraceptive, i.e. Norplant
(6) remove the child from the mother's custody
(7) other (specify)_____
(8) none of the above; our office would not (does not) encourage treatment
     or punishment for fetal abuse

Comments:

(6) How frequent have fetal abuse/endangerment offenses been prosecuted in
    your state (either under formal fetal abuse statutes or under some other
    charging mechanism)?

(A) Over 20 times
(B) 15-20 times
(C) 10-14 times
(D) 5-9 times
(E) 1-4 times
(F) none

Comments:

5

A Gender Analysis of Policy Formation: The Case of Fetal Abuse

JEAN REITH SCHROEDEL & PAUL PERETZ

DESPITE ALMOST TWO DECADES of feminist scholarship, there has been relatively little theoretical analysis of the ways that gender relations are reproduced and reinforced through public policies. Numerous scholars (Boals 1975; Carroll 1979; Silverberg 1990) have commented on the lack of theoretical innovation within the field. Helene Silverberg contends that political science as a discipline has a limited understanding of the concept "gender." By equating gender with sex roles, political scientists have limited the legitimate areas of research to only those that add gender as a predictor variable onto an already existing research agenda or look at women as a case study of some broader area of research.

Political scientists are just beginning to explore the ways that the social construction of gender affects governmental policies. Catharine MacKinnon's 1987 collection of essays on the law was one of the first attempts to use gender as an analytic category. Central to this approach is a study of the intersection between government policy and relations between the sexes. In other words, how do governmental policies reflect, reinforce, and possibly change the balance of power between men and women. MacKinnon showed how legal developments concerning rape, abortion, sexual harassment, and pornography reflect changes in the underlying balance of power between the sexes. In a similar vein, recent feminist critiques of the welfare state have shown how specific policies have reinforced existing social inequalities between men and women (Abramovitz 1988; Gordon 1990; Nelson 1990).

In this chapter we seek to show how the underlying assumptions engendered by a patriarchal society have framed the debate over fetal abuse in a way that places the blame on women when a more appropriate framing would have placed the blame on men or on both sexes. We will show that this framing has had harsh consequences for women and diverted attention from the fetal harms caused by male behaviors.

In the past ten years there has been a sharp increase in the number of infants born with abnormalities traceable to maternal substance abuse during pregnancy. In utero exposure to cocaine has been found to be significantly correlated with premature births, low birth weight, fetal strokes, brain damage, respiratory difficulties, and a host of other physical and developmental abnormalities (Marcotte 1989; Revkin 1989). Babies born to women who drank heavily during pregnancy often have a host of adverse effects ranging from mental retardation to physical deformities (Dorris 1989; Barr, Streissguth, Darby, and Sampson 1990; Bower 1991). The very real social costs of caring for these children, many of whom will never become fully functioning adults, has raised the policy salience of fetal health.

Although prenatal hazards have always existed, this level of awareness of potential risks to fetal well-being is quite new. But even in this new era only certain types of prenatal risks are receiving heightened scrutiny. Many social and environmental hazards that have long been associated with poor birth outcomes, such as poverty, malnutrition, and inadequate medical care, are not part of the current policy debate. Nor do the adverse birth outcomes caused by male behaviors receive significant attention. Instead the current debate about fetal abuse focuses almost exclusively on maternal substance abuse. In this paper we will explore the reasons why this particular policy has been defined in such a narrow manner and why the focus has been exclusively on maternal behaviors rather than on those of their male partners.

We argue that this definition of fetal abuse is a consequence of a generalized system of beliefs about men's and women's natural roles within society. These unconscious beliefs about appropriate sex roles have served to highlight certain behaviors and leave others in the shadows. In what is still a generally patriarchal culture, childbearing and childrearing are seen as primarily female responsibilities, whereas providing for the family's economic well-being is primarily a male responsibility.[1] It follows from this basic division of labor that if harm should come to the fetus or child, one's first instinct is to look to the party primarily responsible for its health—the mother. Behaviors that deviate from the expected norms of female behavior, such as drinking and drug use, are particularly suspect. We argue that these unconscious beliefs about gender-appropriate behavior have resulted in a skewed definition of fetal abuse that focuses almost entirely upon socially inappropriate behaviors of the mothers while ignoring the equally pernicious actions of their male partners. We show how this definition has been generally accepted, even by feminists who have sought to defend the women involved. Finally, we argue that the institutions that placed the issue on the agenda—medicine, law, and the media—have followed long-standing biases in attributing the blame for fetal abuse to women.

Problem Definition

Until very recently there was not such a thing as "fetal abuse." Previous generations attributed adverse birth outcomes to nature. More recently the debate over abortion and advances in medical research have focused attention on conditions affecting the fetus, revising our notions of what is appropriate behavior. As recently as twenty years ago, pregnant women were encouraged to take tranquilizers and drink moderate amounts of liquor (Pollitt 1990:411). Now there is widespread awareness that these behaviors can seriously impair fetal development.

How do new issues such as fetal abuse become defined and how do they change public policy? According to Deborah Stone (1988; 1989), causal stories play a central role in transforming an act of nature into a policy problem: "Problem definition is a process of image making, where the images have to do fundamentally with attributing cause, blame, and responsibility. Conditions, difficulties, or issues thus do not have inherent properties that make them more or less likely to be seen as problems or to be expanded. ... [Political actors] compose stories that describe harms and difficulties, attribute them to actions of other individuals or organizations, and thereby claim the right to invoke government power to stop the harm" (Stone 1989:282).

Although causal stories may or may not tell us much about the "true" causes of particular problems, they tell us a great deal about the power of different groups within society. Causal stories, which are in agreement with dominant cultural values, have a big advantage over those that challenge deeply held beliefs. When medical researchers ask which problems are most important, when prosecutors ask which crimes should receive the most attention, and when the media decide which stories should receive space, they are guided by their embedded values and those in their audience. This gives a great comparative advantage to causal stories that reinforce rather than challenge existing values.

The view that mothers are primarily responsible for children is deeply embedded in our culture. Given this, it is hardly surprising that when society asked who should be blamed for harm to the fetus it turned first to the mother. In a relatively brief period, fetal abuse became defined as adverse birth outcomes caused by the mother's substance abuse. Television and the print media have made it difficult to ignore the suffering of crack babies within the inner cities and the problem of fetal alcohol syndrome on Indian reservations. A typical *New York Times* article, complete with heart-rending photos of babies born to cocaine-addicted mothers, opened with a discussion of the prosecution of a Michigan woman for delivering cocaine to her fetus in utero and went on to say:

> Crack babies seem to be everywhere and they will not go away. Cautionary images of shrieking infants, bug-eyed as if they are watching tape loops from hell, even march across public-service announcements during televised sports events. A frequently cited nationwide study claimed that last year 375,000 children may have been affected by their mothers' drug use during pregnancy. Strokes in utero and respiratory and neurological disorders are only a few of the most common problems plaguing these drastically underweight children. Their suffering, to say nothing of the long term social costs, is so staggering that people understandably want to turn on their perceived torturers, their mothers (Hoffman 1990: 33).

In 1989, 1990, and 1991 the *New York Times* printed thirty-four articles on fetal abuse. Every one framed the problem as caused by women's lifestyle choices. The newspaper devoted a total of 853.5 column inches to the problems of babies harmed by their mothers' use of illegal drugs and/or drinking while pregnant. Almost 200 column inches were devoted to pictures, mostly of the affected infants and children; the remaining 658.5 column inches were text.[2] Less than half of the articles included any discussion of mitigating circumstances, such as a lack of drug treatment facilities for pregnant women, that might argue against a strategy of punishing the mothers. Twenty-two of the articles dealt with the impact of maternal drug abuse on fetuses, seven dealt with the effect of maternal alcohol abuse, and five articles dealt with both. Perhaps the greater attention paid to adverse effects of maternal drug use can be attributed to government's highly publicized war on drugs.

During the same period the *New York Times* printed no articles showing how men's lifestyle choices adversely affect fetal well-being. Not only was there no discussion of the impact of male substance abuse on fetal health, there was no mention even in crime stories of the impact of spousal battering on fetal development. However, in the science section there were two articles that discussed recent scholarly research showing that sperm damage may lead to birth defects. The scientific language of these two articles was in marked contrast to the vilification in most of the articles dealing with women's behavior.

The Effects of Blaming the Mother

The recognition that women's behavior during pregnancy has an impact on the well-being of the fetus has led to assertions of fetal rights. Until recently the rights of the fetus were assumed to coincide with those of the woman. The first attempts to assert fetal rights as distinctly separate from those of the mother evolved out of tort cases involving suits for prenatal injury. Most of these cases involved workplace exposure to harmful chemicals. Employers responded to this climate by establishing fetal protection plans that excluded all women of childbearing age from jobs that would expose them to known teratogens, such as lead. The U.S. Supreme Court's ruling in *International Union, United Auto Workers v. Johnson Controls Inc.*, 111 S. Ct. 1196 (1991)—that these plans were discriminatory—only slowed the attempts to control women's workplace activities.

Legal attempts to control pregnant women's behavior outside of the workplace have continued unabated. Given the one-sided reporting, it should surprise no one that the public perceives fetal abuse in terms that vilify mothers. In a survey commissioned by the *Atlanta Constitution*, 1,500 people from fifteen states were asked whether pregnant women whose drug use injured their babies should face criminal penalties. Seventy-one percent of those polled favored sending the women to jail (Hoffman 1990:33). This public awareness of the social costs of crack babies and fetal alcohol syndrome has led the criminal justice system increasingly to single out pregnant women's use of illegal drugs and alcohol for punishment. In 1987 and 1988 prosecutors in nineteen states and the District of Columbia took criminal actions against women for exposing their fetuses to drugs. Three states have specific laws singling out women who use drugs during pregnancy for additional penalties (Johnsen 1989:211). Some legislators have gone so far as to introduce bills requiring that women using drugs while pregnant be forced to undergo sterilization (Berrien 1990:240). At least eight states define drug exposure in utero as child abuse (Hoffman 1990:34). Some legal scholars (Robertson 1983; Balisy 1987) argue that child abuse laws should be used to not only penalize pregnant women for illegal drug use but also to punish women who smoke or drink alcohol while pregnant.

The Feminist Response

The issue of fetal abuse has placed feminists in an awkward position. On the one hand they are no different from anyone else in having a natural sympathy for the victims of fetal abuse. On the other hand they believe strongly that women are already subject to too many unequal societal constraints and that constraints on women should be loosened rather than tightened.

In many ways feminists were caught off-guard by the framing of fetal abuse as a problem caused by women's lifestyle choices. Everyone wants to protect the health and well-being of babies. It is impossible to see crack or fetal alcohol syndrome babies and not be outraged at the unfairness of their suffering. Along with Michael Dorris, who tells the story of his adopted son with fetal alcohol syndrome in the best-selling book *The Broken Cord*, it is tempting to call for the sterilization or forced incarceration of substance-abusing pregnant women (Dorris 1989).

The emotional power of the causal story blaming the mothers has made it difficult for feminists to confront the issue directly. Instead, most feminists accepted their opponents' framing of the issue of fetal abuse as a problem of women's lifestyle choices and then argued that there were important civil liberties issues at stake as well as a lack of drug treatment facilities that make punishing the mothers an inappropriate strategy. The civil liberties defense of drug- and substance-abusing pregnant women has three parts.

The first component is the standard civil libertarian stance of defending the rights of even those whose conduct one abhors. Prosecuting women for their conduct while pregnant is viewed as a violation of their right to privacy and to equal protection as guaranteed by the Fourteenth Amendment of the U.S. Constitution (Hoffman 1990:35; Field 1989:122; McNulty 1990:35–36; Johnsen 1986:614; Johnsen 1989:182; Gallagher 1987:28–29). Coercion of pregnant women has also been construed to be a violation of their rights to self-determination and bodily integrity, which is protected by the Fourth Amendment's restraints on search and seizure (Gallagher 1987:18–21).

The second component of the civil liberties defense is the argument that even if one could find a "compelling state interest" in promoting fetal health, there is still the "slippery slope" problem. The slippery slope problem refers to the difficulty in finding a logical stopping point in the regulation of pregnant women's activities (Berrien 1990:245; Field 1989:118–119; Johnsen 1986:605–606; Johnsen 1989:192). A wide range of controls on the behavior of pregnant women might be justified on the grounds of a "compelling state interest" in fetal health. Pregnant women or even women who think they might be pregnant may be prohibited from smoking, drinking, using hot tubs, or eating junk foods. Although each of these prohibitions individually might seem justifiable, they add up to a situation that imposes additional burdens on one group of people—women—solely on the basis of their reproductive capacity.

Another civil liberties defense is a variant on the equal protection argument. The argument is that the enforcement of drug abuse laws unfairly singles out poor nonwhite women while allowing substance-abusing white middle-class women to avoid prosecution. One study showed that approximately 70 percent of all pregnant women prosecuted for drug-related fetal abuse were African-American (Chasnoff, Landress, and Barrett 1990:1204). Furthermore, even though pregnant white women were slightly more likely to test positive for drug use, African-American women were ten times more likely to have those results reported to law enforcement officials (Chasnoff, Landress, and Barrett 1990:1204). These studies imply that not only does the social construction of fetal abuse unfairly single out women for prosecution but that it also reinforces society's racial biases.

Finally, many public health officials argue that it is unfair to prosecute pregnant substance abusers when it is almost impossible for them to receive treatment for their addiction. All of the studies looking at pregnant women's access to drug treatment have found that a majority of treatment facilities exclude pregnant women and the ones that admit pregnant women have extremely long waiting lists. There is a catch-22 in this behavior. Because the way in which the issue has been defined makes women responsible for fetal abuse, clinics feel that involvement in treating pregnant drug abusers might make them liable in civil court for birth defects. This in turn makes the problem harder to solve.

For example, in New York City over half of all drug treatment programs refuse to treat any pregnant women and two-thirds refuse to accept pregnant women on Medicaid. Overall, 90 percent of the facilities in the city refused pregnant crack users who were on Medicaid (Chavkin 1990:485). San Diego County has only twenty-six treatment slots available for pregnant addicts; waits of six months or longer for treatment are common (Berrien 1990:249; Field 1989:122). This means that most pregnant substance abusers have only two choices if they decide to have the baby: remain on drugs or go through withdrawal. Either one can result in serious harm to the fetus.

Although these arguments are important, and true as far as they go, they are not points that would seem conclusive to someone with a different viewpoint. One could argue that even if women have a right to legal protection, so do children, who in fact are more in need of societal protection. One can point out that the slippery slope argument could be applied with equal force to many other areas, such as pollution control. One could agree with the equal protection argument but hold that this simply means that the laws must be framed in such a way that they do not discriminate against poor and minority women. One could agree that under current conditions drug treatment and prison are not viable options but argue for programs that would make them more viable.

Further, feminist arguments about protecting civil liberties and equal protection, the slippery slope, and lack of treatment programs are disturbing because of their implicit acceptance of the underlying assumption that fetal abuse is a female crime. When the issue was workplace exposure to harmful toxicants, feminists struggled from the beginning to reframe the debate to include men's behavior. In addition to raising civil liberties and equal protection arguments against fetal protection policies that excluded fertile women from jobs, feminists consistently made the point that male exposure to toxicants also impaired fetal well-being. The discussion of behavior outside the workplace also needs to consider the fetal abuse arising from the actions of males. There are two major ways actions by males can damage the fetus. One is through actions that damage the sperm prior to its uniting with the egg. The other is through the battering of the pregnant mother and her fetus. We examine these in turn.

Male Fetal Abuse—Substance Abuse

Once one concedes the disputable point that unborn children have rights, there are no logical stopping points in judging where fetal harm might originate. Genetically the harm can arise from behavior that damages the egg or the sperm prior to fertilization. After fertilization the fetus can be harmed by actions by the mother or others while it is in the womb. Embryo loss due to genetic defects and post-fertilization problems is extremely high. Fewer than one-third of all embryos conceived actually result in live births. Since most of these losses occur early in the pregnancy, not much is known about the causes of embryo loss (Office of Technology Assessment 1985:5). There is similar ignorance about the causes of birth defects among the embryos that result in live births. At this time, 63 to 67 percent of birth defects are classified as being of unknown origin (Office of Technology Assessment 1985:354).

On the surface it appears reasonable that both maternal and paternal drug abuse might have negative effects on the health of eggs and sperm. If one accepts the causal link, one might expect more damage in groups where drug abuse was more prevalent. Because males are both more likely to become drug addicts and more likely to use a variety of drugs (U.S. Bureau of the Census 1992:128), one would expect there to be a higher likelihood of damage to the sperm than to the egg. The same point can be made about alcohol abuse. Men consume more alcohol and are more likely to become alcoholics (U.S. Bureau of the Census 1992:130). They are also more likely to be exposed to industrial chemicals that are thought to cause genetic damage.

One does not, however, base public policy on reasonable expectations. Is there in fact evidence that substance abuse has such effects? In part because of the way the problem has been framed, research in this area is still in its infancy. It is therefore impossible to reach definitive conclusions but the initial results are interesting. There is some preliminary evidence that substance abuse by males has negative effects on sperm. The few studies looking into male causes of adverse birth outcomes indicate that sperm is very susceptible to chemical exposure. Researchers have identified 1,491 occupational and environmental agents believed to adversely affect the quality of sperm (Davis, Friedler, Mattison, and Morris 1992:290). Despite this finding, there is little indication that firms have instituted policies limiting male exposure to identifiable reproductive hazards (Paul, Daniels, and Rosofsky 1989:267). There is also evidence that men's lifestyle choices, just like women's, can have a detrimental effect on fetal well-being. Alcohol, tobacco, and illegal drugs have been found to adversely impact the morphology of sperm (Office of Technology Assessment 1985:347). But these studies have received very little publicity. In fact, early studies showing a link between male smoking and low birth weight babies were dismissed as "nonsense" and more recent studies showing that tobacco residue is present in the semen of male smokers have also received little attention (Davis 1991:A27).

It is interesting to contrast this minimal research effort with the considerable effort being made to identify the effects of female substance abuse on the fetus. Defining the issue of fetal abuse in a way that relates the problem almost exclusively to the impact of women's activities on the fetus reduces both the attention and funds that are necessary to move an issue higher on the research agenda. A comprehensive approach to preventing adverse birth outcomes would require a consideration of male and female behaviors both before and after fertilization.

Male Fetal Abuse—Battering

It is difficult to accurately estimate the prevalence of male violence toward female partners. The most conservative figures, based on nationwide surveys of
2,000 couples in 1975 and 6,000 couples in 1985, indicate that approximately 1.8
million women every year are beaten by the men with whom they live (Straus
1977–1978:443; Straus and Gelles 1990:96). Other scholars believe that the national
surveys underestimate the actual amount of battering by at least half because
only couples living together were included. By excluding divorced or separated
couples, many of the most violent individuals are left out (Stark, Flitcraft, and
Frazier 1979:461).[3] A report from the U.S. Surgeon General indicated that 2 to 4
million women are physically abused by their partners every year and that domestic violence is the leading cause of injury to women between fifteen and
forty-four years of age (Novello, Rosenberg, Saltzman, and Shosky 1992:3132).

Pregnant women are most likely to be battered and the type of battering they
endure is more intense and more likely to be aimed at the fetus. In fact, pregnant
battered women as a group undergo more severe and frequent beatings than
other battered women (Campbell, Oliver, and Bullock 1992:9). The reasons for
their beatings are also different. When asked to explain why their husbands beat
them, over half of the pregnant battered women gave pregnancy-related reasons
such as anger toward the baby or jealousy of the baby (Campbell, Oliver, and
Bullock 1992:10). Indeed, some batterers are very aware of their own desire to
harm the fetus. The Washtenaw County Sheriff's Department recorded the following account of one man's beating of his wife: "Victim is six months pregnant
at this time. Victim stated accused kept telling victim, 'Bitch, you are going to
lose that baby,' and then accused would beat the victim in the stomach again"
(Eisenberg and Micklow 1979:139). Directing blows and kicks to the woman's abdominal region is characteristic of battering during pregnancy; violence against
nonpregnant women is usually directed at the face or the breasts (Van Stolk
1976:9; Hilberman and Munson 1978:462; Hilberman 1980:1340; Berenson,
Stiglich, Wilkinson, and Anderson 1991:1493). This implies that the men are either
consciously or subconsciously engaging in prenatal child abuse.

Some of the early research on battering indicated that pregnant women were
particularly at risk. Pregnant women seen in emergency rooms were more than
three times as likely as nonpregnant women to indicate that they sought medical treatment for injuries caused by battering (Stark, Flitcraft, and Frazier
1979:472). In the first study designed to explore the relationship between battering and pregnancy, Gelles discovered that almost one-fourth of violent families
reported battering during pregnancy (Gelles 1975:81–86). Subsequent research
indicates that between 14 to 60 percent of battered women retrospectively report
abuse during pregnancy.[4] The wide range in the reported figures is probably due
to differences in the type of populations surveyed. For example, residents of
shelters for battered women have notoriously high rates of abuse during preg-

nancy. Most researchers believe that roughly 4 to 8 percent of all pregnant women are battered during their current pregnancy and that up to 15 percent of other pregnant women must be considered at risk due to previous physical abuse (Helton 1987:5; Amaro, Fried, Cabral, Zuckerman, and Levenson 1988:1; Hillard 1985:186). Others believe that these figures may underestimate the risk, especially among some population groups. A large recent survey of poor black, white, and Hispanic women receiving care at public prenatal clinics found that only 17 percent of the patients had not been physically abused during their current pregnancy (McFarlane, Parker, Soeken, and Bullock 1992:3177).

Since many of the early descriptive studies showed that the abuse began or escalated during pregnancy, some have suggested that pregnancy be included along with drug use and alcoholism as a risk factor associated with battering (Sammons 1981:248; Berenson, Stiglich, Wilkinson, and Anderson 1991:1491). In his analysis of the data from the Second National Family Violence Survey, Richard Gelles found that women under thirty years of age were considerably more at risk than women over thirty. Because most pregnant women are less than thirty, their chances of being battered are higher. Gelles estimates that pregnant women's risk of violence is 35.6 percent higher than that of nonpregnant women (Gelles 1988:844–845). The Surgeon General was so alarmed by the findings of early studies that he recommended that all pregnancies involving spousal abuse be classified as high risk (Campbell, Poland, Waller, and Ager 1992:225).

There are four ways battering can cause adverse birth outcomes. First, there is a strong association between battering and inadequate prenatal care. Battered women are quite often prevented by their partners from receiving medical care while pregnant (Helton 1987:5; Campbell, Poland, Waller, and Ager 1992:225). Second, there is strong anecdotal evidence and some empirical research indicating that the rates of miscarriage and stillbirths among battered women may be up to two times greater than among nonbattered pregnant women (Hillard 1985:189; McFarlane 1989:70; Helton, McFarlane, and Anderson 1986:1338; Helton and Snodgrass 1987:143). Third, one large study showed a significant correlation between low birth weight babies and battering during the pregnancy. This relationship was found to be statistically significant even after researchers controlled for the other major risk factors associated with low birth weight, such as lack of prenatal care and alcohol consumption. A baby's birth weight is a major determinant in the child's survival, growth, and development (Bullock and McFarlane 1989:1153–1155). Finally, there are indications that battering can cause physical injuries to the fetus. After delivering an infant with bruises on its arms, neck, and shoulder, a swollen eye, and intraventricular hemorrhaging caused by prenatal battering, doctors at one hospital urged other physicians to pay closer attention to prenatal battering. Following the baby's death, the physicians wrote to the *Lancet*, "We consider it a delusion to think that the fetus is exempt from the hazards of an environment in which child abuse and spouse abuse are commonplace. Are there others with similar concerns who can help elaborate the battered fetus prototype?" (Morey, Begleiter, and Harris 1981:1294). At this time we know that approximately 6 to 7 percent of pregnancies experience complications due to trauma; only about half of the injuries are caused by auto accidents (Campbell, Oliver, and Bullock 1992:5; Stauffer 1986:91). It is unclear how many of the remaining trauma cases are due to battering but it is probably a high proportion since battering is a major cause of women's treatment in hospital emergency rooms. For all of these reasons battering during pregnancy must be considered a very serious threat to the well-being of the fetus.

Patriarchy and Biases in Problem Definition

We state at the beginning of this essay that the issue of fetal abuse has become defined in a way that blames women despite evidence that men are at least as much to blame for harm to the fetus. We also suggest that the primary reason for this skewed definition is a system of largely unconscious beliefs about women's role in society.

Demonstrating the role of unconscious beliefs is one of the most difficult tasks in the social sciences, despite common agreement that such beliefs are often more powerful than those held at a conscious level. Because they are so seldom articulated it is difficult to find quotes from actors claiming to act from these motives. Since in many cases people will give more socially acceptable reasons for their actions there is usually a wealth of alternative reasons that can be claimed. Given this difficulty we feel that the best that can be done is to show that the actions of the institutions most instrumental in defining the issue are generally consistent with patriarchal values and that the process of problem formation in the case of fetal abuse is also consistent with these values.

What pattern of behavior would we expect to find? A general pattern of discrimination against females by the institutions responsible for framing the issue of fetal abuse, especially when women diverge from the wife-and-mother role prescribed for them. In the area of fetal abuse we would expect that blame for abuse would be placed on the woman, because in a patriarchal society that is where responsibility is assigned.

As to the issue of fetal abuse, the three most instrumental institutions are the medical community, the legal profession, and the media. The actions of all three have been consistent with the hypotheses just outlined.

Bias in the Legal and Scientific Communities

According to Deborah Stone, the legal system and scientific establishment are two of the most powerful institutions involved in problem definition and the legitimation of claims (Stone 1989:294). More than any other institution within our society, the law is devoted to adjudicating competing claims. Case law is the means of transmitting the accumulated wisdom of previous generations to subsequent ones. Thus the legal system plays a powerful role in legitimating claims.

The scientific community plays a similar role in determining cause-and-effect relationships. Having the support of scientific evidence gives a great deal of cultural legitimacy to a claim.

Neither the legal nor scientific communities operate within a cultural vacuum. Both exist within a particular historical and cultural framework. In short, both law and science are social constructions that are undergoing constant modifications as the balance of power between social groups changes. Even though both of these institutions are currently undergoing change, it is important to remember that each in its own way has a long tradition of supporting patriarchal values.

Gender bias is most obvious in the legal system, where under the tradition of coverture married women did not even have a separate legal existence from that of their husbands. One can find evidence of a gender hierarchy within all fields of legal practice. Only within the last twenty years have women been guaranteed the right to serve on juries, to keep their birth names upon marriage, and to serve as executors of estates. Probably the most blatant example of built-in gender bias is seen in the treatment of rape cases. The evidentiary rules are stricter in rape cases and until recently judges routinely gave the following instruction to juries in rape trials: "A charge such as that made against the defendant in this case is one that is easily made and, once made, difficult to defend against, even if the person accused is innocent. Therefore, the law requires that you examine the testimony of the female person named in the information with caution" (Lindgren and Taub 1988:446).

In fact, a large part of the U.S. legal tradition has been based upon the notion of a "reasonable man." In tort cases, juries are often asked to consider what a reasonable man would do in a particular situation. The fact that women have a completely different socialization and are often physically smaller and weaker than men is not taken into account in assessing the reasonableness of a particular action (Gillespie 1989:98–106). The Supreme Court recently recognized that difference in *Harris v. Forklift Systems, Inc.* (1993), where the justices applied a "reasonable person" standard to evaluating whether a work environment was discriminatory.

The explicit gender hierarchy within the law has been under attack since the late 1960s, when the number of women entering into legal practice increased dramatically.[5] The women's movement profoundly affected the way these new attorneys chose to practice law. Female attorneys were at the forefront of the court cases challenging discriminatory legal practices and in establishing groups like the Women's Legal Defense Fund and the ACLU Women's Rights Project (O'Connor 1988:5–6). Today it would be fair to say that the law still has a strong gender bias, but less so than only a few years ago.

The gender bias within the scientific community is significantly less obvious to outsiders and has undergone far fewer challenges. Unless challenged, "normal science," in defining which methods and which areas of research are legitimate, replicates the biases of previous generations. Traditionally the scientific establishment either viewed women simply in terms of their reproductive function or completely ignored them. Within the medical field, women's health care needs are almost totally subsumed under the heading of "maternal and child health," which is primarily devoted to ensuring the well-being of the child (Mitchell 1988:50). Since the broader area of medical research deals almost exclusively with men, women's health care needs are rarely addressed. The best-known illustration of the invisibility of women in scientific research is the study of whether aspirin reduces the risk of heart attacks. Since no women were included in the study, one still does not know whether women have the same physiological response as men do to a daily dose of aspirin. Similar biases can be seen in the research on AIDS, where women are viewed primarily as carriers of the disease (Mitchell 1988:50; Wofsy 1987:2074–2076; Thomas 1987:12). Despite increasing rates of HIV infection among women, researchers routinely exclude women from their drug trials (Levine 1990:448–449).

Responding to complaints about women's exclusion from medical research, the Public Health Service in 1985 did a comprehensive study of women's health care needs. After discovering widespread deficiencies in both research and health care delivery, the U.S. Department of Health and Human Services in 1991 established the Office of Women's Health within the Public Health Service (U.S. Department of Health and Human Services 1991).

Law, Science, and Fetal Abuse

Not surprisingly, given their historic gender bias, both the legal system and the scientific establishment have helped to legitimate the causal story that attributes adverse birth outcomes to women's lifestyle choices. The criminal justice system contributes to this interpretation by extending the child abuse statutes to include fetal exposure to drugs and alcohol delivered in utero, by loosening the standards of criminal intent, and by not prosecuting male battering of the fetus. The scientific community contributes its share by devoting enormous time and energy to studying the effects of women's behavior on the fetus but very few resources to the effects of men's behavior on the fetus. Further, evidence showing a link between male lifestyle choices and fetal well-being is either discounted or ignored.

Out of a desire to coerce pregnant women into avoiding behaviors that might harm the fetus, prosecutors stretch child abuse laws to include fetal exposure to drugs and alcohol in utero. The laws are stretched in two ways: first, the fetus is construed by the courts to be a child; second, a far stricter standard than is normally used in child abuse cases is applied in fetal abuse cases. Usually child abuse laws are only applied in the most extreme situations. As Field put it, "One need not be a model parent to escape charges of abuse and neglect; the statutes come into play only when behavior is truly unacceptable" (Field 1989:115). Because of these problems in applying child abuse statutes to the fetus, women are now being prosecuted for the delivery of drugs to their newborn infants during the few minutes after birth before the umbilical cord is tied off. The mothers are prosecuted under the normal criminal statutes covering the delivery of drugs to another person. In order to accomplish this the normal standards of criminal conduct have to be substantially loosened. Generally, for a person to be found guilty of a criminal offense there needs to be "mens rea" or criminal intent. To prove such intent there needs to be either "objective" evidence showing reck- lessness and/or negligence or "subjective" intent requiring purposeful and knowing action. According to Molly McNulty, any serious attempt to assign criminal intent to these cases is "doomed to failure" because of the social and economic conditions over which a pregnant woman has no control (McNulty 1990:35). For example, this standard would make pregnant women responsible for providing levels of prenatal care that they might not be able to financially or physically obtain.

Despite the difficulty of establishing criminal intent, many states and locali- ties require nothing more than a positive drug test to prosecute the woman and, in some cases, remove the newborn infant from her custody.[6] This is true even though Dr. Ira Chassnoff, head of the National Association of Perinatal Addic- tion, Research, and Education, stated there is no scientific evidence to back up the claim that cocaine is passed to the infant through the umbilical cord before it is clamped (Hoffman 1990:35). In Florida a woman was convicted of a felony punishable by up to thirty years in prison for delivering drugs to her baby through the umbilical cord (Chavkin 1990:484). In a misguided attempt to pro- tect fetal health, judges are increasingly sentencing pregnant women to jail time for offenses that normally would receive probationary sentences (Moss 1988:20; McNulty 1990:34). The irony is that anyone who knows anything about maternal care in prisons would never send a pregnant woman there to protect the fetus. Even though pregnant women need to have a diet high in proteins, vitamins, and nutrients, fourteen out of twenty-six prisons in one survey made no special provisions for providing pregnant inmates with special diets or supplementary vitamins (McHugh 1980:241). Only a few prisons have medical care available for female prisoners round-the-clock and some do not even have contingency plans for overnight medical needs (Holt 1981–1982:526). Furthermore, incarcerat- ing a pregnant woman does not necessarily mean that she will be unable to ob- tain illegal drugs, since many drugs are widely available in prisons.

One way of assessing the suitability of a prison environment for maternal and fetal health is to compare miscarriage rates in prison to the general rate. In Cali- fornia, the general miscarriage rate among fetuses of twenty weeks or more is less than one percent (U.S. Department of Health and Human Services 1990:88).[7] In contrast, the miscarriage rate among pregnant California prisoners is 33.7 percent (Barry 1985:3). There are indications that the situation in county jails is even worse than in state prisons. For example, a study of one county jail showed a miscarriage rate fifty times greater than the rate in the rest of the state.

Of the pregnancies studied, only about one-fifth resulted in a live birth (Barry 1989:202). In short, anyone concerned with increasing the chances of a woman having a healthy live birth should make every effort to keep that woman out of prison.

The scientific community has also contributed to our understanding of fetal abuse as being a female problem. Prior to the thalidomide scare of the 1960s there was very little scientific research into the causes of birth defects. Adverse birth outcomes were usually attributed to nature rather than to human causes. The prevalence of birth defects among children born to mothers who had taken thalidomide while pregnant led to a rethinking of the reasons for birth defects. Once the cause of birth defects moved from being attributable to nature to being a result of human actions, solving the problem became a matter of human intervention. This shift in causal stories led to thirty years of research into maternal causes of fetal damage.

On one level this research emphasis on the mother is understandable. The triggering event, birth defects among thalidomide babies, was the direct result of pregnant women taking a drug. However, there are indications that sexism affected the research in two important ways. First, there appears to be a bias against publicizing research demonstrating that the link between maternal substance abuse and poor pregnancy outcomes is overstated. More than half of the studies from 1980 to 1989 showing that babies born to cocaine-abusing mothers had medical problems were accepted for presentation by the Society for Pediatric Research; better-designed studies showing no connection had a negligible chance of acceptance (Koren, Shear, Graham, and Einarson 1989:1440–1442). In fact, there have been a series of studies indicating that the long-term effects of intrauterine cocaine exposure are unclear and that the early claims of severe and irrevocable brain damage are wildly overblown.[8]

Second, most of the studies have been designed to test for a maternal link rather than a paternal one. For the first fifteen years after the thalidomide scare researchers chose to only use women as research subjects. Even when researchers are interested in exploring the effects of male exposure to a teratogen, the studies have been performed on the wives of the men rather than on the men themselves (Office of Technological Assessment 1985:35). As a result of this bias in research design there have been far fewer studies of the impact of male exposure to teratogens and male lifestyle choices on the fetus (Davis 1991:A27). As one National Academy of Sciences researcher expressed it, "You don't have to be Sigmund Freud to figure out why we have paid so much attention to the female and so little to the male" (Blakeslee 1991:36).

Law, Medicine, and Battering

The reasons for dismissing spousal abuse as a problem rest in society's past acceptance of the practice. The roots of wifebeating in our society can be traced at least back to the Middle Ages, when church doctrine held that wives were to submit themselves to beatings and kiss the rods used against them. One of the first indications that there might be limits on how much violence a man might use against his wife was discovered by Mary Van Stolk in a fifteenth-century sermon where a priest admonished his male parishioners to have more patience with their wives: "You men have more patience with the hen that befouleth thy table but layeth a fresh egg daily, than with thy wife when she bringeth forth a little girl. ... Consider the fruit of the woman, and have patience; not for every cause is it right to beat her" (Van Stolk 1976:12).

English common law considered the wife to have no separate legal existence from that of her husband, who was given responsibility for controlling her actions. When Blackstone was writing in the latter half of the eighteenth century, the exact amount of violence that a man might justifiably use in controlling his wife was undergoing change. Under the old common law tradition a man was allowed to wound his wife severely with whips and fists; by Blackstone's time that amount of "chastisement" was beginning to be viewed as unreasonable (Lindgren and Taub 1988:3). In 1782, one judge held that it was acceptable for a man to beat his wife with a rod the thickness of his thumb, but no larger (May 1978:139).

This explicit legal acceptance of men's right to beat their wives was also part of the U.S. legal tradition. In 1824 North Carolina passed a law allowing a man to beat his wife if he used a switch no thicker than his thumb. It took a half-century for a court to rule that men had no inherent right to beat their wives; however, the court added that unless there was a permanent injury it should be treated as a private matter (Hilberman 1980:1338). State laws explicitly allowing wifebeating survived until the Progressive Era (Bohn 1990:86).

Even today the criminal justice system has a strong tendency to treat spousal abuse as a private matter. In most situations the intentional infliction of physical harm to another person is treated as a crime against society and prosecution is automatic. Only in cases of spouse battering is the criminal prosecution dependent upon the victim vigorously pressing charges against the perpetrator (Eisenberg and Micklow 1979:146–147; Hilberman 1980:1338). Even when women are willing to press charges they find it difficult to do so. Police respond slowly if at all to domestic violence reports and often end up trying to talk the woman out of pressing charges (Dobash and Dobash 1979:207–217; Bohn 1990:94).

The medical system is the only other social institution that has had an opportunity to intervene in spousal-battering cases. Studies have found that most battered women will seek medical treatment in hospital emergency rooms when they are seriously injured but usually will not disclose the true reason for their injuries (Dobash and Dobash 1979:181; Novello, Rosenberg, Saltzman, and Shosky 1992:3132; Sugg and Inui 1992:3158). However, even if the woman's explanation is highly implausible, medical personnel rarely probe to discover the actual reasons for a woman's injuries (Eisenberg and Micklow 1979:155–156; Hilberman 1980:1342; Bohn 1990:95). A primary-care physician explained his reluctance to confront the possibility that his patients were being physically abused in the following manner: "I think that some physicians, and I do the same thing, if you are very busy and have a lot of patients waiting, you just don't ask a question that you know is going to open a Pandora's box. Even if it crosses your mind, you don't ask" (Sugg and Inui 1992:3158).

One study of a large metropolitan hospital showed that emergency room physicians identified only one female patient out of thirty-five as battered; subsequent research revealed that approximately one in four were probably battered (Stark, Flitcraft, and Frazier 1979:466). Until 1992, the American Medical Association had no guidelines instructing their membership to consider domestic violence when treating female patients. This reluctance on the part of medical personnel to uncover spousal abuse reinforces the notion that it is a private rather than a public concern.

Given their history as patriarchal institutions, it should surprise no one that the legal and medical professions act in ways that minimize recognition of the extent of domestic violence against women. By socially sanctioning and, later, by treating spousal abuse differently from other types of assaults, the criminal justice system has contributed to a trivialization of wife battering within our society. The medical profession has contributed to this understatement of the problem by choosing not to follow up on obvious indications that women are being beaten. Not only have both of these institutions sought to minimize the extent of the problem, they have reinforced the social definition of the problem as being private rather than public.

In the past, during prenatal exams medical personnel rarely assessed the likelihood that patients were battered nor looked closely at the causes of miscarriages and stillbirths. This is slowly beginning to change. In 1986 the March of Dimes Birth Defects Foundation launched a major campaign to raise public awareness about the adverse impact of battering on fetal health. The foundation provided funding for a pilot education program, literature for health care providers, a film entitled *Crime Against the Future* with U.S. Surgeon General C. Everett Koop, a video on the battering of pregnant teenagers, and curriculum material for high school students (McFarlane 1989:73–83).

Despite these attempts to raise public awareness the message does not seem to have changed the public perception that fetal abuse is caused by women's actions. Several of the most well-known criminal prosecutions of women for fetal abuse have also involved male battering of the pregnant women. In one Wyoming case a pregnant woman, who went to the hospital because she had been beaten by her husband, was arrested for fetal abuse because she also had been drinking (Pollitt 1990:416). In a nationally publicized California case a woman was prosecuted for failing to provide necessary care to her "pre-born child." The baby was born with severe brain damage and died shortly after birth. One reason for the mother's prosecution was that she had had sexual intercourse in the latter stages of the pregnancy. The fact that the woman was physically beaten by her husband and that the baby's injuries were very likely caused by the beatings was considered irrelevant or not considered at all. The husband was not prosecuted for either the battering nor for violating the doctor's prohibition against having sex with his wife (Berrien 1990:244–246; McNulty 1990:33; Johnsen 1989:208–210; Pollitt 1990:416).

The media has chosen not to publicize fetal abuse caused by violence directed against pregnant women and their fetuses. The failings of the California woman as a parent and as a person received national press attention following the death of her baby, whereas the actions of her husband received very little coverage (Johnsen 1989:208). As we note earlier, between 1989 and 1991 the *New York Times* devoted a total of 853.5 column inches of coverage to fetal abuse brought about by pregnant women's use of illegal drugs and/or drinking. During the same period there was not a single story dealing with adverse birth outcomes due to the physical abuse of pregnant women. There was not even mention of the battering of pregnant women in any of the hundreds of crime stories covered by the newspaper during those three years. Clearly, battering of women and the children within their wombs is an invisible crime. The media's failure to present a gender-inclusive analysis of the causes of fetal abuse is consistent with scholarly research into media bias. The mass media also replicate and reinforce existing social biases, including those against women (Bennett 1988; Kahn and Goldberg 1991; Kahn 1992).

Conclusions

Though clearly an important issue in its own right, the invisibility of male-caused fetal abuse tells us a great deal about the enduring power of our cultural biases. There is no overt conspiracy among lawyers, medical professionals, and journalists to define fetal abuse in a manner that blames the woman and ignores the man. There is simply a predisposition to view the world through analytical lenses that replicate and reinforce existing gender biases. The definition of fetal abuse as a problem of women's behavior occurred through hundreds of individual and seemingly unconnected actions. By choosing to study only maternal causes of adverse birth outcomes, individual scientists contributed to this understanding. The criminal justice system added its part by choosing to ignore battering while zeroing in on pregnant women's substance abuse. Medical practitioners, by choosing not to ask why so many women seek treatment in emergency rooms for traumatic injuries and later by not asking why so many of these same women face difficulties in giving birth to healthy babies, made battering a medical nonissue. And finally, the media played a crucial role by publicizing crack and fetal alcohol syndrome babies while ignoring the effects of battering on the fetuses.

None of the individuals involved in this process was consciously trying to create a one-sided view of fetal abuse. They were simply attempting to deal with a social problem in the best way that they could. However, their cultural predispositions led to a replication of existing gender biases. This tracing of the origins and development of the issue of fetal abuse clearly illustrates the way that policy definitions are socially constructed. Through their seemingly unconnected actions, hundreds of individuals developed a causal story that fit the historic gender biases of the institutions framing the problem.

Notes

This chapter is revised from Jean Schroedel and Paul Peretz, "A Gender Analysis of Policy Formation: The Case of Fetal Abuse," *Journal of Health Politics, Policy and Law* 19(2):335–360 (summer 1994). Reprinted with permission.

1. Scholars have traced this view to a belief in "separate spheres" of responsibility for men and women. Because of the greater power and status ascribed to the male area of responsibility, individuals holding this world view are also often described as having patriarchal beliefs. See Bates et al. (1983) for discussion of the origins and social implications of these beliefs and Cott (1987) for a history of the conflicts between the "separate spheres" ideology and feminism in the United States.

2. Much of the literature on agenda setting utilizes the number of column inches in the *New York Times* as a measure of an issue's salience. For example, in his classic study of agenda setting in the Senate, Walker (1977) uses the number of column inches in the *New York Times* as a means of showing that the public considered traffic safety, coal mine safety, and occupational health and safety to be important problems that warranted governmental action. None of these three issue areas generated anywhere close to the number of column inches devoted to fetal abuse. In the three years prior to passage of the 1966 Highway Safety Act, there were less than 163 column inches devoted to the problem of traffic safety. Coal mine safety generated only thirty-six column inches in the three years prior to the 1969 passage of the Coal Mine Health and Safety Act, and in the three years prior to the 1970 passage of the Occupational Health and Safety Act, there were only twenty-nine column inches dealing with workplace safety.

3. This underreporting of domestic violence against women is especially severe within the African-American community. One recent study of violence against pregnant women reported that only 6 percent of the battering against black women was done by husbands and ex-husbands. Boyfriends, who would not be counted in the national surveys, accounted for a majority of the violence against African-American women (McFarlane, Parker, Soeken, and Bullock 1992:3178).

4. See Campbell, Poland, Waller, and Ager (1992) for a summary of current research dealing with the relationship between pregnancy and battering.

5. In 1960 only approximately 3.8 percent of law school graduates were women. By 1970 that figure had increased to 8.6 percent and ten years later it was up to 33.5 percent (Cook 1983:50).

6. Prosecutors vary a great deal in their willingness to pursue criminal actions against substance-abusing pregnant women. The highest number of criminal prosecutions have occurred in South Carolina, where thirty women were indicted prior to 1992 for drug offenses involving fetal exposure (Strickland and Whicker 1992:6). At least 167 pregnant women from twenty-six states have been arrested and faced criminal charges for endangering their fetuses. Existing statutes dealing with child abuse, child neglect, contributing to the delinquency of a minor, child endangerment, delivering drugs to a minor, assault

with a deadly weapon, manslaughter, and homicide have been used in these prosecutions (Strickland and Whicker 1992:15–17).

7. There are no reliable records of miscarriage rates for fetuses of less than twenty weeks old because many women miscarry before they even know that they are pregnant.

8. Following the publication of the Koren, Shear, Graham, and Einarson (1989) study documenting the bias against publishing studies that showed no adverse effects of cocaine abuse during pregnancy, many of the most respected medical journals published review articles summarizing the current knowledge about the impact of maternal use of cocaine on fetal development. All of these reviews (Neuspiel and Hamel 1991; Mayes, Granger, Bornstein, and Zuckerman 1992; Myers, Olson, and Kaltenback 1992; Zuckerman and Frank 1992) argued that biomedical research had not clearly established whether prenatal exposure to cocaine causes lasting damage to the child. The earlier studies, which documented growth retardation, neonatal behavioral abnormalities and a host of other problems, had serious methodological flaws. The most serious was the failure to control for other confounding factors (the women in the studies also abused other drugs, smoked, drank alcohol, and received minimal prenatal care.) Hence, it is difficult to determine exactly which adverse birth outcomes are attributable to the use of cocaine and which are due to the other risk factors. For an even more up-to-date review of the relevant literature, see Myers, Britt, Lodder, Kendall, and Williams-Petersen's (1993) unpublished manuscript.

References

Abramovitz, Mimi. *Regulating the Lives of Women.* Boston: South End Press, 1988.

Amaro, Hortensia, Lisa E. Fried, Howard Cabral, Barry Zuckerman, and Suzette Levenson. "Violence Toward Pregnant Women and Associated Drug Use." Paper presented at the American Public Health Association Annual Meeting, 1988.

Balisy, Sam S. "Maternal Substance Abuse: The Need to Provide Legal Protection for the Fetus." *Southern California Law Review* 60:1209–1238, 1987.

Barr, Helen M., Ann Pytkowicz Streissguth, Betty L. Darby, and Paul D. Sampson. "Prenatal Exposure to Alcohol, Caffeine, Tobacco and Aspirin: Fine and Gross Motor Performance in 4-Year-Old Children." *Developmental Psychology* 26:339–348, 1990.

Barry, Ellen. "Quality of Prenatal Care for Incarcerated Women Challenged." *Youth Law News* 6(6):1–4, 1985.

———. "Recent Developments: Pregnant Prisoners." *Harvard Women's Law Journal* 12:189–205, 1989.

Bates, Ulku U., Florence L. Denmark, Virginia Held, Dorothy O. Helly, Susan H. Lees, Sarah B., Smith, E. Dorsey, Sue Pomeroy, and Rosenberg Zalk. *Women's Realities, Women's Choices.* New York: Oxford University Press, 1983.

Bennett, W. Lance. *News: The Politics of Illusion.* 2nd ed. New York: Longman, 1988.

Berenson, Abbey B., Norma J. Stiglich, Gregg S. Wilkinson, and Garland D. Anderson. "Drug Abuse and Other Risk Factors for Physical Abuse in Pregnancy Among White Non-Hispanic, Black and Hispanic Women." *American Journal of Obstetrics and Gynecology* 164(6):1491–1499, 1991.

Berrien, Jacqueline. "Pregnancy and Drug Use: The Dangerous and Unequal Use of Punitive Measures." *Yale Journal of Law and Feminism* 2(2):239–250, 1990.

Blakeslee, Sandra. "Research on Birth Defects Shifts to Flaws in Sperm." *New York Times.* 1 January 1991, 1, 36.

Boals, Kay. "Review Essay: Political Science." *Signs* 1(1):161–174, 1975.

Bohn, Diane K. "Domestic Violence and Pregnancy: Implications for Practice." *Journal of Nurse-Midwifery* 35(2):86–98, 1990.

Bower, B. "Alcohol's Fetal Harm Lasts A Lifetime." *Science News* 139:244, 1991.

Bullock, Linda F., and Judith McFarlane. "The Birth-Weight/Battering Connection." *American Journal of Nursing* 89:1153–1155, 1989.

Campbell, Jacquelyn C., Catharine Oliver, and Linda Bullock. "Why Battering During Pregnancy." Unpublished manuscript, 1992.

Campbell, Jacquelyn C., Marilyn L. Poland, John B. Waller, and Joel Ager. "Correlates of Battering During Pregnancy." *Research in Nursing and Health* 15:219–226, 1992.

Carroll, Bernice. "Review Essay: Political Science, Part I: American Politics and Political Behavior." *Signs* 5(2):289–306, 1979.

Chasnoff, Ira J., Harvey J. Landress, and Mark E. Barrett. "The Prevalence of Illicit Drug or Alcohol Use During Pregnancy and Discrepancies in Mandatory Reporting in Pinellas County, Florida." *New England Journal of Medicine* 322(17):1202–1206, 1990.

Chavkin, Wendy. "Drug Addiction and Pregnancy: Policy Crossroads." *American Journal of Public Health* 80(4):483–487, 1990.

Cook, Beverly B. "The Path to the Bench: Ambitions and Attitudes of Women in the Law." *Trial* 19:49–50, 1983.

Cott, Nancy F. *The Grounding of Modern Feminism*. New Haven: Yale University Press, 1987.

Davis, Devra Lee. "Fathers and Fetuses." *New York Times*. 1 March 1991, A27.

Davis, Devra Lee, Gladys Friedler, Donald Mattison, and Robert Morris. "Male-mediated Teratogenesis and other Reproductive Effects: Biologic and Epidemiologic Findings and a Plea for Clinical Research." *Reproductive Toxicology* 6:289–292, 1992.

Dobash, R. Emerson, and Russell Dobash. *Violence Against Wives*. New York: The Free Press, 1979.

Dorris, Michael. *The Broken Cord*. New York: Harper and Row Publishers, 1989.

Eisenberg, Sue E., and Patricia L. Micklow. "The Assaulted Wife: 'Catch 22' Revisited." *Women's Rights Law Reporter* 3:138–161, 1979.

Field, Martha A. "Controlling the Woman to Protect the Fetus." *Law, Medicine and Health Care* 17(2):114–129, 1989.

Gallagher, Janet. "Prenatal Invasions and Interventions: What's Wrong with Fetal Rights." *Harvard Women's Law Journal* 10(9):9–58, 1987.

Gelles, Richard J. "Violence and Pregnancy: Are Pregnant Women at Greater Risk of Abuse?" *Journal of Marriage and Family* 50:841–847, 1988.

Gillespie, Cynthia K. *Justifiable Homicide*. Columbus: Ohio State University Press, 1989.

Gordon, Linda. *Women, the State, and Welfare*. Madison: University of Wisconsin Press, 1990.

Hager, Philip. "Case Against Mothers Spurs Debate on Fetal Abuse." *New York Times*. 17 June 1992, 1, 18.

Helton, Anne Stewart. *Protocol of Care for the Battered Woman*. Houston: March of Dimes Birth Defects Foundation, 1987.

Helton, Anne Stewart, Judith McFarlane, and Elizabeth T. Anderson. "Battered and Pregnant: A Prevalence Study." *American Journal of Public Health* 77(10):1337–1339, 1987.

Helton, Anne Stewart, and Frances Gobble Snodgrass. "Battering During Pregnancy: Intervention Strategies." *Birth* 14(3):142–147, 1987.

Hilberman, Elaine. "Overview: The 'Wife-Beater' Reconsidered." *American Journal of Psychiatry* 137(11):1336–1347, 1980.

Hilberman, Elaine, and Kit Munson. "Sixty Battered Women." *Victimology* 2(3–4):460–470, 1977.

Hillard, Paula J. Adams. "Physical Abuse in Pregnancy." *Obstetrics and Gynecology* 66(2):185–189, 1985.

Hoffman, Jan. "Pregnant, Addicted and Guilty." *New York Times Magazine*. August 19, 1990, 33 et seq.

Holt, Karen E. "Nine Months to Life—The Law and the Pregnant Inmate." *Journal of Family Law* 20:523–543, 1981–1982.

Johnsen, Dawn E. "The Creation of Fetal Rights: Conflicts with Women's Constitutional Rights to Liberty, Privacy, and Equal Protection." *Yale Law Journal* 95:599–625, 1986.

———. "From Driving to Drugs: Governmental Regulation of Pregnant Women's Lives After Webster." *University of Pennsylvania Law Review* 138:179–215, 1989.

Kahn, Kim Friedkan. "Does Being Male Help? An Investigation of the Effects of Candidate Gender and Campaign Coverage on Evaluations of U.S. Senate Candidates." *Journal of Politics* 54:497–517, 1992.

Kahn, Kim Friedkan, and Edie N. Goldberg. "Women Candidates in the News: An Examination of Gender Differences in U.S. Senate Campaign Coverage." *Public Opinion Quarterly* 55:180–199, 1991.

Koren, Gideon, Heather Shear, Karen Graham, and Tom Einarson. "Bias Against the Null Hypothesis: The Reproductive Hazards of Cocaine." *The Lancet* 2:1440–1442, 1989.

Levine, Carol. "Women and HIV/AIDS Research: the Barriers to Equity." *Evaluation Review* 14(5):447–463, 1990.

Lindgren, J. Ralph, and Nadine Taub. *The Law of Sex Discrimination.* St. Paul: West Publishing Company, 1988.

MacKinnon, Catharine A. *Feminism Unmodified: Discourses on Life and Law.* Cambridge, Mass.: Harvard University Press, 1987.

Marcotte, Paul. "Crime and Pregnancy: Prosecutors, New Drugs, Torts Pit Mom Against Baby." *American Bar Association Journal* 75:14 and 16, 1989.

May, Margaret. "Violence in the Family: An Historical Perspective." In *Violence and the Family.* Edited by J.P. Martin. New York: John Wiley and Sons, 1978.

Mayes, Linda C., Richard H. Granger, Marc H. Bornstein, and Barry Zuckerman. "The Problem of Prenatal Cocaine Exposure." *Journal of the American Medical Association* 267(3):406–408, 1992.

McFarlane, Judith. "Battering During Pregnancy: Tip of an Iceberg Revealed." *Women and Health* 15(3):69–84, 1989.

McFarlane, Judith, Barbara Parker, Karen Soeken, and Linda Bullock. "Assessing for Abuse During Pregnancy." *Journal of the American Medical Association* 267(23):3176–3178, 1992.

McHugh, Gerald Austin. "Protection of the Rights of Pregnant Women in Prisons and Detention Facilities." *New England Journal on Prison Law* 6:231–263, 1980.

McNulty, Molly. "Pregnancy Police: Implications of Criminalizing Fetal Abuse." *Youth Law News* Special Issue:33–37, 1990.

Mitchell, Janet L. "Women, AIDS, and Public Policy." *AIDS and Public Policy Journal* 3(2):50–52, 1988.

Morey, Martha A., Michael L. Begleiter, and David J. Harris. "Profile of a Battered Fetus." *The Lancet* 11(8258):1294–1295, 1981.

Moss, Debra Cassens. "Pregnant? Go Directly To Jail." *American Bar Association Journal* 74(11):20, November 1, 1988.

Myers, Barbara J., Heather Carmichael Olson, and Karol Kaltenbach. "Cocaine-Exposed Infants: Myths and Misunderstandings." *Zero to Three* 13(1):1–5, 1992.

Myers, Barbara J., Gena Covell Brit, Diane E. Lodder, Kathy A. Kendall, and Margaret G. Williams-Petersen. "Cocaine Exposure and Infant Development: A Review." Unpublished manuscript, 1993.

Nelson, Barbara J. "The Gender, Race, and Class Origins of Early Welfare Policy and the Welfare State: A Comparison of Workmen's Compensation and Mother's Aid." In *Women, Politics, and Change.* Edited by Louise A. Tilly and Patricia Gurin. New York: Russell Sage Foundation, 1990.

Neuspiel, Daniel R., and Sara C. Hamel. "Cocaine and Infant Behavior." *Developmental and Behavioral Pediatrics* 12(1):55–64, 1991.

Novello, Antonia C., Mark Rosenberg, Linda Saltzman, and John Shosky. "From the Surgeon General, US Public Health Service." *Journal of the American Medical Association* 267(23):3132, 1992.

O'Brien, J.E. "Violence in Divorce Prone Families." *Journal of Marriage and the Family* 33(4):692–698, 1971.

O'Connor, Karen. "Women as Lawyers." In *Women in the Judicial Process*. Edited by Beverly B. Cook, Leslie F. Goldstein, Karen O'Connor, and Susette M. Talarico. Washington, D.C.: American Political Science Association, 1987.

Office of Technology Assessment. *Reproductive Health Hazards in the Workplace*. Washington, D.C.: Government Printing Office, 1985.

Paul, Maureen, Cynthia Daniels, and Robert Rosofsky. "Corporate Response to Reproductive Hazards in the Workplace: Results of the Family, Work, and Health Survey." *American Journal of Industrial Medicine* 16:267–280, 1989.

Pollitt, Katha. "Fetal Rights: A New Assault on Feminism," *The Nation*. March 26, 1990, 409–418.

Revkin, Andrew C. "Crack in the Cradle." *Discover* 10:63–69, 1989.

Roberts, Dorothy. "The Bias in Drug Arrests of Pregnant Women." *New York Times*. 11 May 1990, 25.

Robertson, John A. "Procreative Liberty and the Control of Conception, Pregnancy, and Childbirth." *Virginia Law Review* 69(3):405–464, 1983.

Rosenthal, Elisabeth. "When A Pregnant Woman Drinks." *New York Times Magazine*. February 4, 1990, 30 et seq.

Sammons, Lucy Newmark. "Battered and Pregnant." *American Journal of Maternal Child Nursing* 6:246–250, 1981.

Silverberg, Helene. "What Happened to the Feminist Revolution in Political Science?" *Western Political Quarterly* 43(4):887–903, 1990.

Stark, Evan, Anne Flitcraft, and William Frazier. "Medicine and Patriarchal Violence: The Social Construction of a 'Private Event'." *International Journal of Health Services* 9(3):461–493, 1979.

Starr, Paul. *The Social Transformation of American Medicine*. New York: Basic Books, 1982.

Stauffer, Diane M. "The Trauma Patient Who is Pregnant." *Journal of Emergency Nursing* 12(2):89–93, 1986.

Stone, Deborah A. *Policy Paradox and Political Reason*. New York: Harper Collins Publishers, 1988.

————. "Causal Stories and the Formation of Policy Agendas." *Political Science Quarterly* 104(2):281–300, 1989.

Straus, Murray. "Wife-Beating: How Common, and Why?" *Victimology* 2:443–458, 1977–1978.

Straus, Murray, and Richard J. Gelles. *Physical Violence in American Families*. New Brunswick: Transaction Publishers, 1990.

Strickland, Ruth Ann, and Marcia Lynn Whicker. "Fetal Endangerment Versus Fetal Welfare: Discretion of Prosecutors in Determining Criminal Liability and Intent." Paper prepared for delivery at the 1992 Annual Meeting of the American Political Science Association, 1992.

Sugg, Nancy Kathleen, and Thomas Inui. "Primary Care Physicians' Response to Domestic Violence." *Journal of the American Medical Association* 267(23):3157–3160, 1992.

Thomas, Patricia. "AIDS Agenda Slights Women." *Medical World News*. July 27, 1987, 12–13.

U.S. Bureau of the Census. *Statistical Abstract of the United States: 1992* (112th edition). Washington D.C.: Government Printing Office, 1992.

U.S. Department of Health and Human Services. *Action Plan for Women's Health.* Washington, D.C.: Government Printing Office, 1991.

U.S. Department of Health and Human Services. *Vital Statistics of the United States 1988.* Volume II: Mortality. Washington, D.C.: Government Printing Office, 1990.

Van Stolk, Mary. "Battered Children." *Children Today.* March-April, 1976, 9–12.

Walker, Jack L. "Setting the Agenda in the U.S. Senate: A Theory of Problem Selection." *British Journal of Political Science.* October 1977:421–445.

Wofsy, C. "Human Immunodeficiency Virus in Women." *Journal of the American Medical Association* 257:2074–2076, 1987.

Zuckerman, Barry, and Deborah A. Frank. "Crack Kids: Not Broken." *Pediatrics* 89(2):337–339, 1992.

Punishment, Treatment, Empowerment: Three Approaches to Policy for Pregnant Addicts

IRIS MARION YOUNG

IN THIS ESSAY I use some issues and concepts of feminist ethics, postmodernism, and critical theory to reflect on one very important women's issue: policy approaches to pregnant women who are habitual drug users.[1] Many people, including law enforcement officials, child protection agents, and legislators, think that women who use drugs during pregnancy should be punished for the harm or risks of harm they bring to their babies. I analyze this punishment approach and argue that the situation of pregnant addicts does not satisfy the conditions usually articulated by philosophers to justify punishment. A punishment approach, moreover, may have sexist and racist implications and ultimately operate more to maintain a social distinction between insiders and deviants than to protect children.

Most of those who criticize a punishment approach to policy for pregnant addicts call for meaningful treatment programs as an alternative; I interpret this treatment approach as a version of a feminist ethic of care. For the most part theorizing about the ethic of care has remained at the level of ontology and epistemology, with little discussion of how the ethic of care interprets concrete moral issues differently from more traditional approaches to ethics. By arguing that a treatment approach to pregnant addicts can be justified by an ethic of care, I propose to understand this ethic of care as a moral framework for social policy.

Although I agree with a treatment approach to policy for pregnant addicts, from a feminist point of view there are reasons to be suspicious of many aspects of typical drug treatment. Relying on Michel Foucault's notions of disciplinary power and the operation of "confessional" discourse in therapy, I argue that treatment often operates to adjust women to dominant gender, race, and class structures and depoliticizes and individualizes their situations. Thus I conclude by offering a distinction between two meanings of empowerment in service provision, one that remains individualizing and one that develops social solidarity through consciousness-raising and the possibility of collective action.

Punishment

According to some estimates, as many as 375,000 babies born every year in the United States are affected by their mothers' drug use during pregnancy,[2] though others think the numbers are lower.[3] Some of these babies suffer some disorders and problems at birth, but it is difficult to isolate the mother's drug use from other possible causes such as poverty, poor prenatal care, and depression.[4] The degree of harm to babies is also quite variable. Some children are permanently retarded or physically impaired whereas others are normal and healthy, especially as they grow older.[5] For the purposes of this discussion, however, I will assume that a mother's frequent drug use during pregnancy usually brings some kind of harm, whether short term or long term, to the baby she bears.

Punitive responses to the problem of drug-exposed infants have significant support among policymakers, law enforcement officials, and the general public.[6] Many prosecutors, judges, and legislatures in the United States have acted on these sentiments. Some judges have sentenced pregnant addicts convicted of crimes like theft or shoplifting to much heavier sentences than they would have otherwise.[7]

Punitive legislation regarding pregnant addicts has been considered in more than thirty states and by the U.S. Congress.[8] Although the testimony of legal and medical experts appears to have succeeded in preventing the passage of congressional legislation, at least eight states now include drug exposure in utero in their definitions of child abuse and neglect.[9] In several states without such laws prosecutors have used drug trafficking laws to file criminal charges against women who use cocaine or other controlled substances during pregnancy. By July 1992 at least 167 women in twenty-six states had been arrested and charged criminally because of their use of drugs during pregnancy or because of some other prenatal risk.[10] A number of these women have been found guilty and sentenced to as many as ten years in prison.[11] The overwhelming majority of these cases have involved women of color, even though white women also use illegal drugs.[12] The controversy surrounding this punishment approach to policy for pregnant addicts appears in some of the appeals of these convictions. As of November 1992, twenty-one cases had been challenged or appealed; all were dismissed or overturned.[13]

Even more common than criminal prosecution is court-ordered removal of the baby at birth, without trial or hearing, solely on the grounds that mother and/or infant have a positive drug test at the time of birth. Child removal on these grounds appears to be increasing even though there is a severe shortage of foster homes in many areas of the United States.[14] Despite the complaints of many lawyers and medical professionals that such procedures violate privacy rights and proper medical use of the tests,[15] a number of states require health care professionals to report to the local welfare agency any woman who has or is believed to have used a controlled substance during pregnancy.[16]

As a result of the increasing controversy over punitive policies, some state and local governments have encouraged treatment as a complement or alternative to criminal punishment or child removal. Thus California has enacted a law that requires drug treatment programs to give priority to pregnant women.[17] Connecticut has mandated that outreach workers seek out addicted mothers and mothers-to-be to encourage them to get treatment.[18] In the fall of 1991 New York City instituted a program that allows addicted mothers to take their babies home after birth provided that they enter treatment and agree to weekly visits from a social worker.[19] This program and many others that emphasize treatment over punishment nevertheless retain a punitive tendency in that they coerce women to undergo treatment.

The targeting of women drug users, especially poor women and women of color, for particular surveillance and policies in the U.S. government's "war on drugs" raises questions about sexism and racism implicit in such policies. Most of the municipalities and states that have prosecuted women who give birth to drug-affected babies do not prosecute other women or men for drug use. There is a particular rage often directed at *mothers* in this differential application of punishment, which I suggest reflects an identification with the infant.[20] Dorothy Dinnerstein argues that in a society characterized by mother-dominated infant care both adult men and women often carry an unconscious resentment of their mothers, which is displaced onto women in general. The pre-ego infant is needy and desiring and the mother can never be completely and fully there for it. The lack of the mother—the permanent disappointment that the mother is not always there for me—is the permanent existential trauma of mortality. The social fact of men's relative absence from infant care allows the unconscious to scapegoat women for this existential trauma that is an element in the human condition.[21]

The level of passion directed against pregnant addicts often seems higher than that felt for most ordinary criminals. It is not just anyone who has harmed their baby; it's the child's *mother.* The mother is supposed to be the one who sacrifices herself, who will do anything for her child, who will preserve and nurture it. That's what mothering *means.* The rage directed at pregnant addicts unconsciously recalls the feeling we all had as children—rage toward our mothers who were not always there for us, did not always respond to our needs and desires, and sometimes pursued their own purposes and desires. The mother who harms her child is not merely a criminal—she is a monster.[22]

As Dorothy Roberts argues, the fact that black women are particular targets in the punitive actions of the state against drug-using mothers suggests that we find racism here inextricably tied to sexism. Since the days of slavery, U.S. society has systematically devalued black motherhood. In the tradition of U.S. racial attitudes, black women are by definition not "good" mothers; it would be best if they did not bear children at all. The racism that black women suffer, combined with the fact that their economic status more often brings them into contact with state-run institutions, makes them more likely to be punished than white women. Indeed, their failure to fit society's image of the "good" mother makes their punishment more acceptable.[23]

Most prosecutors and policymakers who pursue punishment of pregnant addicts would deny that racist and sexist biases inform their practices. They claim instead that they are exercising their obligations as state agents to protect infants from harm and to hold accountable those responsible for such harms when they occur. Women who take cocaine or heroin while pregnant are wantonly and knowingly risking the lives and health of future persons and deserve to pay for such immoral harm. Punishing women who give birth to drug-affected babies serves notice to others that the state considers this a grave wrong and thus will deter such behavior. As with most punishments, the primary justifications for punitive policies toward pregnant addicts are deterrence and retribution. Neither justification is well grounded.

The deterrence theory relies on the assumption that people engage in some kind of cost-benefit calculation before taking the actions the policies aim to stop. In some contexts this makes sense. If a city wishes to discourage illegal parking it raises fines and threatens to tow; these policies usually reduce infractions. However, the idea that a pregnant addict weighs the benefits of taking drugs against the costs of possible punishment is implausible because it assumes that she has within her the power to refrain from taking drugs.

Many health professionals argue that punitive policies toward pregnant addicts do deter them from seeking prenatal care.[24] Women are likely to decide to avoid contact with health care providers if they believe that their drug use will be reported to state authorities who will punish them. Because drug-using pregnant women's fetuses and babies are often at particularly high risk, they need prenatal attention even more than most. Experts claim that the harmful effects of drug use on infants can be offset, at least in part, by good prenatal care where health professionals treat drug use in a supportive nonpunitive atmosphere.[25]

In practice, retribution is most often the justification, either implicitly or explicitly, for punitive approaches to pregnant addicts. These women ought to be punished and threatened with punishment because their wrongful actions *deserve* sanction. This retributive justification for a punitive approach must assume that these women are responsible both for their drug use and for their pregnancies; if freedom is a condition for assigning responsibility, however, these are problematic assumptions.

Anyone who starts using drugs is responsible for that use. But the concept of addiction implies a limitation on the free agency, and hence the responsibility, of the addicted person. There are paternalistic dangers in promoting a model of addiction that depicts the habitual drug user as completely irrational, unaware, out of control. But there are equal dangers in denying the reality of a substance dependence so ingrained in a person's habits, way of life, and desire that she is not responsible for her continuing use. Virtually no one uses drugs with the aim of becoming dependent. Indeed, affirming the norm of self-control, they deceive themselves into thinking that they can avoid addiction and too often refuse to admit a dependence. Most experts agree that, once a person has become dependent on a substance, stopping is very difficult and cannot be accomplished by mere act of will. Beginning with a series of acts, drug dependence has become a condition she is in rather than something she does. Criminal law should punish people for acts, not conditions. In recognizing this distinction, legal precedent has found that criminalizing drug addiction violates a prohibition against cruel and unusual punishment.[26]

Most states that pursue punitive policies toward pregnant addicts do not prosecute people for drug use alone; in such cases, women are essentially being punished for carrying a pregnancy to term.[27] This presupposes that women are responsible for being pregnant, ignoring several social conditions that limit women's choices to be or not be pregnant. Ours is still a society where women often are not free in their sexual relations with men. Access to contraception, moreover, is not easy for many women, especially the poor or young. And, of course, contraception sometimes does not work. With rapidly decreasing access to abortion for all women in the United States, especially the young and poor, fewer and fewer women can freely choose whether to carry a pregnancy to term.[28]

Proponents of the punishment approach sometimes justify it primarily as a means to encourage or force women into drug treatment. Keeping in line with earlier arguments, one might say that a pregnant addict is morally blameworthy for harming her child only if she does not seek help in dealing with drug use. But even though in recent years small steps have been taken to increase the availability of drug treatment for pregnant women and design programs specifically for their needs, for the most part access to more than perfunctory drug treatment is very limited. Most programs either do not accept pregnant women or have waiting lists that extend long beyond due dates. Most private health insurance programs offer only partial reimbursement for treatment, and in many states Medicaid will reimburse only a portion of the cost of drug treatment. Most treatment programs are designed with men's lives in mind and very few have child care options.[29] Moreover, mandatory reporting laws and other procedures that force women into treatment create an adversarial and policing relationship between health care providers and the women they are supposed to serve, thereby eroding the patient trust most providers believe is necessary for effective drug therapy.[30]

These arguments against application of a punishment approach to policy for pregnant addicts do not mean that pregnant addicts have no obligations regarding the fetuses they carry. There are many matters about which people think that there are obligations and responsibilities, even though they are not held criminally liable.[31] But we need to remember that women's freedom in respect to these responsibilities is often quite circumscribed, though not absent.

Philosophers typically base the retributive theory of punishment on the social contract between the individual and the state. Laws express a compact among citizens, a common commitment to limit personal desires and interests to create a mutually respecting community of citizens. Social membership depends on such regulation and mutual respect, and one who claims social membership and benefits from it implicitly promises to obey the rules. The lawbreaker violates this implied promise, forfeits membership in society, and deserves punishment as a way of paying a debt for a broken promise.

Jeffrie Murphy argues that this retributive theory of punishment implies a conception of society as a relationship among equals with shared values and ways of looking at the world. A retributive justification only works morally to legitimate punishment if those subject to punishment are indeed equal citizens who receive the social benefits that oblige them to obey the rules in return. Murphy points out, however, that most people whom capitalist societies define as criminals and punish are not equal citizens. They are poor and working-class people who do not participate in setting the rules or enjoy the benefits of social participation that the theory supposes.[32]

Murphy argues that if punishment is applied to those excluded from the full benefits of social membership its actual function is to reinforce that exclusion. Either you obey the rules or you are marked as deviant and punished. The law-abiding citizen is not needy, works hard, is independent, has relations with others through contracts of mutual exchange, and exhibits temperance and self-control. Those who do not conform to this model—the needy, irrational, dependent, those who are unwilling or unable to work, do not exercise self-control, or for whom there are no benefits in the legitimate market exchange game—are deviant and deserve punishment. As Michel Foucault theorizes, the system of modern law itself creates the category of "delinquents" whose actions its punishments are designed to curtail and recreates them in subjecting them to the carceral system.[33] Since punishing the pregnant addict does next to nothing to prevent the birth of babies harmed by the chronic drug use of their mothers, punishment seems only to have the function of marking her as deviant, publicly reaffirming her exclusion from the class of clear upstanding citizens.

Ethics of Care and Treatment

Critics of a punishment approach to addicts in general, and pregnant addicts in particular, argue that addiction is a health problem rather than a problem of criminal justice. The problem of substance-using mothers should be the province of health care and social service agencies, not the law and the courts. Like any other needy people, pregnant addicts should be cared for, nurtured, and helped to be made well and independent. The American Medical Association, along with many other organizations that represent service providers, has taken the position that punitive policies toward pregnant addicts, including coerced treatment, interfere with the professional-client relation and inhibit effective rehabilitative treatment services.[34]

Arguments for an approach that emphasizes supportive treatment appeal to values much like the ethic of care conceptualized by feminist moral theorists.[35] The ethic of care emphasizes contextualized issues of harm and suffering rather than a morality of abstract principle. It directly criticizes two aspects of the model relation between individual and society that underlies the punishment approach: its assumption of the moral self as independent and its assumption that social relations are entered into voluntarily and can be understood as exchanges among equals.

I suggested earlier that the usual arguments justifying punishment as retribution presume a contractualist model of society where individuals are autonomous and independent. Under this conception social obligations consist of little more than traffic rules to ensure that a person pursuing personal interests will not crash into the others. This picture of atomized selves ignores and devalues the interdependence and multivariant relationships that structure human cultures and practices. As Annette Baier argues, reliance on the formalistic ethic of rights that this atomistic picture generates does little "to ensure that the people who have and mutually respect such rights will have any other relationships to one another than the minimal relationship needed to keep such a 'civil society' going."[36]

Those developing an ethic of care argue that relationships of inequality and dependence call for different standards of moral responsibility than the equality presumed by the atomist contractualist picture. Many social relations are between unequals, where one party is dependent on the other. According to many theorists of an ethic of care, the relation of parent and child is paradigmatic; other hierarchical relations of dependency, such as between teacher and student or doctor and patient, have a similar structure. Moreover, in contrast to the relations assumed in the contract model of society, these unequal relations of dependence are often involuntary; they are relations of kinship or community that cannot be severed by mutual agreement. The structure of moral obligation and responsibility in such relations operates more through empathy and the acknowledgement of pregiven interdependence and connectedness than through contracts and promises.

Ethic of care theories have been influential among feminist psychologists and therapists. Some have developed theories and practices of service provision and therapy that emphasize empathy and understanding the context of social relationships in which a client's self and problems are embedded.[37] Some of the few drug treatment programs that have been set up specifically to serve pregnant addicts claim to operationalize an ethic of care distinct from more confrontational and achievement-oriented models typical of therapeutic techniques.[38] Although there is much to praise about such efforts, there are reasons to be suspicious of many therapeutic practices for pregnant addicts, including those that explicitly take themselves to be using an ethic of care.

For the most part, debate over the ethic of care has located the model of obligation and responsibility in face-to-face personal relationships.[39] In my view, the values of an ethic of care can and should be extended to the interconnections of strangers in the public world of social policy and its implementation. A few feminist theorists have suggested that the ethic of care can serve as a general ethical theory to ground a normative conception of politics and policy.[40]

Despite these promising beginnings, feminist ethics in general, and the ethic of care in particular, have done little to apply insights to the pressing social policy issues of justice and need that face all societies in the world. At the very least this would mean interpreting the reasons for welfare and publicly funded social services very differently from the dominant interpretation in the United States.

Public support and assistance for the needy is most often understood as merely beneficent rather than obligatory, except where the recipient has earned them through productive contribution. Thus in the United States unemployment compensation and social security are generally regarded as entitlements, whereas other forms of public assistance are regarded as handouts—mere charity that the public dispenses at its pleasure and convenience and not because it has a moral responsibility to do so. This distinction between types of benefits rests on an implicit contractual model of social relations. The society "owes" welfare to those who have paid for it through working but owes nothing to those who are simply needy.[41]

If one instead substitutes a hierarchical model of social relations, in which some persons are vulnerable with respect to the actions of others by virtue of institutional structures and relations of power, a different basis for obligation emerges. In relations of inequality some persons are potentially subject to coercion because they are needy. The privileged and the powerful have a duty to refrain from taking advantage and a duty to protect the vulnerable from the consequences of their compromised situation.[42]

Therefore, an ethic of care for pregnant addicts means greatly expanded public and private funding for therapeutic drug treatment and social services specifically aimed at pregnant women, mothers, and their children. Services should include prenatal, obstetrical, and other health care. Whether residential or outpatient, services should include child care so that mothers are not inhibited from seeking or staying in treatment. Treatment services for pregnant addicts must be designed with women's lives specifically in mind.[43] For example, programs should directly address the issues of incest, sexual abuse, and battery, which are part of the life history of many addicted women.[44]

In 1989 Lucia Meijer reported that there was nearly zero funding for such services anywhere in the United States.[45] Since then both the federal government and a few states have helped develop and funded drug treatment programs specifically designed for pregnant women and mothers. The extent of such services, however, remains meager. As of fall 1991, for example, Pennsylvania funded only four treatment centers to provide residential treatment for women and their children. Pittsburgh has one of these centers, which houses seventeen women and their children. The state funds a few more outpatient programs, which serve a larger number of women. The Maternal Addiction Program in Pittsburgh, for example, serves about sixty women; one-and-a-half counselors see these women three times a week in private and group sessions and the center is unable to provide child care. In Pittsburgh the ratio of women who need such services to space available may be as high as ten-to-one; the problem is probably more dire in other cities.

The United States has lately seen a period of conservative retrenchment, in which all forms of public services have been curtailed. We have been moving away from caring for needy people. Social problems like poverty and drug abuse have been growing as a result, creating the punitive response toward people that we see typified in policies toward pregnant addicts. Adopting a genuinely caring approach in our policy for pregnant addicts will be expensive, although one can argue that taking care of drug-affected babies is even more expensive. But publicly supported treatment policies and programs for all substance-dependent people must be on the agenda for a restructured health care system in the United States.

Foucaultian Suspicions of Treatment

Although some feminist theorists doubt the utility of Foucault's analyses of power and society in understanding women's situations,[46] many others have found his work important as a tool of feminist analysis.[47] Relying on Foucault's notions of disciplinary power and the confessional discourse of therapies, I argue in this section that there are reasons to be suspicious of many typical aspects of drug treatment therapies from the viewpoint of feminist values. This disciplinary power can be conceived on a continuum, from military-like forms of rules and obedience paternalistically enforced "for the patient's own good" to more caring humanistic practices. Many punitive, paternalistic treatment practices, as well as some more caring humanistic practices, are suspicious in that they redefine a client's problem through the categories of expert knowledge, inhibit the client's freedom through surveillance, and attempt to normalize her life and behavior in ways that reinforce privilege and individualize the source of her problem and its solution.

According to Foucault, disciplinary power—as distinct from political and juridical power—is enacted in the everyday microprocesses of many institutions of state and civil society, including schools, factories and other workplaces, the enlightened rehabilitative prison, hospitals, mental institutions, and social service agencies. This power is largely constituted through application of the knowledge of humanistic and social science disciplines, such as medicine, psychology, social work, criminology, public administration, pedagogy, and scientific management. The authority of disciplinary power comes not from commands of a sovereign, upheld and enforced through law, but from the rules that experts claim as natural—the normal structure of operation of human subjects. Disciplinary practices of medical treatment, exercise, therapy, school and workplace examinations, and the like aim to constitute subjects in conformity with those norms. Through systems of surveillance and self-examination disciplinary power enlists the subject's agency in the formation and reformation of self.[48]

The relation of pregnant addicts to the institutions and experts who administer treatment is certainly one of unequal power. Whether she has entered treatment voluntarily or under threat, her situation is usually one of dependence, vulnerability, and need. The relation of power is often obscured by the neutral knowledge and skills that providers possess and by their real intentions to be helpful and caring. The combination of expertism and care often produces situations of paternalistic power and discipline.

This often requires that women in drug treatment programs obey a set of more or less onerous rules and be subject to various forms of surveillance. There is a range of treatment models, some of which are more rigid than others. Clients must not have drugs on the premises and must remain drug-free while in treatment (enforced by random drug tests). Residential programs frequently dictate how people spend their time and determine the kinds and amounts of possessions patients may have. Both residential and outpatient programs often discourage the formation of bonds of friendship and especially sexual bonds between clients. Thus programs sometimes have dress codes forbidding sexually revealing clothes and forbid pairs to walk alone. Surveillance by experts may also be a normal part of the outpatient experience for pregnant addicts. In the New York City outreach program, to retain custody mothers must agree to treatment and allow a social worker to visit their homes at least once a week to check on the progress of their babies and the conditions of their homes. Many of the women resent these visits and consider them onerous surveillance.[49] Although drug treatment programs and other services rarely impose rules or engage in surveillance practices arbitrarily (they usually articulate reasons that involve the good of the client), this does not usually change the fact that clients experience the rules and surveillance as imposed disciplines.

Most drug treatment programs claim to enlist the participation of the client in determining the course of her therapy. Like social service practices more generally, however, the introduction of the expert knowledge of social service disciplines often functions to reinscribe her needs and experience in a foreign language. The normalizing language of therapy defines her history and the particular attributes of her situation as a "case," that is, as a particular instance of generalized concepts of norm and deviance, health and disorder, self-fulfillment and self-destruction. The organizations and providers often attach expert labels to these general conditions and behaviors, which then generate for them the service response.[50]

The object of treatment is to change behaviors and ultimately to transform the very self of the client. Drug treatment is nearly always medicalized insofar as this transformation is conceived as moving the client from a position of disorder to a position of greater health. When the subject of such healing is the mind or spirit rather than the body, however, therapeutic norms easily become infiltrated with *social* norms that function to enforce and reproduce relations of privilege and oppression. A treatment approach toward pregnant addicts may often work to adjust her to dominant social norms of being a "good" woman and a "good'" worker in ways designed to adjust her to the prevailing structures of domination and exploitation.[51]

There are some mothering virtues that pertain to the objective caring that children receive; mothers can and should be faulted for neglecting the care of their children. Often, however, superficial and culturally biased evaluations add to or substitute for such legitimate evaluations. A woman's progress toward normality in a treatment program may be measured according to her development of a demure comportment, a pleasant voice, a cheerful presence. She may be encouraged to develop modestly feminine habits of personal attire. I spoke with the director of a residential drug treatment program for women; he mentioned that he and his staff try to teach clients not to dress and wear makeup in a manner he associated with prostitutes but rather to dress in a respectably feminine way. To take another example, mothers will often be encouraged to develop mothering and housekeeping styles that may in fact devalue their own cultural and neighborhood family styles and norms of housekeeping. A woman may "earn" the right to live with her children by demonstrating a proper self-sacrificing attitude, orienting her concern away from her own needs and pleasures, and adopting a work ethic where pleasure can and should be delayed, pursued in small amounts, and always kept under control. Much of her therapy will consist in developing her as a competent and compliant worker: developing habits of getting up and getting to work on time, following orders and meeting deadlines, learning proper self-presentation in interview settings, and so on. Drug treatment programs often include a certain amount of job training but usually only for basic skills suited for low-wage work that may be quite sex-typed (a woman will be taught basic secretarial skills, for example).

Caring service providers usually do not consciously aim at adjusting their clients to societal structures of domination and oppression. Yet institutional racism, sexism, and classism are reproduced partly by the application of unconscious norms and stereotypes in a range of interactions, especially between social unequals in disciplinary settings. My point is that it is nearly inevitable for service providers to reproduce these structures in their interactions with pregnant addicts unless they become conscious of how social norms can enter their work and try to resist the tendency to reinforce and reproduce them.

Drug treatment programs and similar services vary in the manner and degree to which they consciously or unconsciously impose disciplines and surveillances on women and in the manner and degree to which they normalize clients and adjust them to dominant structures of privilege and oppression. Many therapists and social workers are critical of the expertism, tendencies toward disrespect, creation of a punitive atmosphere, and paternalism, which nevertheless remain the norm in service provision, especially toward those defined as deviant, such as addicts and poor people. Another element that Foucault finds in modern educative and therapeutic practices is much more standard: the use of confessional discourse.

According to Foucault, the genealogy of modern therapeutic practices can be traced to Christian practices of caring and making the self by means of a confessional narrative that plumbs the depths of the soul, seeking to root out illusion and self-deception: "Each person has the duty to know who he is, that is, to try to know what is happening inside him, to acknowledge faults, to recognize temptations, to locate desires, and everyone is obliged to disclose these things either to God or to others in the community and hence to bear public or private witness against oneself."[52] In traditional and early modern Christianity the goal of such confessional discourse was renunciation of the self. Modern therapeutic practices transform and develop these confessional techniques to a new end—the fashioning of a new self. According to Nikolas Rose, twentieth-century therapeutic practices refine and multiply these confessional technologies with the goal of producing a transparently autonomous self, where the individual has internalized the skills and disciplines of self-inspection and self-direction that assure her independence and self-control.[53]

Whether residential or outpatient, most clients in drug treatment spend their time in therapeutic talk. Typically a client participates in both individual and group counseling. Some of these meetings are educative (for example, addressing the effects of drug use and proper nutrition). Much of this individual and group talk, however, is confessional. It aims to help the patient discover and express the deep truth about her self. She constructs a narrative of her history that uncovers aspects of her self that account for her drug dependence. Often she finds relationships with others or fears about her capacities that she has been denying, repressing, and hiding from herself, which she brings forward through talk and vows to overcome. Group counseling sessions in drug treatment programs are often modeled on the twelve-step techniques first developed in Alcoholics Anonymous. The confessional model in twelve-step programs is direct. Group members are exhorted to give over their selves to a higher power and plumb their souls' depths while the others bear witness to their discourse. The confessional narrative often includes an element of resolution, a forward-looking conversion toward new understandings and actions and a construction of the means needed to achieve these goals.

The goal of therapeutic talk in most drug treatment programs is for the patient to bring herself under direction, to make herself an autonomous, independent agent. In this way typical drug treatment programs retain the atomistic and individualizing model of the relation of the person and society that underlies the punishment approach to pregnant addicts, which I have argued the ethic of care rejects.

The problem with the confessional talk typical of drug therapy, as well as most other therapies, is that it tends to be depoliticizing and individualizing. It enlists the patient's own complicity in her adjustment to existing institutions and relations of privilege and oppression by encouraging her to construct her self, or her family, as the source of her pain and her problems. This self-reflective exercise diverts her from locating her life in the context of wider social institutions and problems and also discourages her from forming dialogic bonds with others in relations of solidarity and resistance. The solution to each addict's problems lies solely or primarily in herself, in her ability to develop coping skills for managing her reaction and those around her to the dangers and disturbances in her life.[54] Some drug treatment theoreticians and practitioners recognize this depoliticized nature of the therapeutic tradition and have attempted to modify therapeutic practice to include more discussion of the oppressive social causes of personal distress. But an individualized model of self-discovery and conversion remains typical.

I have labeled a typical treatment approach to the problem of pregnant addicts "suspicious," but to suspect them is not to condemn them outright. Support for treatment is still the only viable alternative for a policy approach to the problem of drug-exposed infants. Indeed, some of the causes of surveillance or paternalistic practices in drug treatment programs may lie in insufficient resources for the programs. The grounds for suspicion, moreover, apply to many kinds of therapy and service provision besides drug treatment. What we can learn from Foucault, Fraser, Rose, and others is how to view with suspicion precisely those liberal, humanistic, service-providing practices that seem to be an alternative to overtly dominative practices like criminal punishment. Contemporary structures of domination and oppression appear as often in the bureaucracy of the welfare state as in the prison, though not in the same form.

Empowerment as an Alternative

Empowerment is like democracy: Everyone is for it, but rarely do people mean the same thing by it. For Jack Kemp, former secretary of the U.S. Department of Housing and Urban Development, "empowering" poor public-housing tenants meant turning over management and/or ownership of their old, deteriorating, and poorly maintained buildings while providing little in the way of resources to help renovate, run, and maintain them. The term "empowerment" appears frequently in literature on the philosophy of social service provision. Although usages vary, I identify two primary meanings. For some therapists and service providers, empowerment means the development of individual autonomy, self-control, confidence; for others empowerment refers to the development of a sense of collective influence over the social conditions of one's life. I think that the second definition works better because it includes both personal empowerment and collective empowerment and suggests that the latter is a condition of the former.

In the previous section I pointed out that therapeutic service centers are often sites for the exercise of power in modern societies, which normalizes individuals and adjusts them to the demands of the dominant oppressive institutions, often with their own complicity through confessional talk. Social service theorists who use the first definition of empowerment challenge the more overtly dominative forms of power that sometimes appear in drug treatment programs. They challenge models of service provision that make the service provider an expert and authority and that rely on rules and surveillance.[55] They advocate instead what Tom Wartenberg calls a "transformative" use of power by the service provider in relation to the client. As Wartenberg describes it, in a transformative use of power, the superior exercises power over the subordinate in such a way that the subordinate agent learns certain skills that undercut the power differential between her and the dominant agent. The transformative use of power seeks to bring about its own obsolescence by means of the empowerment of the subordinate agent.[56]

This concept of empowerment fits with a certain parental model of an ethic of care. The parent, teacher, or service provider may exercise some disciplinary power in relation to the child, student, or client, but only for the sake of the development of skills and resources that will lead to autonomy and equality. Thus John L. Forth-Finegan defines empowerment as "taught by giving choices, and images to hold only, to help define a self."[57] Some theorists who use empowerment in this sense also derive their conception of the self that is so defined from the self-in-relation theory of the ethic of care. They argue that a woman's sense of autonomy must be structured not in an effort to separate from others, as in many male-oriented concepts of autonomy, but established in a context of caring and supportive relationships. For this reason many therapists using this conception of empowerment encourage approaching a client in the context of her family system or other important relationships. Thus Janet Surrey defines empowerment as the "mobilization of the energies, resources, strengths, or powers of each person through a mutual, relational process. Personal empowerment can be viewed only through the lens of power through connection, that is, through the establishment of mutually empathic and mutually empowering relationships."[58]

According to my analysis in the previous section, this sort of caring therapy may not be subject to the more obvious criticisms of disciplinary practices. It nevertheless remains suspect to the degree that it operates with a confessional model of therapeutic talk, as distinct from the dialogical model I will describe below, wherein the client is encouraged to look into herself and express her inhibitions and resolutions as others bear witness. Despite its understanding of the self as constituted in the context of relationships, this meaning of empowerment tends to remain individualistic. It envisions the development of personal skills and resources through which a person can learn to "be on her own," "get on her feet," and cope with the situations and responsibilities she encounters. This meaning of empowerment tends to stop short of a politicized understanding of the social structures that condition an individual's situation and the cultivation of effective action in relation to those structures.

The second definition of empowerment used by social service theorists, which I endorse, evolves from ideals of participatory democracy, critical self-reflection, and collective action. I define this meaning of empowerment as: A process in which individual and relatively powerless persons dialogue with each other and thereby come to understand the social sources of their powerlessness and see the possibility of acting collectively to change their social environment. In this process each participant is personally empowered and undergoes some personal transformation in the context of a reciprocal aiding of others in doing so in order that they might together be empowered to engage in effective collective action.[59]

Empowering treatment involves a kind of talk very different from the therapeutic confessional talk I described earlier, a kind of talk political movements have called "consciousness-raising." Confessional therapeutic talk needs other people—the therapist and sometimes fellow confessors. Their function is to encourage the confession, bear witness, and absolve. Confessional talk, however, is monological: Even though it requires the presence of others, it remains one individual reciting her individual story. Consciousness-raising talk, by contrast, it dialogical. Through the give and take of discussion participants construct an understanding of their personal lives as socially conditioned—constrained in ways similar to that of others by institutional structures, power relations, cultural assumptions, and economic forces. The consciousness-raising group "theorizes" this social account together, moving back and forth between individual life stories and social analysis to confirm or disconfirm both. The members of the group propose interpretations of one another's life stories and propose accounts of the social structures and constraints conditioning those lives; these proposals are tested through discussion. Participants in the discussion are equal in the sense that they all have an equal right to speak, to criticize the accounts of others, and to have their accounts criticized.[60]

Consciousness-raising is empowering because it develops in people the ability to be reflective and critical about the situated social basis of individual action. Such reflection and criticism enable people to move from an acceptance of institutional forms as natural and given to seeing them as human constructs that are changeable, however difficult that may be. Especially when this reflection and criticism occurs in dialogue with others, group solidarities can form that portend the further empowerment that can come with collective action. The final aspect of empowerment, then, is organization: the establishment or joining of democratic collectives that foster bonds of solidarity and bring the actions of many individuals together toward some end of social transformation.

Ruth J. Parsons described a Head Start mothers program in which she works that embodies some of these ideas of empowerment. The mothers program was started to address the fact that their children were identified by the Head Start workers as "discipline problems." However, instead of defining this problem as one concerning the mothering practices of the women and developing in them skills to better manage and care for their children, the program encouraged the mothers to come together in free-ranging dialogue about their children and their lives. The women discussed the problems in their neighborhood and their frustration in their interactions with schools, health care organizations, and the like that made parenting difficult for them. Through this group dialogue, the women began to see ways that they could work together to address some of these community and social problems that pressed on their lives as parents. Together they persuaded local community mental health centers to make home visits and to alter their services in ways the women would find more helpful.[61]

Presumably drug treatment is a special case of service provision. Substance-dependent women sometimes have lost the ability to function in daily life at a basic level, are usually self-deceiving about their dependence, and often are emotionally damaged from physical or psychological abuse. These special circumstances may make it more difficult to provide empowering services for them than for women like those described by Parsons, but with sufficient care and resources it should be possible to do so. Many drug treatment professionals are aware of tendencies to normalize and individualize in therapeutic practice and aim in their own practices for more dialogical relationships with clients. But as Joel Handler points out, the good intentions of individual providers are not enough to make drug treatment programs or other social services empowering.[62] The structure, rules, and institutional relationships of programs in many cases must be redesigned to produce more institutional equality between providers and clients and connect provider activities in treatment programs with wider community activity. I will close with some general proposals for how designers of drug treatment programs might think about the structure of those programs.

I have already discussed why drug treatment programs for pregnant addicts should provide prenatal and obstetrical services, child care, and gender-specific counseling that addresses issues of sexual abuse. This makes programs minimally caring. Several other structured program elements are necessary to make services empowering. Many of these are not specific to services for women or mothers but should apply to all service provision that aims to empower. Although a few drug treatment programs contain some of these elements, my research leads me to believe that programs that contain all of them are almost nonexistent.

1. Programs should structure at least some therapeutic group sessions on the dialogic model of consciousness-raising in which the goal is for the group collectively to identify social sources of individual pain and habit in structures of power and privilege. Such consciousness-raising dialogue can also seek to cultivate a positive culture of gender, racial, and class solidarity.[63]

2. Programs should include structured client participation and evaluation of the program, including the evaluation of individual providers. If programs have rules that clients must follow, then clients should participate in making the rules. Rather than merely asking clients for suggestions about services or encouraging them individually to voice complaints, programs can have regular periods of structured self-evaluation in which client representatives formally and collectively participate. The power hierarchy between providers and clients can be reduced, finally, by formal evaluation of providers by clients, perhaps similar to the way that students now evaluate teachers in most colleges. My research leads me to believe that client participation in rulemaking and the formal evaluation of programs and providers is extremely rare.

3. Meaningful work is another element of empowering programs. Those addicts who have careers or satisfying jobs can be encouraged to continue them during treatment. Others should be provided meaningful work, by which I mean work that issues in recognizable results, which develops the skills of the worker and from which the worker derives significant benefits. Drug treatment programs, even those serving unemployed persons or persons working sporadically in unskilled jobs, do not usually include meaningful work. Such programs could try to link with community development programs in order to provide such work. For example, in many cities nonprofit development agencies rehabilitate dilapidated housing largely through the labor of future low-income residents, trained and supervised by skilled workers.

This suggestion links to the last:

4. Empowering drug treatment programs needs to be part of a wider network of participatory community organizations in which people work to politicize their needs and address community problems, much as in the Head Start mothers program Ruth Parsons described. Dialogue about the social sources of indi-

vidual problems and the formation of bonds of group solidarity become merely abstract if those who discover such problems are not organized to take action to address them. The dominant tendency in drug treatment programs is to isolate clients from community networks and for programs themselves to be self-contained. The goal of removing clients from the influence of those who would encourage them to continue their drug use is laudable. But this goal is better achieved by linking drug treatment with broader strategies of community control over networks and services through a set of interlocked institutions. I have argued that a punishment approach is both unjust to addicted mothers and largely ineffective in preventing harm to babies. A caring treatment approach is far superior to punishment. When caregiving people and institutions deny or ignore the facts of their power, however, they often operate in normalizing ways that strive primarily to adjust clients to existing social structures and expectations. These structures and expectations usually reinforce relations of privilege and oppression. An approach to treatment and policy for pregnant addicts aimed at empowering them is best. I have no doubt that a great many service providers wish to empower their clients. However, if Foucault is correct in stating that bureaucratic and therapeutic institutions are usually normalizing, providers should recognize that empowering clients is very difficult within service providing institutions. An empowering approach to policy for pregnant addicts entails struggle—by service providers, by clients to whom they listen, and by the rest of us who seek a more just world for women.

Notes

This chapter is revised from Iris Young, "Punishment, Treatment, Empowerment: Three Approaches to Policy for Pregnant Addicts," *Feminist Studies* 20(1):33–57 (Spring 1994). Reprinted by permission of Feminist Studies, Inc., c/o Women's Studies Program, University of Maryland, College Park, Md 20742.

1. I am grateful to Claire Cohen, Nancy Fraser, Nancy Glazner, Michelle Harrison, Kary Moss, Shane Phelan, Rayna Rapp, Dorothy Roberts, Jana Sawicki, Joan Tronto, Tom Wartenberg, and anonymous referees for *Feminist Studies* for helpful comments on earlier versions of this paper. Thanks to Terrence Raftery, Amy Marlo, and Carrie Smarto for research assistance.

2. See Jan Hoffman, "Pregnant, Addicted—and Guilty," *New York Times Magazine*, Sunday, August 19, 1990, 24. Some estimate that as many as 11 percent of women in labor test positive for illegal drugs; see Benjamin A. Niel, "Prenatal Drug Abuse: Is the Mother Criminally Liable?" *Trial Diplomacy Journal* 15(3):129 (May–June 1992).

3. In a personal communication, Kary Moss of the American Civil Liberties Union Reproductive Rights Project tells me that these government statistics are badly sampled and do not adequately distinguish types of drug use.

4. See Michelle Harrison, "Drug Addiction in Pregnancy: The Interface of Science, Emotion and Social Policy," *Journal of Substance Abuse Treatment* 8:261–268 (1991). See also Wendy K. Mariner, Leonard H. Glantz, and George J. Annas, "Pregnancy, Drugs and the Perils of Prosecution," *Criminal Justice Ethics* 7:30–41 (Winter-Spring 1990).

5. Emmalee S. Bandstra, M.D., "Medical Issues for Mothers and Infants Arising from Perinatal Use of Cocaine," in *Drug Exposed Infants and Their Families: Coordinating Responses of the Legal, Medical and Child Protection System* (American Bar Association Center on Children and the Law, Washington, D.C., 1990). See also Joseph B. Treaster, "Plan Lets Addicted Mothers Take Their Newborns Home," *New York Times*, 19 September 1991.

6. A survey of 15 Southern states by the *Atlanta Constitution* found that 71 percent of the 1,500 people polled favored criminal penalties for pregnant women whose illegal drug use injured their babies; see Mark Curriden, "*Roe v. Wade* Does Not Prevent Criminal Prosecution of Prenatal Child Abuse," *ABA Journal* 16:51–53 (March 1990). A National Law Journal Lexis poll found that the majority say a mother should be held criminally responsible when she abuses substances during pregnancy and as a result gives birth to an impaired child; see "Courts Disagree on Mother's Liability," *National Law Journal* 13:30 (May 13, 1991).

7. Curriden, "*Roe v. Wade* Does Not Prevent Criminal Prosecution," 52; Ellen M. Barry, "Pregnant, Addicted, and Sentenced," *Criminal Justice* 5:22–27 (Winter 1991); Davidson, "Drug Babies Push Issue of Fetal Rights," *Los Angeles Times*, 25 April 1989.

8. ACLU Memo, October 3, 1989, in *Drug Exposed Infants and Their Families: Coordinating Responses of the Legal, Medical and Child Protection System* (American Bar Association Center on Children and the Law, Washington, D.C., 1990); Dorothy E. Roberts, "Punishing Drug Addicts Who Have Babies: Women of Color, Equality, and the Right of Privacy," *Harvard Law Review* 104(7):1419–1482 (May 1991).

9. These states include Illinois, Indiana, Minnesota, Nevada, Florida, Oklahoma, Rhode Island, and Utah. See Dorothy Roberts, "Drug Addicted Women Who Have Babies," *Trial*, April 1990, 56–61.

10. See Ruth Ann Strickland and Marcia Lynn Whicker, "Fetal Endangerment Versus Fetal Welfare: Discretion of Prosecutors in Determining Criminal Liability and Intent," Chapter 4 of this volume.

11. Alison B. Marshall, "Drug Addiction, Pregnancy and Childbirth: Legal Issues for the Medical and Social Service Communities," in *Drug Exposed Infants and Their Families: Coordinating Responses of the Legal, Medical and Child Protection System* (American Bar Association Center on Children and the Law, Washington, D.C., 1990); Hoffman, "Pregnant, Addicted—and Guilty"; "Greenville Woman Sentenced to Prison," *Charleston Observer*, 19 October 1990.

12. Roberts, "Punishing Drug Addicts Who Have Babies"; Deborah S. Pinkey, "Racial Bias Found in Drug Abuse Reporting," *American Medical News* 32:4 (October 6, 1989); Ira J. Chasnoff, Harvey J. Landress, and Mark E. Barrett, "The Prevalence of Illicit Drug or Alcohol Use During Pregnancy in Pinellas County, Florida," *New England Journal of Medicine* 322(17):1202–1207 (April 26, 1990). Despite similar rates of substance abuse among black and white women, black women were ten times more likely to be reported than white women; poor women were also more likely to be reported.

13. Mark Hansen, "Courts Side with Moms in Drug Cases," *ABA Journal* 78:18 (November 1992).

14. In June 1989 a survey of five major cities found that there were 304 "boarder" babies, most of whom were born to drug-using mothers. Josephine Gittler and Merle McPherson, "Prenatal Substance Abuse," *Children Today* 19:3–7 (July-August 1990).

15. See Wendy Chavkin, "Drug Addiction and Pregnancy: Policy Crossroads," *American Journal of Public Health* 80(4):483–487 (April 1990).

16. These states include Massachusetts, Minnesota, Oklahoma, and Utah. See Roberts, "Punishing Drug Addicts Who Have Babies," 1430; Bonnie I. Robin-Vergeer, "The Problem of the Drug Exposed Newborn: A Return to Principled Intervention," *Stanford Law Review* 42:745–809 (February 1990).

17. Judith Larson, "Creating Common Goals for Medical, Legal and Child Protection Communities," in *Drug Exposed Infants and Their Families: Coordinating Responses of the Legal, Medical and Child Protection System* (American Bar Association Center on Children and the Law, Washington, D.C., 1990).

18. Judy Mann, "Cure an Addict, Save a Child," *Washington Post*, 5 April 1991, C3.

19. Treaster, "Plan Lets Addicted Mothers Take Their Newborns Home."

20. Harrison, "Drug Addiction in Pregnancy," 262.

21. Dorothy Dinnerstein, *The Mermaid and the Minotaur* (New York: Harper and Row, 1975).

22. See Edwin M. Shur, *Labeling Women Deviant: Gender, Stigma and Social Control* (Philadelphia: Temple University Press, 1983). Allegations of "unfit" motherhood stand against the understanding that a woman who undertakes parenthood subordinates her own needs, desires, and priorities to the welfare of the child.

23. Roberts, "Punishing Drug Addicts Who Have Babies."

24. Alan I. Tracktenberg, M.D., testimony to House Select Committee on Children and Families, April 19, 1990. Ellen M. Barry claims that research shows that the threat of incarceration has no significant deterrent effect on the behavior of substance-dependent women and tends to deter women from getting prenatal care. Barry, "Pregnant, Addicted and Sentenced."

25. Andrew Skolnick, "Drug Screening in Prenatal Care Demands Objective Medical Criteria, Support Services," *Journal of the American Medical Association* Vol. 264 (July 18, 1990). Researchers conclude that care provided in the framework of support, rather than judgment, can improve the outcome for drug-abusing pregnant women.

26. See *Robinson v. California,* 370 U.S. 660 (1962); cited by Roberts.

27. See Lynn M. Paltrow, "When Becoming Pregnant is a Crime," *Criminal Justice Ethics* 7:41–47 (Winter-Spring 1990); Mariner, Glantz, and Annas, "Pregnancy, Drugs and the Perils of Prosecution," 30–41; Roberts, "Punishing Drug Addicts Who Have Babies," see especially 1445–1456; Roberts argues that prosecutions of drug-addicted mothers infringe on two aspects of the right to individual choice in reproductive decision making: (1) the freedom to continue a pregnancy, which she claims is essential to an individual's personhood and autonomy, and (2) they impose an invidious government standard for the entitlement to procreate.

28. See Tamar Lewin, "Hurdles Increase for Many Women Seeking Abortions," *New York Times,* 15 March 1992.

29. See "Substance Abuse Treatment for Women: Crisis in Access," *Health Advocate,* no. 160 (Spring 1989); see also Josette Mondonaro, *Chemically Dependent Women* (Lexington, Mass.: Lexington Books, 1989), especially Chapters 1–3.

30. Wendy Chavkin, "Mandatory Treatment for Drug Use During Pregnancy," *Journal of the American Medical Association* 260(11):1556–1561 (September 18, 1991).

31. See Thomas H. Murray, "Prenatal Drug Exposure: Ethical Issues," in *The Future of Children* 1(1):105–112 (Spring 1991).

32. Jeffrie Murphy, "Marxism and Retribution," in *Retribution, Justice and Therapy* (The Hague: D. Reidel, 1979), 93–115.

33. Michel Foucault, *Discipline and Punish* (New York: Harper and Row, 1977).

34. "Legal Interventions During Pregnancy: Court-ordered Medical Treatment and Legal Penalties for Potentially Harmful Behavior by Pregnant Women," *Journal of the American Medical Association* 264(20) (November 28, 1990), 2663–2670. Also see Skolnick, "Drug Screening in Prenatal Care," who reports a study that showed that when pregnant addicts were in a supportive atmosphere and not threatened with punishment 83 percent of patients who tested positive for drug use agreed to counseling and 61 percent of the women

in counseling discontinued their drug use. See also Chavkin, "Mandatory Treatment for Drug Use During Pregnancy."

35. A burgeoning literature in philosophy and political theory on the ethics of care has become too vast to enumerate. Carol Gilligan's *In a Different Voice* (Cambridge: Harvard University Press, 1982) is the seminal starting point. Other important works in addition to those I will cite below are: Seyla Benhabib, "The Generalized and the Concrete Other," in Seyla Benhabib and Drucilla Cornell, eds., *Feminism as Critique* (Minneapolis: University of Minnesota Press, 1987); the articles in *Women and Morality*, ed. Diana Meyers and Eva Kittay (Totowa, N.J.: Rowman and Littlefield, 1986); and Marilyn Friedman, "Beyond Caring: The De-Moralization of Gender," in *Science, Morality and Feminist Theory*, ed. Marsha Hanen and Kai Nielsen (Calgary: University of Calgary Press, 1987).

36. Annette Baier, "The Need for More than Justice," in *Science, Morality and Feminist Theory*, ed. Marsha Hanen and Kai Nielsen (Calgary: University of Calgary Press, 1987), 47.

37. The Wellesley College Stone Center for the Study of the Psychology of Women has pioneered transferring the insights of Gilligan and other theorists of caring into a general theory of self-in-relation that can be applied in therapeutic situations. See Judith Jordan et al., *Women's Growth in Connection* (New York: The Guilford Press 1991); see also Emily K. Abel and Margaret K. Nelson, eds., *Circles of Care: Work and Identity in Women's Lives* (Albany: SUNY Press, 1990).

38. See Gillian Walker, Kathleen Eric, Anita Purick, and Ernest Crucker, "A Descriptive Outline of a Program for·Cocaine-Using Mothers and Their Babies," *Journal of Feminist Family Therapy* 3(3 & 4):7–17 (1991).

39. Nell Noddings, *Caring: A Feminine Approach to Ethics and Moral Education* (Berkeley: University of California Press, 1984); Lawrence Blum, *Love, Friendship and Altruism* (London: Routledge and Kegan Paul, 1981).

40. Virginia Held, "Non-Contractual Society: A Feminist View," in *Science, Morality and Feminist Theory*, ed. Marsha Hanen and Kai Nielsen (Calgary: University of Calgary Press, 1987), 111–138; Bernice Fisher and Joan Tronto, "Toward a Feminist Theory of Caring," in *Circles of Care*, ed. Emily K. Abel and Margaret K. Nelson, 35–62; Selma Sevenhuijsen, "Justice, Moral Reasoning, and the Politics of Child Custody," in *Equality, Politics and Gender*, ed. E. Meehan and S. Sevenhuijsen (London: Routledge, 1991).

41. See Theodore M. Benditt, "The Demands of Justice: The Difference that Social Life Makes," in *Economic Justice*, ed. Kenneth Kipnis and Diana T. Meyers (Totowa, N.J.: Rowman and Allenheld, 1985), 108–120. Nancy Fraser points out that the distinction between benefits that recipients have rights to and those that are merely gifts of charity is gendered in the U.S. welfare system, as it is in many others. Such a gender division in social service, she suggests, perpetuates the second-class citizenship of women. See "Women, Welfare and the Politics of Need Interpretation," in her *Unruly Practices: Power, Discourse and Gender in Contemporary Social Theory* (Minneapolis: University of Minnesota Press, 1988); see also Carole Pateman, "The Patriarchal Welfare State," in her *The Disorder of Women* (Stanford: Stanford University Press, 1989).

42. See Robert Goodin, *Protecting the Vulnerable: A Re-Analysis of Our Social Responsibilities* (Chicago: University of Chicago Press, 1985); see also Robert Goodin, *Reasons for Welfare* (Princeton: Princeton University Press, 1989), Chapters 5 and 6.

43. G. M. Beschner, B. G. Reed, and J. Jondonaro, *Treatment Services for Drug Dependent Women* (National Institute on Drug Abuse, Rockville, Md., U.S. Department of Health and Human Services, 1981).

44. John L. Forth-Finegan, "Sugar and Spice and Everything Nice: Gender Socialization and Women's Addiction—a Literature Review," *Journal of Feminist Family Therapy* 3(3 & 4):25 (1991). A number of studies find a high correlation between women's substance abuse and a history of sexual abuse.

45. Lucia Meijer, testimony before the House Select Committee on Children, Youth and Families on Substance Abuse Treatment and Women, April 27, 1989; see also "Substance Abuse Treatment for Women: Crisis in Access," *Health Advocate* 160 (Spring 1989).

46. See Nancy Hartsock, "Foucault on Power: A Theory for Women," in *Feminism/Postmodernism*, ed. Linda Nicholson (New York: Routledge, 1990), 157–175. Nancy Fraser expresses skepticism about Foucault's conception of biopower in her essay "Foucault's Body Language: A Posthumanist Political Rhetoric," in *Unruly Practices*. However, many of her papers on women and the welfare state from the same volume, which I rely on later in this section, are informed by Foucaultian insights as well as insights from critical theory.

47. See Jana Sawicki, *Disciplining Foucault: Feminism, Power and the Body* (New York: Routledge, 1991); Shane Phelan, "Foucault and Feminism," *American Journal of Political Science* 34(2) (May 1990); Chris Weedon, *Feminist Practice and Poststructuralist Theory* (London: Basil Blackwell, 1987), Chapter 5; Sandra Bartky, "Foucault, Femininity, and the Feminization of Patriarchal Power," in *Femininity and Domination* (New York: Routledge, 1990); Susan Bordo, "The Body and the Reproduction of Femininity: A Feminist Appropriation of Foucault," in *Gender/Body/Knowledge: Feminist Reconstructions of Being and Knowing*, ed. Susan Bordo and Alison Jaggar (New Brunswick: Rutgers University Press, 1986), 13–33.

48. See Foucault, *Discipline and Punish*; see also Michel Foucault, *Power/Knowledge* (New York: Pantheon, 1980), 93–108. For an insightful summary and analysis of disciplinary power, see Mary Rawlinson, "Foucault's Strategy: Knowledge, Power, and the Specificity of Truth," *The Journal of Medicine and Philosophy* 12:371–395 (1987).

49. Treaster, "Plan Lets Addicted Mothers Take Their Newborns Home."

50. Nancy Fraser, "Women, Welfare, and the Politics of Need Interpretation" and "Struggle Over Needs: Outline of a Socialist Feminist Critical Theory of Late Capitalist Political Culture," both in *Unruly Practices*; Joel Handler, "Dependent People, the State and the Modern/Postmodern Search for the Dialogic Community," *UCLA Law Review* 35(6):999–1113 (August 1988); Ann Weick, Charles Rapp, W. Patrick Sullivan, and Walter Kisthardt, "A Strengths Perspective for Social Work Practice," *Social Work* 34:350–354 (July 1989).

51. See Fraser, *Unruly Practices*; Handler, "Dependent People, the State and the Modern/Postmodern Search for the Dialogic Community." Also see Nikolas Rose, *Governing the Soul: The Shaping of the Private Self* (New York: Routledge, 1990), 224–237.

52. Michel Foucault, *Technologies of the Self*, ed. Luther H. Martin, Huck Gutman, and Patrick Hutton (Amherst: University of Massachusetts Press, 1988), 40; cf. Foucault, *History of Sexuality*, Vol. 1 (New York: Random House, 1978), 60–67.

53. Rose, *Governing the Soul: The Shaping of the Private Self*, especially Chapters 16–20.

54. See Fraser, *Unruly Practices*; Ellen Luff, "Using First Amendment and Title VII to Obtain Woman Centered Drug/Alcohol Treatment Programs," Proceedings of the Second Conference of the Institute for Women's Policy Research, Washington, D.C., June 1990, 1–7; Bette S. Tallen, "Twelve Step Programs: A Lesbian Feminist Critique," *NWSA Journal* 2(3):390–407 (Summer 1990).

55. See Patricia Pasick and Christine White, "Challenging General Patton: A Feminist Stance in Substance Abuse Treatment and Training," *Journal of Feminist Family Therapy* 3(3 & 4):87–102 (1991); Judy Kopp, "Self-Observation: An Empowerment Strategy in Assessment," *Social Casework: The Journal of Contemporary Social Work* 70:276–279 (May 1989).

56. Thomas Wartenberg, *The Forms of Power: From Domination to Transformation* (Philadelphia: Temple University Press, 1990), Chapter 9.

57. Forth-Finegan, "Sugar and Spice and Everything Nice," 36.

58. Janet L. Surrey, "Relationship and Empowerment," in Judith V. Jordan, Alexandra G. Kaplan, Jean Baker Miller, Irene P. Stiver, and Janet L. Surrey, *Women's Growth in Connection* (New York: The Guilford Press, 1991), 164.

59. For statements of this sort of meaning of empowerment, see Ruth J. Parsons, "Empowerment: Purpose and Practice Principle in Social Work," *Social Work in Groups* 14(2):7–21 (1991); Lorraine M. Gutierrez, "Working with Women of Color: An Empowerment Perspective," *Social Work* 35(2):149–153 (March 1990).

60. Handler, "Dependent People, the State and the Modern/Postmodern Search for the Dialogic Community," 1083–1111; Fraser, "Women, Welfare, and the Politics of Need Interpretation," in *Unruly Practices*, 156–158.

61. Parsons, "Empowerment: Purpose and Practice Principle in Social Work."

62. Handler, "Dependent People, the State and the Modern/Postmodern Search for the Dialogic Community."

63. James Jennings reports a study that concludes that the nurturing of social and racial solidarity deters drug use in some African-American communities. Laurence Gary et al., "Some Determinants of Attitudes Toward Substance Use in an Urban Ethnic Community," *Psychological Reports* 54(2):539–545 (1984), cited in James Jennings, "Blacks, Politics and the Human Service Crisis," in *Blacks, Politics and Economic Development*, ed. James Jennings (London: Verso, 1992).

References

Abel, Emily K., and Margaret K. Nelson, eds. *Circles of Care: Work and Identity in Women's Lives*. Albany: SUNY Press, 1990.

ACLU Memo, October 3, 1989. In *Drug Exposed Infants and Their Families: Coordinating Responses of the Legal, Medical and Child Protection System* (American Bar Association Center on Children and the Law, Washington, D.C., 1990).

Baier, Annette. "The Need for More than Justice." In *Science, Morality and Feminist Theory.* Edited by Marsha Hanen and Kai Nielsen. Calgary: University of Calgary Press, 1987.

Bandstra, Emmalee S., M.D. "Medical Issues for Mothers and Infants Arising from Perinatal Use of Cocaine." In *Drug Exposed Infants and Their Families: Coordinating Responses of the Legal, Medical and Child Protection System* (American Bar Association Center on Children and the Law, Washington, D.C., 1990).

Barry, Ellen M. "Pregnant, Addicted, and Sentenced." *Criminal Justice* 5:22–27 (Winter 1991).

Bartky, Sandra. *Femininity and Domination*. New York: Routledge, 1990.

Benditt, Theodore M. "The Demands of Justice: The Difference that Social Life Makes." In *Economic Justice*, 108–120. Edited by Kenneth Kipnis and Diana T. Meyers. Totowa, N.J.: Rowman and Allenheld, 1985.

Benhabib, Seyla. "The Generalized and the Concrete Other." In *Feminism as Critique*. Edited by Seyla Benhabib and Drucilla Cornell. Minneapolis: University of Minnesota Press, 1987.

Beschner, G. M., B. G. Reed, and J. Jondonaro. *Treatment Services for Drug Dependent Women*. National Institute on Drug Abuse, Rockville, Md., U.S. Department of Health and Human Services, 1981.

Blum, Lawrence. *Love, Friendship and Altruism*. London: Routledge and Kegan Paul, 1981.

Bordo, Susan. "The Body and the Reproduction of Femininity: A Feminist Appropriation of Foucault." In *Gender/Body/Knowledge: Feminist Reconstructions of Being and Knowing*, 13–33. Edited by Susan Bordo and Alison Jaggar. New Brunswick: Rutgers University Press, 1986.

Chasnoff, Ira J., Harvey J. Landress, and Mark E. Barrett. "The Prevalence of Illicit Drug or Alcohol Use During Pregnancy in Pinellas County, Florida." *New England Journal of Medicine* 322(17):1202–1207 (April 26, 1990).

Chavkin, Wendy. "Drug Addiction and Pregnancy: Policy Crossroads." *American Journal of Public Health* 80(4):483–487 (April 1990).

———. "Mandatory Treatment for Drug Use During Pregnancy." *Journal of the American Medical Association* 260(11):1556–1561 (September 18, 1991).

"Courts Disagree on Mother's Liability," *National Law Journal* 13:30 (May 13, 1991).

Curriden, Mark. "*Roe v. Wade* Does Not Prevent Criminal Prosecution of Prenatal Child Abuse," *ABA Journal* 16:51–53 (March 1990).

Davidson, "Drug Babies Push Issue of Fetal Rights." *Los Angeles Times,* 25 April 1989.

Dinnerstein, Dorothy. *The Mermaid and the Minotaur.* New York: Harper and Row, 1975.

Fisher, Bernice, and Joan Tronto. "Toward a Feminist Theory of Caring." In *Circles of Care: Work and Identity in Women's Lives,* 35–62. Edited by Emily K. Abel and Margaret K. Nelson. Albany: SUNY Press, 1990.

Forth-Finegan, John L. "Sugar and Spice and Everything Nice: Gender Socialization and Women's Addiction—a Literature Review." *Journal of Feminist Family Therapy* 3(3 & 4):25 (1991).

Foucault, Michel. *Discipline and Punish.* New York: Harper and Row, 1977.

———. *History of Sexuality,* Vol. 1. New York: Random House, 1978.

———. *Power/Knowledge.* New York: Pantheon, 1980.

———. *Technologies of the Self.* Edited by Luther H. Martin, Huck Gutman and Patrick Hutton. Amherst: University of Massachusetts Press, 1988.

Fraser, Nancy. *Unruly Practices: Power, Discourse and Gender in Contemporary Social Theory.* Minneapolis: University of Minnesota Press, 1988.

Friedman, Marilyn. "Beyond Caring: The De-Moralization of Gender." In *Science, Morality and Feminist Theory.* Edited by Marsha Hanen and Kai Nielsen. Calgary: University of Calgary Press, 1987.

Gilligan, Carol. *In a Different Voice.* Cambridge, Mass.: Harvard University Press, 1982.

Gittler, Josephine, and Merle McPherson. "Prenatal Substance Abuse." *Children Today* 19:3–7 (July–August 1990).

Goodin, Robert. *Protecting the Vulnerable: A Re-Analysis of Our Social Responsibilities.* Chicago: University of Chicago Press, 1985.

———. *Reasons for Welfare.* Princeton: Princeton University Press, 1989.

Gutierrez, Lorraine M. "Working with Women of Color: An Empowerment Perspective." *Social Work* 35(2):149–153 (March 1990).

Handler, Joel. "Dependent People, the State and the Modern/Postmodern Search for the Dialogic Community." *UCLA Law Review* 35(6):999–1113 (August 1988).

Hansen, Mark. "Courts Side with Moms in Drug Cases." *ABA Journal* 78:18 (November 1992).

Harrison, Michelle. "Drug Addiction in Pregnancy: The Interface of Science, Emotion and Social Policy." *Journal of Substance Abuse Treatment* 8:261–268 (1991).

Hartsock, Nancy. "Foucault on Power: A Theory for Women." In *Feminism/Postmodernism,* 157–175. Edited by Linda Nicholson. New York: Routledge, 1990.

Held, Virginia. "Non-Contractual Society: A Feminist View." In *Science, Morality and Feminist Theory,* 111–138. Edited by Marsha Hanen and Kai Nielsen. Calgary: University of Calgary Press, 1987.

Hoffman, "Pregnant, Addicted—and Guilty"; "Greenville Woman Sentenced to Prison." *Charleston Observer,* 19 October 1990.

Hoffman, Jan. "Pregnant, Addicted—and Guilty." *New York Times Magazine.* August 19, 1990, 24.

Jennings, James. "Blacks, Politics and the Human Service Crisis." In *Blacks, Politics and Economic Development.* Edited by James Jennings. London: Verso, 1992.

Jordan, Judith et al. *Women's Growth in Connection*. New York: The Guilford Press, 1991.

Kopp, Judy. "Self-Observation: An Empowerment Strategy in Assessment." *Social Casework: The Journal of Contemporary Social Work* 70:276–279 (May 1989).

Larson, Judith. "Creating Common Goals for Medical, Legal and Child Protection Communities." In *Drug Exposed Infants and Their Families: Coordinating Responses of the Legal, Medical and Child Protection System* (American Bar Association Center on Children and the Law, Washington, D.C., 1990).

"Legal Interventions During Pregnancy: Court-ordered Medical Treatment and Legal Penalties for Potentially Harmful Behavior by Pregnant Women." *Journal of the American Medical Association* 264(20):2663–2670 (November 28, 1990).

Lewin, Tamar. "Hurdles Increase for Many Women Seeking Abortions." *New York Times*, 15 March 1992.

Luff, Ellen. "Using First Amendment and Title VII to Obtain Woman Centered Drug/Alcohol Treatment Programs." Proceedings of the Second Conference of the Institute for Women's Policy Research, Washington, D.C., June 1990, 1–7.

Mann, Judy. "Cure an Addict, Save a Child." *Washington Post*, 5 April 1991, C3.

Mariner, Wendy K., Leonard H. Glantz, and George J. Annas. "Pregnancy, Drugs and the Perils of Prosecution." *Criminal Justice Ethics* 7:30–41 (Winter-Spring 1990).

Marshall, Alison B. "Drug Addiction, Pregnancy and Childbirth: Legal Issues for the Medical and Social Service Communities." In *Drug Exposed Infants and Their Families: Coordinating Responses of the Legal, Medical and Child Protection System* (American Bar Association Center on Children and the Law, Washington, D.C., 1990).

Meijer, Lucia. Testimony before the House Select Committee on Children, Youth and Families on Substance Abuse Treatment and Women, April 27, 1989.

Meyers, Diana and Eva Kittay, eds. *Women and Morality*. Totowa, N.J.: Rowman and Littlefield, 1986.

Mondonaro, Josette. *Chemically Dependent Women*. Lexington, Mass.: Lexington Books, 1989.

Murphy, Jeffrie. *Retribution, Justice and Therapy*. The Hague: D. Reidel, 1979.

Murray, Thomas H. "Prenatal Drug Exposure: Ethical Issues." In *The Future of Children* 1(1):105–112 (Spring 1991).

Niel, Benjamin A. "Prenatal Drug Abuse: Is the Mother Criminally Liable?" *Trial Diplomacy Journal* 15(3):129 (May-June 1992).

Noddings, Nell. *Caring: A Feminine Approach to Ethics and Moral Education*. Berkeley: University of California Press, 1984.

Paltrow, Lynn M. "When Becoming Pregnant is a Crime." *Criminal Justice Ethics*, Winter-Spring 1990, 41–47.

Parsons, Ruth J. "Empowerment: Purpose and Practice Principle in Social Work." *Social Work in Groups* 14(2):7–21 (1991).

Pasick, Patricia, and Christine White. "Challenging General Patton: A Feminist Stance in Substance Abuse Treatment and Training." *Journal of Feminist Family Therapy* 3(3 & 4):87–102 (1991).

Pateman, Carole. *Disorder of Women*. Stanford: Stanford University Press, 1989.

Phelan, Shane. "Foucault and Feminism." *American Journal of Political Science* 34(2) (May 1990).

Pinkey, Deborah S. "Racial Bias Found in Drug Abuse Reporting." *American Medical News* 32:4 (October 6, 1989).

Rawlinson, Mary. "Foucault's Strategy: Knowledge, Power, and the Specificity of Truth." *The Journal of Medicine and Philosophy* 12:371–395 (1987).

Roberts, Dorothy E. "Drug Addicted Women Who Have Babies," *Trial*, April 1990, 56–61.

———. "Punishing Drug Addicts Who Have Babies: Women of Color, Equality, and the Right of Privacy." *Harvard Law Review* 104(7):1419–1482 (May 1991).

Robin-Vergeer, Bonnie I. "The Problem of the Drug Exposed Newborn: A Return to Principled Intervention." *Stanford Law Review* 42:745–809 (February 1990).

Rose, Nikolas. *Governing the Soul: The Shaping of the Private Self.* New York: Routledge, 1990.

Sawicki, Jana. *Disciplining Foucault: Feminism, Power and the Body.* New York: Routledge, 1991.

Sevenhuijsen, Selma. "Justice, Moral Reasoning, and the Politics of Child Custody." In *Equality, Politics and Gender.* Edited by E. Meehan and S. Sevenhuijsen. London: Routledge, 1991.

Shur, Edwin M. *Labeling Women Deviant: Gender, Stigma and Social Control.* Philadelphia: Temple University Press, 1983.

Skolnick, Andrew. "Drug Screening in Prenatal Care Demands Objective Medical Criteria, Support Services." *Journal of the American Medical Association,* Vol. 264 (July 18, 1990).

"Substance Abuse Treatment for Women: Crisis in Access." *Health Advocate,* no. 160, Spring 1989.

Surrey, Janet L. "Relationship and Empowerment." In Judith V. Jordan et al., *Women's Growth in Connection.* New York: The Guilford Press, 1991.

Tallen, Bette S. "Twelve Step Programs: A Lesbian Feminist Critique." *NWSA Journal* 2(3):390–407 (Summer 1990).

Treaster, Joseph B. "Plan Lets Addicted Mothers Take Their Newborns Home." *New York Times,* 19 September 1991.

Tracktenberg, Alan I., M.D. Testimony to House Select Committee on Children and Families, April 19, 1990.

Walker, Gillian, Kathleen Eric, Anita Purick, and Ernest Crucker. "A Descriptive Outline of a Program for Cocaine-Using Mothers and Their Babies." *Journal of Feminist Family Therapy* 3(3 & 4):7–17 (1991).

Wartenberg, Thomas. *The Forms of Power: From Domination to Transformation.* Philadelphia: Temple University Press, 1990.

Weedon, Chris. *Feminist Practice and Poststructuralist Theory.* London: Basil Blackwell, 1987, 93–108.

Weick, Ann, Charles Rapp, W. Patrick Sullivan, and Walter Kisthardt. "A Strengths Perspective for Social Work Practice." *Social Work* 34:350–354 (July 1989).

7

The ACLU Philosophy and the Right to Abuse the Unborn

PHILLIP E. JOHNSON

A 1984 CALIFORNIA COURT DECISION provides a good example of the appropriate role and inherent limits of the criminal law in maternal child abuse cases. The defendant in *People v. Pointer*[1] adhered to an extremely rigorous macrobiotic diet and imposed it upon her young children, ignoring the protests of their father and the repeated advice of physicians that the diet was permanently damaging the health of the children. When the younger child was near death a doctor finally called the police, who took the infant boy to the hospital where his life was saved by emergency procedures. During the enforced hospitalization the mother surreptitiously brought her son unsuitable food despite warnings not to do so and continued to breast-feed him even after being told that her milk contained high levels of sodium that endangered his health.

The boy was placed in a foster home. The mother was allowed to visit and used the opportunity to abduct the child because she did not like the idea of his "getting fat." She took him and her older boy to Puerto Rico, where she continued to provide both with an inadequate diet until authorities brought the family back to California. There medical examinations showed that the older brother was seriously underdeveloped and the younger one had suffered severe growth retardation and permanent neurological damage.

The mother was convicted of willful child endangerment, a felony punishable by up to four years imprisonment, and placed on probation. The conditions of probation were that she serve a year in the county jail; that she participate in an appropriate counseling program; that she lose custody of the children and have no unsupervised visits with them; and that she not conceive another child during the five-year probationary period. The mother appealed the last condition on the ground that it violated her constitutional right to procreate. The court of appeals, in a thoughtful opinion written by Justice J. Anthony Kline, agreed with her. Former advocate for the poor and minorities at San Francisco's leading "public interest" law firm and chief legal adviser for Governor Jerry Brown, Justice Kline had to decide whether humanitarian concerns can ever limit the asserted fundamental right to procreate.

He distinguished the case from others that invalidated no-pregnancy conditions on the grounds they were unrelated to the underlying crime (robbery, for instance). The defendant in *Pointer* had continually and deliberately abused her children by malnutrition and had given every indication of intending to do the same in the future whenever she had the opportunity. Moreover, she was unwilling to practice birth control and thus was likely to become pregnant again. Taking present and future children out of her custody was not a sufficient remedy because of the likelihood that her diet would "cause severe damage to conceived but unborn children." Justice Kline agreed that protection of the health of unborn children was a legitimate governmental objective and acknowledged that the trial judge had imposed the no-pregnancy condition in furtherance of that "salutary purpose." In other words, an expectant mother has no constitutional right to maintain a diet that causes severe prenatal damage to her child. The no-pregnancy condition had to be modified, however, because of its likely effect if the defendant violated the condition by becoming pregnant. To avoid going to prison she would have to procure a secret abortion—a condition coercive of abortion is improper. The trial court should therefore have ruled instead that, if Pointer became pregnant, "she be required to follow an intensive prenatal and neonatal treatment program monitored by both the probation office and by a supervising physician."

With the benefit of hindsight, it is clear that Ruby Pointer should have been sent to a secure institution until her childbearing years were over; a few years later she repeated this tragedy with children born after the events described in Judge Kline's opinion. On June 21, 1991, authorities in Santa Cruz, California, removed girls aged two, four, and six from a trash-strewn apartment after neighbors finally got police to respond to their stories of screams and beatings. The police found the children in pathetic condition amid unspeakable squalor. Ruby Pointer begged them not to take her children away from her.[2]

Such cases should be addressed with compassion, but the California courts were absolutely right to say that expectant mothers have some duty towards their children and that the duty may be enforced with criminal sanctions if necessary. If a mother has a legal and moral duty to refrain from deliberately starving her infants after the moment of birth then there is no reason to exempt her from that duty during pregnancy, when the likelihood of damage to the child's current and future health is just as great. A person who deliberately neglects a duty of care and thereby causes a child permanent injury commits egregiously harmful conduct, whether the neglect occurs before or after birth. Society may decide not to prosecute such cases for various utilitarian policy reasons or because of a compassionate understanding of the plight of the mother, but the principle is clear: There is no right to abuse children, born or unborn, in the third trimester of pregnancy or the first.[3]

Some confusion on this point may be due to the U.S. Supreme Court's abortion decisions, which say that the mother's right to privacy in choosing abortion is limited by no interest in preserving fetal life before the third trimester. Although in some states a third person is guilty of murder if he kills an unborn child at any stage of development without the consent of the mother,[4] the expectant mother herself may destroy the fetus for any reason she considers appropriate, at least up to the point of viability. Why, then, may she not abuse it short of death by withholding nourishment or ingesting drugs? One answer is that the power to kill does not include the power to inflict wanton abuse, even in the case of a convicted murderer who may be sentenced to death. Another answer is that there is a societal interest in protecting the health of unborn children who will one day be citizens.

Although there is no right to abuse a fetus and the state possesses a legitimate interest in protecting its future citizens from disabling maltreatment, it does not follow that criminal punishment is ordinarily an effective way of dealing with parental child abuse—whether of the born or the unborn. Parents who abuse their children physically are frequently persons who were abused themselves as children, and often the criminal process is invoked merely in order to coerce them to cooperate with a program of therapy and supervision. Expectant mothers who use crack cocaine or other damaging substances are harming themselves as well as their children, and they often are victims of circumstances that cry out for compassionate treatment. If such a person wants to enter a treatment program and cure her addiction, at least for as long as it takes to complete the pregnancy, it makes sense to provide treatment rather than send her to jail. Similar principles apply to drug use generally when pregnancy is not involved. The fact that conduct may be criminal does not mean that prosecutors or police should seek opportunities to do something silly about it.

One can find instances where headline-seeking or callous law enforcement officials have singled out some unfortunate woman for prosecution without sufficient reason. If such cases are the norm rather than the exception, then they make good examples for refusing to criminalize maternal abuse of the unborn as a matter of legislative policy. No doubt it is unrealistic to expect all pregnant women to follow medically established standards for prenatal behavior, although it would be worth a great deal of effort to encourage and empower them to do so. Yet at the same time there may be a substantial number of cases like *Pointer,* where the mother repeatedly and defiantly pursued a course of misconduct that demonstrably caused severe damage to her children. Criminal prosecution in such cases may or may not succeed in preventing further damage, but it serves the purpose of demonstrating that the community has certain norms of behavior and takes them seriously.

Reading various papers on this subject that reflect what I think of as the "ACLU philosophy" leaves me with the impression that the writers begin with a valid argument and then drive its logic to the point of moral insanity. For example, ACLU attorney Lynn M. Paltrow thinks that many or most crack mothers and pregnant drug abusers are victims of social conditions who merely want treatment for their addiction, cannot get it, and are charged under statutes that the legislatures never intended to apply to their situations.[5] To the extent that this is what is going on, I agree wholeheartedly that the mothers should receive their treatment and the overreaching prosecutors should be censured.

Paltrow seems to have something more on her agenda than exposing instances of prosecutorial abuse, however. She insists that prosecutions of drug-using expectant mothers *in principle* "penalize a woman solely because of her decision to continue a pregnancy" and asserts hyperbolically that "allowing criminal sanctions moves us toward turning pregnancy itself into a crime since no woman can provide the perfect womb."[6] More disturbing still is her (incorrect) declaration that "at no stage of development are fetuses persons with rights separate from the woman."[7] Implicit in her statements is that a mother has a right to abuse her fetus in any way she likes, whatever the circumstances. Even animals have legal protection against wanton cruelty, yet not unborn children. Abusing them is one of the mother's American Civil Liberties.

Paltrow's position is not idiosyncratic. According to Dr. George J. Annas,[8] to impose any standard of care whatever upon expectant mothers is to treat them as "fetal containers" and therefore "nonpersons." Dawn Johnsen,[9] who like Paltrow is from the ACLU's Reproductive Freedom Project, states, "A pregnant woman can affect her future child's quality of life, albeit to a limited extent." The possibility that a mother might impose "limited" damage upon her child by, say, crack cocaine use causes Johnsen to concede that she has "a moral obligation to act responsibly during pregnancy." This obligation only requires her to "consider" adverse effects upon the fetus, however, and not necessarily to give such considerations any particular weight. Because there is no conceivable standard for evaluation, we must accept whatever the mother chooses to do as morally correct. If we are tempted to criticize we should remember that pregnant women are influenced by a multitude of factors in deciding whether to use substances like alcohol, drugs, and tobacco; that women "should not and cannot make these decisions solely on the basis of what is most likely to reduce the chances of harming the fetus"; and that "the risk [to the fetus] posed by any single decision is usually extremely small."

The ACLU philosophy proceeds from a tenable legal position (prosecutions of pregnant drug abusers are unauthorized by existing statutes and may cause more harm than good) to a monstrous moral conclusion (pregnant women have a right to use drugs or engage in other conduct that severely and permanently damages a developing unborn child). Perhaps all this is just rhetorical overkill and the writers will back off their extreme position once someone points out the consequences of their logic. But perhaps the ACLU philosophy does not recognize that conduct can be morally outrageous even though for practical reasons it is beyond the power of the criminal law to control. To show the importance of distinguishing between what is moral and what is merely legal, I must make a few elementary points about the moral basis of family life.

One of the most important things that adults do is to prepare the next generation for the joys and responsibilities of life. To do this they must ensure to the best of their ability that their children are born healthy. Following birth children must be nurtured and educated in moral behavior by loving parents, preferably *two* parents. That is why it is important for lovers to regard marriage as a sacred bond rather than as a contractual arrangement to be terminated at the convenience of either party. That is also why mothers in a sane society regard pregnancy as both an opportunity and a responsibility rather than primarily as an encumbrance that men impose in order to make women unhappy and impede their pursuit of wealth, power, and pleasure. Similarly, fathers in a sane society regard their offspring from the beginning of pregnancy as their own flesh so that they become enthusiastic providers and conurturers rather than the unwilling objects of child support orders. Through its educational and legal institutions, a sane state does what it can to foster these healthy attitudes so that there may be enough productive and responsible citizens around to do the essential work and to take care of the minority of unfortunate persons who did not get a proper start in life.

In contemporary America, the moral bonds that hold families together have been loosened as people have come to think of themselves as rights-bearing and pleasure-seeking individuals who form and sever relationships with other people according to their own convenience. In such a society fathers can be taught to see the unborn child in the womb as the mother's sole property and hence her sole responsibility. With divorce available upon request and no social stigma, the norm for family life may become single mothers struggling alone with the problems of raising and supporting their children. The law can promise to collect child support from irresponsible fathers but it will not be able to keep this promise with any consistency. Mothers themselves may be tempted to give up on their responsibilities and pursue pleasure instead. After all, if pregnant women can affect the quality of life of their future children only "to a limited extent," and if it is the responsibility of the state to provide for the children thereafter, why should anyone be such a fool as to sacrifice the best years of her life for a stranger that has invaded her body?

The law relating to family life is not important because of its direct effect in coercing compliance. If people no longer believe that marriage should be a permanent arrangement, that unborn children are developing human beings worthy of love and respect, or that fathers should care for mothers and children as their own flesh and blood, then it is futile to try to compel them to comply with discarded norms by threatening to send them to jail. Family life rests upon personal commitment and willing acceptance of responsibility, not upon state compulsion.

Law cannot compel virtue, but the state of the law can tell us something important about the kind of people we have become. The crack-mother prosecutions reveal a nation desperately trying one thing after another to slow (or at least protest) an alarming disappearance of personal and family norms of behavior that preceding generations were able to take for granted. Criminal prosecutions are no solution, of course, but neither are ACLU proposals to stop the breakdown by subsidizing it with ever higher levels of government spending at the expense of increasingly exasperated voting taxpayers who are to understand that the behavior of the people who receive the subsidy is none of their business. Rights are excellent concepts if placed within a larger framework of personal responsibility, but a philosophy that pays no attention to anything but rights is a license for self-indulgence.

The great-grandparents of today's crack mothers and absent fathers had a religious morality that enabled them in most cases to provide an admirable family life during the Great Depression, when poverty and discrimination were everywhere and no one imagined that child care was the federal government's business. The old theology taught previous generations that poverty is no excuse for irresponsibility and that it is possible to maintain dignity in the face of oppression. The ACLU philosophy teaches the current generation that people should do pretty much as they please and that some abstraction called "society" is to blame and must pay up if anything goes wrong. Anyone who has traded the old theology for the new philosophy had better submit the bill for damages soon, while there is still enough social capital in society's bank account to keep the checks from bouncing.

Notes

This chapter is revised from Phillip E. Johnson, "The ACLU Philosophy and the Right to Abuse the Unborn," *Criminal Justice Ethics* 9(1):48–51 (Winter/Spring 1990). Reprinted by permission of The Institute for Criminal Justice Ethics, 899 Tenth Avenue, New York, N.Y., 10019.

1. 151 Cal. App. 3d 1128, 199 Cal. Rptr. 357 (1st Dist. 1984).

2. "3 Malnourished Children Found in Trash-filled Home," *Los Angeles Times*, 22 June 1991, A27.

3. I forbear mention in the text of *U.A.W. v. Johnson Controls, Inc.*, 111 S.Ct. 1196 (1991), because the case involves complex statutory and social policy considerations that go far beyond the scope of this essay. The decision invalidated a battery manufacturer's "fetal protection policy," which excluded all women who might conceivably become pregnant from work in areas of high lead exposure. The holding is controversial because it gives little

weight to the interest in preventing fetal and birth defects. Before the Supreme Court handed down the *Johnson Controls* decision, the circuits (including the 7th Circuit, which decided in favor of Johnson Controls' fetal protection policy) had indicated that an overwhelming majority of federal appellate judges would strenuously deny that a pregnant woman has a right to risk the health of her fetus by working in an area of high lead exposure, even though her own interest in obtaining or retaining the employment opportunity may be substantial.

4. A closely divided Minnesota Supreme Court recently upheld an indictment for murder of an "unborn child" that alleged the defendant had shot and killed a woman who was twenty-eight days pregnant. *State v. Merrill*, 450 N.W.2d 318 (Minn. 1990). The Minnesota court noted that, of the seventeen states that have codified the crime of murder of an unborn child, thirteen impose criminal liability only if the fetus is viable. Two non-code states have expanded their definition of common law homicide to include viable fetuses. Arizona and Indiana impose criminal liability for causing the death of a fetus at any stage, but with a maximum penalty of five years and two years, respectively.

5. Lynn M. Paltrow, "When Becoming Pregnant Is a Crime," *Criminal Justice Ethics* 9:41 (Winter-Spring 1990).

6. Ibid., at 43.

7. Ibid., at 44.

8. See George J. Annas, "Pregnant Women as Fetal Containers," *Hastings Center Report* (December 1986), 13–14. Dr. Annas is Utley Professor of Health Law, Boston University School of Medicine, and Chief of the Health Law Section, Boston University School of Public Health. I do not know if Dr. Annas has any formal connection with the ACLU, but his article reflects the same philosophy as the articles by Dawn Johnsen and Lynn Paltrow of the ACLU's Reproductive Freedom Project.

9. Dawn Johnsen, "A New Threat to Pregnant Women's Autonomy," *Hastings Center Report* 17(4):33 (August 1987).

8

The Trope of the Dark Continent in the Fetal Harm Debates: "Africanism" and the Right to Choice

LISA C. BOWER

THIS CHAPTER EXPLORES how the fetal harm debate is sustained by a tropological dependence on race. In this debate, the focus on the substance-abusing mother—who is frequently described as single, black, and deficient—suggests how perceptions about fetal abuse are supported by the trope of the dark continent, the notion that female sexuality is a dark and unexplored territory. Rhetorically, this trope is constructed by a metonymic chain that links disease, sexuality, female sexuality, and racial otherness.

The trope of the dark continent is mirrored in representations of race or what Toni Morrison has recently referred to as "Africanism."[1] To explore how race is suppressed and expressed in this debate, this chapter considers problems raised by conventional defenses of substance-abusing pregnant women, specifically defenses that rest upon the language of reproductive rights. Concerns about surrogacy, in vitro fertilization, and new reproductive technologies have, in conjunction with the doctrinal unravelling of *Roe v. Wade*, generated justifiable alarm regarding women's ability to control their reproductive futures. For some feminists, the erosion of reproductive autonomy provides an opportunity to rethink the contours and limitations of the right to privacy, the doctrinal principle animating the right to choice.[2] Others have reasserted the intimate connection between mother and fetus as an antidote to fetal rights advocates who claim the primacy of the rights of the fetus. Drawing on Carol Gilligan's work, one variant of this theme posits that women's close physical and psychological relationship to the fetus constitutes a distinctive "moral vision" that supports the importance (and appropriateness) of women's decision making during pregnancy.[3] Some claim that the criminalization of pregnant women who abuse drugs is exacerbated by the erosion of the (mother's) right to choice, specifically by the effects of the more recent *Webster v. Reproductive Health Services* decision, which granted fetuses the status of legal personhood.[4]

Framing the debate in terms of reproductivity, however, reinscribes a core legal fiction developed in several cases involving reproductive rights. On close examination, the legal fiction of "choice" turns out to be sustained by (even as it creates) an oppositional interdependence: As Morrison teaches, the construction of a white, independent subject depends upon the simultaneous invocation of a black, dependent subject.[5]

The problems that reproductive choice raises are those of how to talk about identity and agency. Examining the symbolic labor that arguments about reproductive choice perform, I suggest that accounts of the harm caused by the criminalization of substance-abusing mothers can be subverted in a number of ways. First, a framework that foregrounds questions of choice and rights suppresses the more salient issues of race and class. And when statistical evidence is marshalled to support claims that pregnant women who are criminalized for their substance abuse are disproportionately women of color, the effect is to make race and its relationship to gender and class invisible factors in this debate. The use of statistical data summons forth an analytic framework, social science discourse, which is presumed to be neutral but actually sustains the erasure of difference except as a deviant outlier. Without a sustained analysis of the ways in which race frames the fetal harm debate, women of color are reinscribed as objects of analysis rather than as subjects with agency.[6]

Secondly, and this is a more complex problem underscoring the problem of talking about differences: The figural and unstable nature of language militates against overt and transparent claims. Arguments that simply mention the obligatory triad of race, class, and gender depend on traces and slippages in rhetorical meaning that evoke a chain of unconscious associations and linkages: "verbal patterns, metaphors, replacements and similar tropes become outward, consciously unintended manifestations of wishes and fears, desires and terrors that have been driven inward."[7] Thus if language is sustained by a series of unconscious associations, then the incorporation of race as an analytic element and the articulation of the "other's" situation, life history, and complexity is a risky business at best. As Marianna Torgovnick explains, the manner in which the other functions as "a screen upon which we project our deepest fears and desires" means that the "best of intentions" are always circumscribed by the play of unconscious forces.[8]

For example, the racism and sexism manifested in policies aimed at punishing the pregnant addict may be, as Iris Young suggests, supported by an unconscious resentment of the mother. She argues that "the targeting of woman drug users, especially poor women and women of color," points to a particular rage directed at mothers that "reflects an identification with the infant."[9] I am making a related but broader claim. One of the difficulties this debate presents is the ongoing problem of how to incorporate race, class, and gender into feminist analyses of legal and public policy issues. These difficulties are compounded by unconscious forces related to the (m)other that affect men and women in general and infect the formulation of public policy and feminist analyses.[10]

The instability of language and the psychological complexities involved in "othering" demonstrate the intractability of racism at the rhetorical and unconscious level. Both problems suggest that the terms and levels of analysis that are required for analyzing multilayered problems such as fetal harm must become objects of criticism in their own right. Moreover, the intersectionality of race, class, gender, ethnicity, sex, and so on must be rethought at the critical juncture where theory and practice can fruitfully inform renewed agendas for political change.

Tracing out how race is imbricated in the fetal harm debate and how the legal fiction of individual choice suppresses the articulation of race in accounts of the prosecution of substance-abusing mothers is the task of the following essay.

Contexts, Frameworks, Terms

My point of departure for thinking about the role of race in the fetal harm debate is an article by Patricia Williams, in which she notes the penchant for a popular New York newspaper "to run stories about how single black mothers, the universal signifiers for poverty, irresponsibility, drug addiction, and rabbit-like fertility, are causing the downfall of Western civilization."[11] Williams explores the connections among the historical legacy of blackness as property, questions of maternal-fetal connection, and the human despair animating acts that pit the fetus and mother against each other.

She juxtaposes the story of a pregnant inmate in a Missouri prison who sued the state on behalf of her fetus against another unusual case in which a pregnant women in Washington, D.C. was incarcerated so that she would be "out of drug-temptation's way, ostensibly in order to protect her fetus."[12] "What a cycle of absurdity," she notes, "protecting the fetus from the woman by putting her in jail, then protecting the fetus from jail by asserting the lack of due process accorded the fetus in placing it there." This "absurdity" reminds Williams of what she describes as "a madperson's metaphor for maternalism"—the story of Melody Baldwin, "who injected her baby with her toxic antidepressant medication ... to protect the infant from the toxin of life's despair."[13]

What intrigues me about Williams' analysis is her suggestion that the signifying power of the black single mother is integral to the public articulation of fetal harm and abuse. Throughout her essay, she alludes to how a signifying chain—black, single, poor, drug-addicted, sexually promiscuous, natally absent—is constructed through a series of discursive moves that are instigated within familiar institutional settings such as medicine, law, drug enforcement agencies, and so on. The construction of the sexualized, drug-abusing mother is enabled by social problems such as urban poverty, AIDS, and crack addiction. And proposed solutions such as the war on drugs feed into the already complex identity of the single, drug-abusing mother.

Although each problem and its solution is integral to the construction of fetal harm as a public policy issue, each also calls up the trope of the dark continent and an "intricate historical articulation of the categories of racial and sexual difference."[14] In the fetal harm debate, this trope returns to perform a familiar task. By linking together poverty, disease, sexuality, and race, the reappearance of the imagery of the dark continent invites a return to a colonialist imagination and a familiar set of stereotypes.

The Trope of the Dark Continent

Some of the elements for understanding the historical uses to which this trope has been put, including its subliminal effectiveness in the fetal harm debate, derive from Freud's observation that "the sexual life of women is a dark continent," a phrase that he borrowed from Victorian colonialist texts that used the term to refer to Africa. Both Mary Ann Doane and Sander Gilman trace out the way in which black women's sexuality, based frequently on meticulously recorded biological "difference," has been linked to abnormal (read primitive) sexuality.[15] White female sexuality (and the purity of white women) is constructed as the polar opposite of the "animality" of black women who are, in the eighteenth century, increasingly associated with prostitution and, in the nineteenth century, with "syphilophobia." Black females, as Gilman explains, "do not merely represent the sexualized female, they also represent the female as the source of corruption and disease."[16]

In the late twentieth century, the construction of pregnant women of color as substance-abusing addicts is enabled by the reactivation of a complex historical relationship between racial and sexual differences. Frequently allied with problems of the decaying inner city, linkages among sexually deviant behavior, race, intravenous drug use (including crack addiction), and AIDS are tightly drawn. Conceptions of "pollution" and disease are joined to differences of race, class, and sex and reinscribed by the discourses that construct AIDS.

Rhetoric surrounding AIDS also rests on an allusion to the trope of the "dark continent." In *AIDS and Its Metaphors,* Susan Sontag explains that AIDS is "thought to have started in the dark continent and then spread to Haiti, then to the United States and Europe."[17] The unconscious associations made to racial otherness coupled with the "many hypotheses that have been fielded about possible transmission from animals cannot help but activate a familiar set of stereotypes about animality, sexual license and blacks."[18] The symptoms of AIDS, as Simon Watney argues, are identifiable as "some innate Africanness—lassitude, extreme weight loss, huge staring eyes—the only too familiar signs of famine," but in this case "supposedly caused by excessive sexual appetite."[19]

The relationship between AIDS and unnatural sexual drives is further inter-twined with what Watney refers to as the "maternal fecundity of Africa." Much of the rhetoric depicting Africa as the source of AIDS relies not only on an image of Africa as "a wild and gorgeous apparition of a woman"[20] but also reinscribes African women as the cause and origin of the disease. This rhetoric suggests that African women's maternal instincts are innately flawed precisely because their "sexuality cannot be classified within the terms of Christian monogamy." Accordingly, any woman whose sexuality doesn't fit this standard is "a prostitute and deserves to die. Moreover, she is the author of her own destruction, rather than someone who has herself been infected by a man."[21] The discourses that are integral to the construction of AIDS further define the substance-abusing mother as both promiscuous and worthy of punishment.

Closer to home, the emergence of the pregnant drug-abusing woman draws on the historical devaluation of black women as mothers. The description of African-American women as "bad mothers" is rooted in the "unique experience of slavery, perpetuated by complex social forces"[22] and sustained by a series of rhe-torical displacements such as the trope of the dark continent. Frequently blamed for the devastating effects of poverty and abuse on their children, the scapegoating of black mothers emerges in public policy decisions and legal decisions. For example, the disproportionate number of black mothers who lose custody of their children through the welfare system is a result of racist policies that judge the validity of the black family and black women's capacity for mothering in terms of the norm of the white nuclear family.[23] Similarly, women of color are often caught in the double-bind of giving up their welfare benefits if they refuse sterilization. Under current government policy, sterilization is paid for by Medicaid, yet information about and access to other contraceptive techniques and abortion is frequently not available.[24] The "myth of the black Jezebel," as Dorothy Roberts puts it, has been joined to "the contemporary image of the lazy welfare mother who breeds children at the expense of taxpayers in order to increase the amount of her welfare check."[25] The familiar strategy of configuring whiteness and good mothering in relation to blackness and bad mothering suggests the return of a colonialist imaginary that draws on the legacy of slavery and allied images of deficient black maternity.

Race and Africanism

Just as the trope of the dark continent helps us understand how race and gender are rhetorically related in the fetal harm debate, so numerous scholars' redefinition of "race" highlights the rhetorical instability of this term. Race, as some contemporary redefinitions suggest, has lost its credibility as a meaningful category of analysis in the biological sciences. As Henry Louis Gates Jr. describes it, race is a dangerous trope that functions to "inscribe and describe differences of language, belief systems, artistic tradition and gene pool, as well as all sorts of supposedly natural attributes."[26] Race's status as an empty signifier, as a concept "virtually vacuous in its own right,"[27] means that it can perform a myriad of functions. Metaphorically, it works as a way of referring to, without explicitly naming, class division or social and economic decay, suggesting that in contemporary parlance race is always standing in for something else.

Toni Morrison's analysis of the metaphysical and ideological dimensions of Africanism suggests that one task that race is called upon to perform is the simultaneous articulation of both white and black identities. Morrison uses the term Africanism to capture the "denotative and connotative blackness that African peoples have come to signify as well as the entire range of views, assumptions, readings, and misreadings that accompany Eurocentric learning about these people."[28] "Africanism," Morrison argues, is metaphysically necessary to the configuration of an "Americanism": A masked representation of an Africanist presence provides, in a variety of different ways, "the staging ground and arena for the elaboration of the quintessential American identity."[29]

In the fetal harm debates, Africanism, understood as stereotypic views of blackness connected to substance-abusing women of color, functions "metaphysically" to reaffirm white maternal identities that have been seriously eroded. A concern with fetal harm, like contemporary debates about family values, single mothers, and homosexualities, is a reaction to the unsettling of "natural" categories of sexed, gendered identities. One question animating these diverse debates is how to (re)configure white maternal identities once they have been undermined by technological changes, medical discourses, and, ironically, by feminist and legal rhetoric that has redefined women's roles independent of mothering.

Yet the ideological appeal of Africanism stems from the way in which a subordinated "black population" is conceived as opposite to notions of freedom and individualism in American culture. In other words, when a black population is configured as stereotypically dependent, it effectively confirms the ideology of individualism as an identifying feature of the white population. In effect, Morrison shows how the binary opposition white/black functions in language as a vehicle for a white identity that knows "itself as not enslaved, but free."[30]

This opposition is, I suggest, constructed anew by legal discourse in a number of familiar cases involving reproductive rights. These cases articulate a freely choosing subject whose identity depends on the exclusion of race and class. By relying on legal definitions of subjectivity, analyses of fetal harm reinscribe the dynamic that Morrison describes, that is, representations of white subjectivity are recreated by a dependence on a suppressed Africanist presence.

Reliance on legal configurations of women's identity is a familiar strategy within legal feminist and feminist argumentation. Indeed, it is precisely because law makes available competing rhetorical modes and categories of identity that it is so seductive as a discourse of change.[31] However, the turn to the law creates a number of strategic dilemmas and paradoxes. As Butler describes it, some of these are peculiar to the nature of juridical power, specifically the way in which it "inevitably 'produces' what it merely claims to represent. ... In effect, the law produces and then conceals the notion of a 'subject before the law' in order to invoke that discursive formation as a naturalized foundational premise that subsequently legitimates the law's own regulatory hegemony."[32] Yet legal constructions of subjectivity are produced by a set of exclusionary practices that appear to constitute the grounds of a natural identity. These subject positions rely on a "metaphysics of substance," a core fiction of identity that assumes a reasoning subject who is capable of exercising moral judgment. Moreover, this core identity rests on the notion, in Mary Poovey's words, that "the social contexts or relationships in which the person engages are ... external and incidental to the inner essence."[33] Legal discourse thus has the effect of excluding race and class. These exclusions, as I argue below, return to haunt feminist theories and practices that fail to interrogate how legal definitions of women's identity are both constituted and deployed.

The Legacy of *Roe v. Wade* and the "Metaphysics of Substance"

At the center of some feminist criticisms of the legal sanctioning of substance-abusing mothers that rely on arguments about reproductive rights is a complex of so-called liberty rights that includes the "right to privacy." Under the right to privacy falls the right to bodily integrity,[34] the right of parents to control the care and education of their children,[35] and the right to make decisions about childbearing.[36] This last right, often interpreted as the "right to choice," was not stated as such in *Roe v. Wade.* Parsed from the broader notion of the right to privacy, the U.S. Supreme Court never suggested that women could make decisions about whether or not to bear a child independent of a state interest. The privacy of the pregnant woman was always circumscribed by the state's interests in potential human life or maternal health.

The problem of shifting definitions of viability that plagued the *Roe* decision from the beginning made it difficult to establish bright-line distinctions between mother and fetus. Nevertheless, as Poovey has observed, the Court used the relative clarity of the fundamental rights guaranteed by the Fourteenth Amendment "to simplify the pregnant woman into a single subject during the first trimester of the pregnancy, at the same time that it elaborated the viable fetus into a 'person' during the last." The effect was to "divide one legal person into two, the mother and the fetus."[37] The legal identity of the woman in *Roe* was based on the capacity for exercising reason as a freely willing individual. In contrast, the fetus was assigned by the language of *Roe* to the category "potential person" and acquired (in the latter stages of pregnancy, at least) the right to protection.

Ironically, by creating these two competing legal fictions about subjectivity, *Roe* laid the groundwork for the fetal harm debate. In *Webster v. Reproductive Health Services,* the Court refused to find unconstitutional that part of the Missouri statute that stated "the life of each human being begins at conception" and "unborn children have protectable interests in life, health, and well-being." By doing so the Court opened the door to an enlarged conception of the freely choosing subject. By expanding the language of *Harris v. McRae* to uphold the ban on the use of public facilities and employees, *Webster* effectively foreclosed choice for many women, particularly women of color.[38] Nevertheless, the decision created, within legal discourse, the presumption that women's decisions about abortion would remain "unaffected." The core identity of the legal subject, defined independently of material contexts, was reinforced, whereas the opportunity to foreground a multiple notion of subjectivity that shows how race, socio-economic status, and gender are interrelated was suppressed.

The fetal harm debate is sustained by the legacy of *Roe* and *Webster* in two ways. First, critics of a tough-minded prosecutorial approach clearly wish to refute the legal fictions that created the mother-fetus divide initially. At the same time, the fetal harm debate presents an opportunity to extend the right to choice that sustains the legal fiction of woman as "choosing subject." In the context of this debate, the question of choice is not about "whether or not a woman wants to continue her pregnancy—the abortion question—but rather her decision regarding how to conduct her life during pregnancy."[39] Arguably, this notion of choice is a radical attempt to move beyond *Roe* and *Webster* to establish—based on the core legal fiction created by these cases—a subject with a more extensive range of choice.

However, the terms derived from *Roe* that are being defended anew by feminists in the fetal abuse debate, such as "choice" and "rights," assume a definition of personhood that resituates the choosing subject of liberal individualism and forecloses the expression of racial and class differences. The right to choice in the fetal harm debate is again supported by the fiction of a substantive core that appears to be a "natural" ground for the choosing subject. Yet it is legal discourse itself that creates this notion of a core identity, as I suggested above.

As cases like *Webster* and *Harris v. McRae* intimate, the Court is willing to reaffirm the primacy of this core identity underlying the notion of individual choice. The problem is that it does so with a vengeance. For example, in *Webster* the Court found that the language of the Missouri statute that refers to the fetus as a person "does not by its terms regulate abortion or any other aspect of appellee's medical practice" and therefore does not "burden women's choice." Neither did the Court's failure to support the provision of Medicaid payments for medically necessary abortions in *Harris v. McRae* "burden women's choice." The language of "managerial formalism"[40] that extracts definitions of legal personhood from questions of social and economic context facilitates the articulation and recognition of only certain claims. The expression of rights and restrictions in cases like *Webster* and *Harris* highlights the instability of legal terms such as "rights" and "privacy." These cases also show how a focus on rights, which are always created in light of fictional categories of identity, glosses over the social and economic conditions that set boundaries to rights and delimit access to them.

Feminist arguments about reproductive choice can thus circumscribe access to choice for those who do not fall within the definition of personhood created by legal discourse. Analyses that depend on the right to choose to defend substance-abusing pregnant women from prosecution foreclose attention to how Africanism sustains and differentiates white identities—caricatured as the freely choosing subject—from the dependent, unfree, subject position of the black substance-abusing mother. The ideological appeal of references to race can be seen in the way black women are frequently figured as the victims of harm and systemic discrimination that is beyond their control. Yet their status as "victims" renders them agents without choice, a choicelessness reinforced by their drug-dependent status.

Both within the fetal harm debate and the larger debate about reproductive rights, the suppression of race as a constituent element of identity suggests the necessity for rethinking the terms in which arguments have been cast. A focus on abstractions like "individual choice" makes it rhetorically difficult to address the differences that social and material contexts create, particularly when they are already sustained in terms of polar opposites such as white/black, free/unfree.

Revisions and "Remedies"

As we have seen, the fiction of the "core identity" created by reproductive rights discourse suggests the fixity of legal definitions of personhood. When race is used to reframe the fetal harm debate, however, the choosing subject of liberal discourse can be redefined for more heterogenous political practices. Race, the suppressed term in this debate, can be used to disrupt the legal fiction of the choosing (white) subject. In other words, the "metaphysics of substance" at the center of arguments about reproductive choice can be evoked with the goal of opening up this category as a "site of permanent political contest."[41]

To this end, recent arguments such as Roberts' extended treatment of the fetal harm debate change the terms of analysis from gender as "the primary locus of oppression" to a framework showing that poor black women have been selected for punishment as a result of the "inseparable combination of their gender, race, and economic status."[42] Beginning with the perception that the criminalization of substance-abusing pregnant women is defined by complex interrelationships among race, class, and gender, Roberts contests the legal standards governing reproductive choice and, by extension, discussions of fetal harm. Articulating the problem of fetal harm from the perspective of black women offers the following advantages: It shows how the fetal harm debate is defined by an Africanist presence; it enables the redefinition of "choice" from the perspective of black women; and, as Roberts suggests, it both enlarges and disrupts legal understandings of reproductive freedom and the right to privacy.[43] By adopting a framework that takes seriously the manner in which race, class, and gender are simultaneously articulated, the legal fiction of individual choice can be redefined.

Roberts argues that the equal protection principle and the right to privacy, both of which have formed the centerpiece of feminist arguments about reproductive rights, can be configured to grant black women's reproductive choices full respect and protection. Her reworking of legal doctrine entails two moves. First, she argues that the equal protection of the Fourteenth Amendment, which embodies an ideal of racial equality, falls short as an analytical tool because the dominant standard, the antidiscrimination view, identifies "the primary threat to equality as the government's failure to treat black people as individuals without regard to race."[44]

This vision of equality sees racism as the result of individual actors rather than the effect of institutional and discursive power that reinscribes the devaluation of black women as natally deficient, sexually promiscuous, and diseased. In contrast, an "antisubordination principle" mandates "that equal protection law concern itself with the concrete ways in which government policy perpetuates the inferior status of black women."[45]

Secondly, Roberts argues that when race is made a critical factor in understanding reproductive rights it changes our perception of the right to privacy. For example, when white middle-class women's concerns predominate, a focus on abortion rights is theorized as the center of reproductive freedom. One result is that choices otherwise available to them, for example to use contraception and to pay for abortions, are merely burdened. Such a focus obscures the concerns of poor women and women of color—the "material conditions of poverty and oppression that restrict their choices."[46] The legal conception of privacy can be rethought, Roberts argues, to insist that government has an "affirmative duty" to protect conceptions of personhood from degradation and to facilitate the processes of choice and self-determination.[47] Roberts' creative retooling of the "right to privacy" suggests that it can be used to support a principle of self-definition for black women.[48] The concept of personhood embodied in the right to privacy can be used to affirm black women's construction of their own multiple and contested identities.

In the context of the fetal harm debate, the elimination of racial categories of exclusion requires an analysis that begins with race and outlines the historical work that racial and sexual differences have produced. More generally, it requires thinking about how the "deep grammar"[49] that defines the expression of racist discourse can be undermined. Further, the mechanisms whereby social subjects come to identify themselves as raced and to discriminate against those who are racially other must become objects of analysis and criticism. Finally, the paradoxical nature of legal discourse—its inherent instability *and* its tendency to fix conceptions of identity—provides an opportunity to highlight the constructed nature of core legal fictions and the exclusions they sustain. Although dismantling unitary definitions of identity is a first step, the resilience and insidiousness of racism requires attention to the specificity of racist practices and their manifestations in both theory and practice.

Notes

1. Toni Morrison, *Playing in the Dark: Whiteness and the Literary Imagination* (Cambridge: Harvard University Press, 1992).

2. Frances Olsen, "Unraveling Compromise," *Harvard Law Review* 103:105–135 (November 1989); Catharine MacKinnon, "Reflections on Sex Equality Under Law," *Yale Law Journal* 100:1281–1328 (1990).

3. "Rethinking (M)otherhood: Feminist Theory and State Regulation of Pregnancy," *Harvard Law Review* 103:1325–1343 (1990); Joseph Losco, "Fetal Rights and Feminism," in *Feminist Jurisprudence: the Difference Debate,* ed. Leslie Goldstein (Lanham, MD: Rowman and Littlefield, 1992).

4. Dawn Johnsen, "From Driving to Drugs: Governmental Regulation of Pregnant Women's Lives after Webster," *University of Pennsylvania Law Review* 138:179–215 (1989).

5. Morrison, *Playing in the Dark.*

6. Conversations with Kristin Koptiuch helped clarify my thinking on this point.

7. John Bender and David E. Wellbery, "Rhetoricality: on the Modernist Return of Rhetoric," in *The Ends of Rhetoric,* ed. John Bender and David E. Wellbery (Stanford: Stanford UP, 1990), p. 131.

8. Mariana Torgovnick, *Gone Primitive: Savage Intellects, Modern Lives* (Chicago: University of Chicago Press, 1990), 247.

9. See Chapter 6 of this volume.

10. See my "'Mother' in Law: Conceptions of Mother and the Maternal in Feminism and Feminist Legal Theory," *differences: a Journal of Feminist Cultural Criticism* 3:20–38 (Spring 1991); Julia Creet, "Daughter of the Movement: the Psychodynamics of Lesbian S/M Fantasy," *differences: a Journal of Feminist Cultural Studies* 3:135–159 (Summer 1991), and Homi Bhabha, "The Other Question," *Screen* 24(6):34 (1983), where he notes: "darkness signifies at once both birth and death; it is in all cases a desire to return to the fullness of the mother, a desire for an unbroken and undifferentiated line of vision and origin."

11. Patricia Williams, "Fetal Fictions: an Exploration of Property Archetypes in Racial and Gendered Contexts," *University of Florida Law Review* 42:86 (1990).

12. Williams, "Fetal Fictions," 92.

13. Williams, "Fetal Fictions," 93.

14. Mary Ann Doane, *Femmes Fatales: Feminism, Film Theory, Psychoanalysis* (New York: Routledge, 1992), 212.

15. Sander Gilman, "Black Bodies, White Bodies: Toward an Iconography of Female Sexuality in Late Nineteenth Century Art, Medicine and Literature," in *"Race," Writing and Difference,* 223–261, ed. Henry Louis Gates (Chicago: Chicago University Press, 1986).

16. Gilman, "Black Bodies, White Bodies," 250.

17. Susan Sontag, *AIDS and Its Metaphors,* (New York: Anchor, 1989), 139.

18. Sontag, *AIDS and Its Metaphors*, 140.

19. Simon Watney, "Missionary Positions: AIDS, 'Africa,' and Race," *differences: a Journal of Feminist Cultural Criticism* 1:91 (Winter 1989).

20. Watney, "Missionary Positions." Watney borrows this phrase from Joseph Conrad's *Heart of Darkness*.

21. Watney, "Missionary Positions," 85.

22. Dorothy Roberts, "Punishing Drug Addicts Who Have Babies: Women of Color, Equality, and The Right to Privacy," *Harvard Law Review* 104:1424 (May 1991).

23. Ibid.

24. Ibid.

25. Ibid.

26. Henry Louis Gates, "Introduction: Writing "Race" and the Difference It Makes," in *"Race," Writing and Difference*, ed. Henry Louis Gates (Chicago: Chicago University Press, 1986), p. 5.

27. David Theo Goldberg, *Racist Culture: Philosophy and the Politics of Meaning* (Cambridge: Blackwell, 1993), 210.

28. Morrison, *Playing in the Dark*, 5.

29. Ibid.

30. Ibid.

31. For example, see my "Unsettling 'Woman': Competing Subjectivities in No-Fault Divorce and Divorce Mediation," *Feminist Jurisprudence: the Difference Debate*, ed. Leslie Goldstein (Lanham, MD: Rowman and Littlefield, 1992), where I suggest that it is the "coexistence of competing rhetorical modes in law that supports the feminist construction of conceptions of woman as simultaneously nurturing subject and rights-bearing citizen."

32. Judith Butler, *Gender Trouble: Feminism and the Subversion of Identity* (New York: Routledge, 1990), 2.

33. Mary Poovey, "The Abortion Question and the Death of Man," in *Feminists Theorize the Political*, ed. Judith Butler and Joan Scott (New York: Routledge, 1992), 241.

34. As the author of "Maternal Rights" observes, "courts and commentators have recognized, in a variety of contexts, that an individual has a right to make decisions that affect her body." "Maternal Rights and Fetal Wrongs: the Case Against the Criminalization of 'Fetal Abuse,'" *Harvard Law Review* 101:1001. This "right" can be derived from the Fourth Amendment's prohibition against unreasonable searches—the court has used it to prohibit government from "pumping the stomachs of suspects" or allowing the state "to force civilly committed patients to take antipsychotic drugs."

35. See *Pierce v. Society of Sisters* (1925) where the Supreme Court invalidated a statute that required parents to send their children to public schools.

36. Two cases preceding *Roe v. Wade* laid the groundwork. *Griswold v. Connecticut* (1965) struck down a Connecticut law that prohibited married couples from using contraceptive devices. In *Griswold*, Justice Douglas stated that various constitutional guarantees located in the "penumbras" of the first, third, fourth, fifth and ninth amendments created "zones of privacy." In *Eisenstadt v. Baird* (1972), the Court found the right to privacy, the right to be free of "unwarranted governmental interference," was applicable to the individual, married or single. In *Eisenstadt*, the Court struck down a statutory prohibition against distributing contraceptives to unmarried persons.

37. Poovey, "The Abortion Question and the Death of Man," 245.

38. As early as 1977 in *Maher v. Roe* and then in 1980 in *Harris v. McRae*, the Court made it clear that mandatory federal funding was not available for abortions. *Webster*, of course, expanded this reasoning.

39. "Maternal Rights and Fetal Wrongs," 997.

40. See Rand Rosenblatt's discussion in "Social Duties and the Problem of Rights in the Welfare State," in *The Politics of Law*, ed. David Kairys (New York: Pantheon, 1990).

41. Judith Butler, *Bodies That Matter: On the Discursive Limits of Sex* (New York: Routledge, 1993), 222.

42. Roberts, "Punishing Drug Addicts Who Have Babies," 1424. Although few articles dealing with fetal harm and reproductivity analyze the interrelationships among race, class, and gender as succinctly as Roberts does, the following address similar themes: In "Reproductive Laws, Women of Color and Low-Income Women," *Women's Rights Law Reporter* 11:14 (1989), Laurie Nsiah-Jefferson analyzes the reproductive needs of women of color; in "Abusive Prosecutors: Gender, Race & Class Discretion and the Prosecution of Drug-Addicted Mothers," *Buffalo Law Review* 39:737 (1991), Dwight L. Greene discusses how prosecutorial discretion is influenced by gender, color, and class; and in "Furthering the Inquiry: Race, Class and Culture in the Forced Medical Treatment of Pregnant Women," *Tennessee Law Review* 59:487 (1992), Lisa Ikemoto argues that analyses of cases involving court-ordered medical treatment often focus exclusively on gender. Ikemoto suggests that a "gender only" model supports an ideology of good motherhood that is implicitly "white and middle class" (510–511).

43. Roberts, "Punishing Drug Addicts Who Have Babies," 1435.

44. Ibid.

45. Ibid.

46. Ibid.

47. Ibid.

48. Ibid.

49. Goldberg, *Racist Culture*, 225.

References

Bender, John and David E. Wellbery. "Rhetoricality: On the Modernist Return of Rhetoric." In *The Ends of Rhetoric*, 113–142. Edited by John Bender and David E. Wellbery. Stanford: Stanford UP, 1990.

Bhabha, Homi. "The Other Question." *Screen*. 24(6):18–36 (1983).

Bower, Lisa C. " 'Mother' in Law: Conceptions of Mother and the Maternal in Feminist and Feminist Legal Theories." *differences: a Journal of Feminist Cultural Criticism* 3:20–38 (Spring 1991).

———. "Unsettling 'Woman': Competing Subjectivities in No Fault Divorce and Divorce Mediation." *Feminist Jurisprudence: the Difference Debate*, 209–230. Edited by Leslie Goldstein. Lanham, MD: Rowman and Littlefield, 1992.

Butler, Judith. *Bodies That Matter: On the Discursive Limits of Sex*. New York: Routledge, 1993.

———. *Gender Trouble: Feminism and the Subversion of Identity*. New York: Routledge, 1990.

Creet, Julia. "Daughter of the Movement: the Psychodynamics of Lesbian S/M Fantasy." *differences: a Journal of Feminist Cultural Studies* 3:135–159 (Summer 1991).

Doane, Mary Ann. *Femmes Fatales: Feminism, Film Theory, Psychoanalysis*. New York: Routledge, 1992.

Gates, Jr. Henry Louis. "Introduction: Writing "Race" and the Difference It Makes." In *"Race," Writing and Difference*, 1–20. Edited by Henry Louis Gates. Chicago: Chicago University Press, 1986.

Gilman, Sander. 1986. "Black Bodies, White Bodies: Toward an Iconography of Female Sexuality in Late Nineteenth Century Art, Medicine and Literature." In *"Race," Writing and Difference*, 223–261. Edited by Henry Louis Gates. Chicago: Chicago University Press, 1986.

Goldberg, David Theo. *Racist Culture: Philosophy and the Politics of Meaning.* Cambridge: Blackwell, 1993.

Greene, Dwight L. "Abusive Prosecutors: Gender, Race & Class Discretion and the Prosecution of Drug-Addicted Mothers." *Buffalo Law Review* 39:737 (1991).

Ikemoto, Lisa. "Furthering the Inquiry: Race, Class and Culture in the Forced Medical Treatment of Pregnant Women." *Tennessee Law Review* 59:487 (1992).

Johnsen, Dawn. "From Driving to Drugs: Governmental Regulation of Pregnant Women's Lives after Webster." *University of Pennsylvania Law Review* 138:179–215 (1989).

Losco, Joseph. "Fetal Rights and Feminism." In *Feminist Jurisprudence: the Difference Debate*, 231–262. Edited by Leslie Goldstein. Lanham, MD: Rowman and Littlefield, 1992.

MacKinnon, Catharine. "Reflections on Sex Equality Under Law." *Yale Law Journal* 100:1281–1328 (1990).

"Maternal Rights and Fetal Wrongs: The Case Against the Criminalization of 'Fetal Abuse.'" *Harvard Law Review* 101:994–1012.

Morrison, Toni. *Playing in the Dark: Whiteness and the Literary Imagination.* Cambridge: Harvard University Press, 1992.

Nsiah-Jefferson, Laurie. "Reproductive Laws, Women of Color and Low-Income Women." *Women's Rights Law Reporter* 11:14 (1989).

Olsen, Frances. "Unraveling Compromise." *Harvard Law Review* 103:105–135 (November 1989).

Poovey, Mary. "The Abortion Question and the Death of Man." *Feminists Theorize the Political*, 239–256. Edited by Judith Butler and Joan Scott. New York: Routledge, 1992.

"Rethinking (M)otherhood: Feminist Theory and State Regulation of Pregnancy." *Harvard Law Review* 103:1325–1343 (1990).

Roberts, Dorothy. "Punishing Drug Addicts Who Have Babies: Women of Color, Equality, and the Right to Privacy." *Harvard Law Review* 104:1419–1482 (May 1991).

Rosenblatt, Rand. "Social Duties and the Problem of Rights in the American Welfare State." *The Politics of Law*, 90–114. Edited by David Kairys. New York: Pantheon, 1990.

Sontag, Susan. *AIDS and Its Metaphors.* New York: Anchor, 1989.

Torgovnick, Marianna. *Gone Primitive: Savage Intellects, Modern Lives.* Chicago: University of Chicago Press, 1990.

Watney, Simon. "Missionary Positions: AIDS, 'Africa,' and Race." *differences: a Journal of Feminist Cultural Criticism* 1:83–100 (Winter 1989).

Williams, Patricia. "Fetal Fictions: an Exploration of Property Archetypes in Racial and Gendered Contexts." *University of Florida Law Review* 42:81–92 (1990).

9

"Surrogate Mothering" and Women's Freedom: A Critique of Contracts for Human Reproduction

MARY LYNDON SHANLEY

FEMINIST THEORISTS AND STUDENTS of public policy are deeply divided over the question whether the so-called surrogate motherhood contract—by which a woman agrees to undergo artificial insemination, bear a child, and relinquish that child upon birth to someone else (usually its biological father and his wife)—is liberating or oppressive to women. Some supporters of contract pregnancy regard a woman as having a right to enter a contract to bear a child and receive money for her service; they view the prohibition or nonenforcement of pregnancy contracts as illegitimate infringements on a woman's autonomy and self-determination.[1] Others focus on the desire for a child that motivates those who hire a woman to bear a child; they argue that to prohibit or fail to enforce pregnancy contracts violates the commissioning party's "right to procreate."[2] Those who oppose pregnancy contracts, by contrast, see such contracts as oppressive to the childbearing woman, particularly if she enters the contract out of dire economic need or is forced to fulfill the contract against her will.[3] These differing viewpoints reflect a dispute even as to what to call such a pregnancy: proponents tend to accept the term surrogate motherhood, whereas those with reservations resist calling a woman who bears a child a "surrogate" mother (although some regard her as functioning as a "surrogate wife" to a man who commissions the pregnancy).

Although contract pregnancy clearly can be viewed from the perspective of those who commission a pregnancy as well as from that of the woman who

save : prostitute v sex worker.

bears the child, I place the childbearing woman at the center of my analysis.[4] In doing so I seek to focus discussion directly on the issue of women's freedom, because differing understandings of whether pregnancy contracts enhance or violate a woman's freedom deeply divide feminists and because the ways in which proponents and opponents describe the gestational mother reveal important but largely unarticulated differences in their views of two clusters of considerations that extend beyond contract pregnancy. The first is the importance we give to human embodiment in our understandings of the "self" and its freedom; the second is the tension between the exercise of individual choice through contract, on the one hand, and the recognition and preservation of noncontractual human relationships on the other.

Because these considerations raise issues of individual autonomy, freedom, and contract, they are important for liberal feminist theory in general. Starting our analysis of contract pregnancy from women's experiences and perspectives compels us to see how some forms of liberal theory have ignored or misunderstood what it means to be "free" and "autonomous" as physically embodied and gendered beings. Contract pregnancy sheds important light on the necessity for any adequate account of human freedom to attend to the conditions under which we form, sustain, and develop within relationships—including sexual and reproductive relationships—that are central to human existence. Contract pregnancy raises issues that are important not only for the children, mothers, and fathers who are directly touched by them, but also for all those concerned with the meaning of new reproductive practices for the common life we shape together through public discourse and law.

"Woman's Body, Woman's Right": Considerations in Favor of Pregnancy Contracts

It is no wonder that many feminists have welcomed contract pregnancy as a way to illustrate that childbearing and child rearing are two quite distinct human functions and that child rearing need not and should not be assigned exclusively to the woman who bears a child. A woman's agreement to bear and then to relinquish custody of a child offers concrete resistance to the overly close connection that law and social practice have often made between women's childbearing capacity and other aspects of their personalities. Motherhood has often been taken as women's preeminent, even defining, characteristic and possession of a womb deemed reason enough to disqualify women for most activities of public life.[5] Separating the responsibilities of parenthood from gestational activity allows us to see childbearing as one thing a woman may choose to do, but by no means as the definition of her social role or legal rights. In a somewhat parallel fashion, a man who commissions a pregnancy undertakes "fatherhood" quite consciously and might be expected to be more involved in caring for the child than men traditionally have been. Thus Marjorie Shultz believes that contract pregnancy is a way to make the assumption of parental responsibilities more gender-neutral; it can "soften and offset gender imbalances that presently permeate the arena of procreation and parenting" (Shultz 1990, 304).

By emphasizing that not all women who bear children (or who have the capacity to bear children) need to be thought of as mothers, surrogacy allows women who cannot bear children to assume the responsibilities of parenthood. This can also be done through foster care and adoption, of course, but a contract pregnancy allows a couple to take responsibility for a child even before conception; in a heterosexual couple it enables at least the man and sometimes the woman to have a genetic relationship to the child. The "heightened intentionality" of contract pregnancy makes it possible for any number of persons of either sex to commission a pregnancy. Although most known contracts to date have involved married couples, there is no technological reason why anyone, male or female, married or not, could not provide or purchase sperm and, using artificial insemination, impregnate a "surrogate" to obtain a child by contractual agreement; this would encourage a plurality of family forms in which parents would share a deep commitment to raising children (Shultz 1990, 344).

Carmel Shalev regards the gestational mother's obligation to relinquish the child she bore for the commissioning party as an expression of her freedom to undertake whatever work she chooses. She argues that "the refusal to acknowledge the legal validity of surrogacy agreements implies that women are not competent, by virtue of their biological sex, to act as rational, moral agents regarding their reproductive activity." Like other defenders of contract pregnancy, Shalev places great emphasis on the consent which is at the heart of any valid contract. "If the purpose is to increase the voluntariness of the decision, attention should focus on the parties' negotiations before conception. If conception is intentional and the surrogate mother is an autonomous agent, ... why should she not be held responsible for the consequences of her autonomous reproductive decision?" (Shalev 1989, 11–12, 96). The same liberty that should protect a woman from any governmental effort to prohibit birth control or abortion or to force sterilization also protects her freedom to agree to carry a child for someone else. The slogan "woman's body, woman's right" succinctly captures the notion that a woman herself—not a husband, not a doctor, not the state—must make the procreative decisions that affect her.

Those who see contract pregnancy as an exercise of freedom particularly emphasize that consent is given prior to conception: "The surrogate consciously enters into the agreement and voluntarily consents to give up the child even before she becomes pregnant. Rather than being unwanted, the pregnancy is actively sought" (Katz 1986, 21). Or again, "If autonomy is understood as the deliberate exercise of choice with respect to the individual's reproductive capacity, the point at which the parties' intentions should be established is before conception" (Shalev 1989, 103). Defenders of contract pregnancy seek to distinguish

[handwritten margin note: entered into prior to conception - before 'product' exists.]

it from baby-selling, arguing that it is not the child or fetus for whom the woman receives payment but the woman's gestational services.

How can one be sure a woman's agreement is really voluntary, her consent truly informed? Advocates of contract pregnancy propose a variety of safeguards to help ensure that pregnancy contracts will be fair and noncoercive. For example, so that women fully understand what kind of physical and emotional experiences to expect from pregnancy, the law could allow only women who have previously given birth to contract to bear a child for someone else. To facilitate adjustment to this new mode of family formation, all parties to a contract pregnancy could be required to undergo counseling before the conception, during the pregnancy, and after the birth. And to avoid financial exploitation of poor or economically vulnerable women, only those with a certain level of financial resources could be allowed to enter a pregnancy contract.[6] The emphasis in all these proposals is on the combination of reason and will that are involved in consent. "In contract law, intent manifested by a promise and subsequent reliance provides the basis for enforceable agreements. Typically, the mental element is the pivotal element in determining legal outcomes" (Stumpf 1986, 195). If the choice is a free one, argues Shultz, then "the principle of private intention [should] be given substantial deference and legal force" (Shultz 1990, 398). Attention should focus on whether conditions under which the mind can be held to have freely acceded to the bargain pertained when the contract was made.

Feminist proponents of contract pregnancy argue that those who would allow a surrogate to change her mind about relinquishing custody fall into the age-old trap of assuming that women are not as rational as men or that their reason can be overridden by instinct or sentiment. "The paternalistic refusal to force the surrogate mother to keep her word denies the notion of female reproductive agency and reinforces the traditional perception of women as imprisoned in the subjectivity of their wombs"(Shalev 1989, 121). One surrogate mother quoted approvingly by Lori Andrews insisted "A contract is a contract. ... It's dangerous to say that we are ruled by our hormones, rather than our brains. You don't have a right to damage other people's lives [i.e., those of the expectant couple deprived of a child when a surrogate reneges] because of your hormones." Robin Bergstrom, a legislative aide in the New York State Senate, remarked in the same vein, "I truly can't understand the feminists who are now arguing against women's rights [i.e., to prohibit payment to surrogates and to make pregnancy contracts revocable]. ... Women's rights have been cut back in the past based on male perceptions that women are incompetent to make decisions, but this time women will be putting it on themselves" (Andrews 1989, 92, 223).

It is important to notice that these arguments about a woman's free consent to bear a child assume, implicitly or explicitly, that the "work" of pregnancy is analogous to other kinds of human labor. What distinguishes allowing a surrogate to renege on her contract from state interference in women's contractual capacity implicated in protective labor legislation? In the early twentieth century many feminists supported legislation to protect women from oppressive working conditions, although the U.S. Supreme Court had struck down protective labor legislation for men as a violation of freedom of contract (Sklar 1986, 25–35). But by the 1990s most advocates of women's rights had come to argue that women should not receive protections unavailable to men, with the possible exception of maternity leave so that they, like men, could become parents without forfeiting their jobs (many feminists, of course, advocated gender-neutral parental leave policies; Finley 1986, 118–182; Littleton 1987, 1043–1059). Many argued that, even when work involved substances that might cause fetal damage, pregnant women should not be barred from such jobs. If, after appropriate medical and psychological counseling, a woman freely consents to a pregnancy contract, then allowing her later to renege on her agreement and keep custody of the child she bears—or to share custody with its biological father—smacks of the legal paternalism that many feminists have long opposed. Is it not antithetical to all that feminists have worked for, ask proponents, to argue that women's reproductive experiences should be the grounds for allowing the law to treat their contracts concerning pregnancy as less binding than other contracts? Does it not suggest that women are less bound than others by their freely given words?

Defenders of contract pregnancy assume not only that gestation of a fetus is work that is analogous to other forms of wage labor, but also that selling one's labor for a wage is a manifestation of individual freedom. From this perspective, prohibiting a woman from receiving payment for bearing a child denies her the full and effective proprietorship of her body. Lisa Newton, director of the Program of Applied Ethics at Fairfield University, has argued that surrogacy is a service that is "simply an extension ... of baby-sitting and other child-care arrangements which are very widely practiced" and that it is "irrational" to allow payment for the latter services and not for pregnancy (Andrews 1989, 267).[7] Shalev similarly believes that "the transaction under consideration is ... for the sale of reproductive services. ... A childless couple is regarded as purchasing the reproductive labor of a birth mother." Banning the sale of procreative services will "reactivate and reinforce the state's power to define what constitutes legitimate and illegitimate reproduction," whereas allowing payment will "recognize a woman's legal authority to make decisions regarding the exercise of her reproductive capacity" (Shalev 1989, 157, 94).

The consequence of prohibiting pregnancy contracts or banning payment for gestational services is suggested by the question of the surrogate who asked, "Why am I exploited if I am paid, but not if I am not paid?" (Andrews 1989, 259). When the state forbids payment for contract pregnancy it treats reproductive activity as it has traditionally treated women's domestic labor—as unpaid, noneconomic acts of love and nurturing rather than as work and real economic contributions to family life. Even Margaret Radin, who opposes pregnancy contracts, acknowledges that prohibiting paid pregnancy creates a double-bind. Contract pregnancy could "enable a needy group—poor women—to improve their relatively powerless, oppressed condition, an improvement that would be beneficial to personhood" (Radin 1987, 1916). To forbid people to labor or be paid for using their bodies as they choose when no harm is done to others seems extraordinarily hard for a liberal polity to justify, a point that proponents of the decriminalization of prostitution never tire of repeating.[8] Proponents of contract pregnancy emphasize the value of allowing individuals to determine their activities and life courses as they choose. When the contract between the gestational mother and the commissioning parents reflects the procreative intentions of both parties, enforcement of the contract is the only way to give force to the desire and commitment of those who seek to raise a child *and* to recognize the autonomy of the gestational mother.

Although I deeply value self-determination, I believe that pregnancy contracts should not be enforceable. I would not, however, prohibit "gift surrogacy" in which only payment of medical and living expenses would be allowed. Such surrogacy agreements could be treated like pre-adoption agreements that leave the birth mother free to decide not to relinquish custody at birth. I am ambivalent about whether any further payment should ever be permitted.[9] I take up only the enforceability of contracts in detail here.

"Our Bodies, Our Selves": Considerations Against Irrevocable Contracts

Perhaps the most salient problem with the notion that women's freedom is reflected in and protected by a contract signed prior to the conception of a child is that the woman carries to term a fetus that did not exist at the time the agreement was struck. As we have seen, most advocates of contract pregnancy insist that the payment the gestational mother receives is not for the child but for gestational services.[10] This distinction, however, seems hard to sustain when the fetus develops from the gestational mother's ovum. In such cases, the woman is contributing more than the labor of her womb; she is also selling her genetic material and it becomes difficult to see how the exchange escapes the charge of baby-selling.[11] In addition, as Radin has pointed out, selling an ovum along with gestational services entails pricing all of a woman's personal attributes—race, height, hair color, intelligence, artistic ability—as well as reproductive capacity. And in a society in which women's bodies are already highly commodified by advertisers, pornographers, and promoters of prostitution, the dangers of commodification of women's attributes are palpable and pressing (Radin 1987, 1933).

When the childbearing woman has no genetic relationship with the fetus the assertion that the commissioning couple is purchasing only gestational services is stronger. To date there are some eighty known cases in which an embryo has been introduced into another woman's womb for gestation after having been fertilized in vitro (*New York Times*, August 12, 1990, 1). In the recent California

commodified society.

case in which Anna Johnson bore a child conceived by in vitro fertilization from the ovum and sperm of Crispina and Mark Calvert and sued to have her contract declared invalid, Judge Richard N. Parslow awarded custody to the genetic parents and commented that the contract was binding: "I see no problem with someone getting paid for her pain and suffering. ... They [gestational mothers] are not selling a baby; they are selling pain and suffering" (Mydans 1990, A14).[12] To Judge Parslow the contract appeared to be an agreement about work, and his remarks raise the question of how the "pain and suffering" of pregnancy are analogous to the physical and psychological demands of other kinds of labor.

Arguments for contract pregnancy depend, it seems to me, on a strong analogy between the "work" of pregnancy and forms of wage labor with which we are already familiar. The analogy seems to rest on two main considerations: pregnancy involves the body, culminating in the extraordinary physical exertion of "labor" and giving birth; and pregnancy ends with the appearance of something new in the world, a tangible "product" of gestational work.

Human gestation is distinguished from other kinds of productive work, however, by the ways in which it involves both a woman's physical and psychological being and by the difference between the human being that results from a pregnancy and other kinds of products. I concentrate here on the woman's experience and on how a rich account of pregnancy might inform our judgment about the claim that only enforcing pregnancy contracts properly recognizes women's freedom and autonomy.

Women's accounts of pregnancy point out the complexity of women's childbearing experiences and the ways in which a woman's self, not simply her womb, may be involved in reproductive labor. Iris Young offers one such account in a phenomenological examination of pregnancy and embodiment. She notes that in our culture "pregnancy does not belong to the woman herself. It either is a state of the developing foetus, for which the woman is a container; or it is an objective, observable process coming under scientific scrutiny; or it becomes objectified by the woman herself, as a 'condition' in which she must 'take care of herself.' " Young points out that we almost never see the pregnant woman as Julia Kristeva does, as "the subject, the mother as the site of her proceedings" (Young 1990, 160). The mother's body is the "environment" in which the fetus grows, but most arguments in favor of contract pregnancy seem to posit no more intrinsic relationship between them than there would be between an artificial womb and a fetus that might develop within it. Even our everyday language reflects the distinctness of mother and fetus: pregnant women are said to be "expecting" the babies that doctors "deliver" to them (Rothman 1989, 100; Young 1990, 167).

Mother and fetus, however, are not yet, or are not in every way, distinct entities. Neither are they the same being. In her 1945 poem about abortion, "The Mother," Gwendolyn Brooks cries out against the inability of language to express the relationship between mother and fetus: "You are dead./Or rather, or instead,/You were never made./ But that too, I am afraid,/Is faulty: oh, what shall I say, how is the truth to be said?" (Brooks 1989, 2505). In her stunning analysis of "The Mother," Barbara Johnson notes that "the poem continues to struggle to clarify the relation between 'I' [the woman] and 'you' [the fetus]," but in the end "[the language of the] poem can no more distinguish between 'I' and 'you' than it can come up with a proper definition of life" (Johnson 1987, 190). Like Brooks, Adrienne Rich testifies to her experience of the fluidity of the boundary between self and other during pregnancy. "In early pregnancy, the stirring of the foetus felt like ghostly tremors of my own body, later like the movements of a being imprisoned within me; but both sensations were *my* sensations, contributing to my own sense of physical and psychic space" (Rich 1976, 47). Iris Young points out that whereas pregnancy may appear to observers to be "a time of waiting and watching, when nothing happens," to the pregnant subject "pregnancy has a temporality of movement, growth and change. ... The pregnant woman experiences herself as a source and participant in a creative process. Though she does not plan and direct it, neither does it merely wash over her; rather, she *is* this process, this change" (Young 1990, 167). Mother and fetus are simultaneously distinct and interrelated entities, and this fundamental fact of human embodiment means that to speak of the "freedom" of the mother as residing in her intention as an "autonomous" agent misunderstands both the relationship between woman and child and of the woman to her ongoing self.

The interrelatedness of mother and fetus makes it difficult to specify exactly what gestational labor entails. Unlike other work, gestational labor is not consciously controlled; the bodily labor of pregnancy goes on continuously, even while the pregnant woman is asleep. Whether the "work" is done badly or well is only marginally within the mother's control; she can refrain from smoking, drinking, and drug use, eat properly, and get sufficient exercise, but whether the fetus grows to term, has a safe birth, and is free of genetic abnormalities is otherwise largely beyond her control.

In her critique of contract pregnancy, Carole Pateman argues that although all wage labor involves selling some aspect of oneself to some degree, the alienation involved in selling gestational services is so extreme as to make it illegitimate. In Pateman's view, wage labor rests on a fundamentally flawed notion of the proprietary self that assumes that it is possible to separate labor power or capacities from the person of the worker "like pieces of property." But "the worker's capacities are developed over time and they form an integral part of [the worker's] self and self-identity" (Pateman 1988, 150). Although this is true of all workers, some forms of labor involve the worker's sense of self more directly and intimately than do others. Labor that leaves no time for other pursuits, deadens the mind through boring and repetitive chores, warps the spirit by requiring unethical behavior, or enfeebles the body by unhealthy practices involves a forfeiture of the self greater than that experienced by more fortunate workers. Contract pregnancy entails a very high degree of self-alienation because the work of pregnancy involves women's emotional, physical, and sexual experiences and understandings of themselves as women. Pateman argues that the "logic of contract as exhibited in 'surrogate' motherhood" sweeps away "any intrinsic relation between the female owner, her body and reproductive capacities. She stands to her property in exactly the same external relation as the male owner stands to his labour power or sperm" (Pateman 1988, 216). This objectifies women's bodies and their reproductive labor in a manner and to a degree that is wholly unacceptable.

Elizabeth Anderson echoes this point when she argues that any form of paid pregnancy involves "an invasion of the market into a new sphere of conduct, that of specifically women's labor—that is, the labor of carrying children to term in pregnancy." In her view, "treating women's labor as just another kind of commercial production process violates the precious emotional ties which the mother may rightly and properly establish with her 'product,' the child." When a woman is required "to repress whatever parental love she feels for the child, these [economic] norms convert women's labor into a form of alienated labor." The forfeiture of self involved in contract pregnancy is an extreme instance of the diminution of the self involved in many labor contracts. Market norms may be legitimate and useful in their proper sphere, but when "applied to the ways we treat and understand women's reproductive labor, women are reduced ... to objects of use" (Anderson 1990, 75, 82, 81, 92).[13]

It is also important to take into account that payment for gestational service does not occur in some neutral market environment but in a society in which many of our institutions and interactions are shaped by relationships of domination and subordination between men and women. To talk about the freedom of the self-possessing individual to do what she will with her own body while ignoring gender structures in her society distances such arguments from the world of lived experience. I think it is possible (barely) to imagine conditions in which it would be legitimate for a woman to receive payment for bearing a child to whom she had no genetic relationship, provided always she retained the power to assert custodial rights before or at birth. At a minimum, such conditions would include an economy free from wage labor undertaken in order to survive; rough economic equality between men and women; a culture in which the "ideology of motherhood," which asserts that childbearing is women's natural and preeminent calling, did not contribute to some women deriving their sense of self-worth from being pregnant; a society free from the objectification and commodification of women's sexuality; and a politics uninfluenced by gender hierarchy. Descriptions of contract pregnancy that depict the practice as nothing more than womb rental in a supposedly neutral market fail to take account of the profoundly gendered nature of the structures that surround the transaction. Viewed in its social context, contract pregnancy can as appropriately be described as enabling economically secure men to purchase women's procreative labor and custodial rights as allowing women the freedom to sell procreative labor. And in this context payment should be prohibited.

These reflections lead me to think that pregnancy contracts might as usefully be compared to contracts for consensual slavery as to other kinds of employment contracts. Discussions of slave contracts force us to ask whether certain kinds of contracts are illegitimate, whether people can be held to have agreed to certain stipulations that limit in fundamental ways freedoms essential to human dignity, autonomy, and selfhood or whether some kinds of freedom are inalienable.

In both contract pregnancy and consensual slavery, fulfilling the agreement, even if it appears to be freely undertaken, violates the ongoing freedom of the individual in a way that does not simply restrict future options (such as whether I may leave my employer) but does violence to the self (my understanding of who I am). Both John Locke and John Stuart Mill assert that consensual slavery is illegitimate. Locke argues that "a man, not having the power of his own life, *cannot*, by compact, or his own consent, *enslave himself* to any one" (Locke [1690] 1980, sec. 23, p.17).[14] In a much-quoted passage of *On Liberty*, Mill asserts that to agree to be a slave might look like an exercise of freedom in the present but, since such a contract removed the possibility of free exercise of freedom in the future, "freely choosing" to be a slave was incoherent. "By selling himself for a slave, [a person] abdicates his liberty; he forgoes any future use of it beyond that single act." But, says Mill, this act "defeats ... the very purpose which is the justification of allowing him to dispose of himself." One limitation on freedom is that one cannot "be free not to be free. It is not freedom, to be allowed to alienate his freedom" (Mill [1859] 1975a, 126).

The analogy of consensual slavery to enforceable pregnancy contracts may seem flawed because slavery is for a lifetime whereas human gestation lasts for about nine months. But the time involved in a pregnancy depends upon how one regards pregnancy and childbirth in relationship to a woman's identity and self-understanding. If the baby is an extrinsic "product" of her gestational work, then the gestational mother simultaneously fulfills her contractual obligation and regains her freedom in turning the baby over to the commissioning parent(s). If, however, she and the fetus were beings-in-relationship during pregnancy and she perceives herself as (at least one of) its mother(s), then a law that denies her all custodial rights will deprive her of any lived expression of her relationship to that child for her entire lifetime. Writing about the lower court decision that denied the gestational mother custody in the Baby M. contract pregnancy case, Patricia Williams notes "Mary Beth Whitehead's powerlessness came about as a result of a contract that she signed at a discrete point of time—yet which, over time, enslaved her by depriving her of freedom to assert custodial rights" (Williams 1988, 15).

Shifting understandings of divorce are also related to the questions of whether the freedom to choose at one point in time captures what is most important about human freedoms in a liberal society. Concern for what it means for a person to exercise freedom over time have dramatically altered divorce laws in Anglo-American jurisdictions during the past century. Most U.S. states now permit no-fault divorce, which entails releasing people upon their request from the promise to be husband or wife "until death do us part." The views of John Stuart Mill are again salient: Mill frequently refers to marriage as "slavery" because nineteenth-century marriage law bound a woman for life to a man who gained possession of all her property, whose consent was necessary for her to make any valid contract or will, who decided where she would live, who had legal custody of their children, and who could not be prosecuted for rape or sexual assault against her. Mill is ambivalent about divorce but unequivocally believed that the act of consent with which a woman entered marriage—consent often joyfully and lovingly given—did not and could not legitimate the terms of such a marriage contract (Mill [1869] 1975b, 425–548).

Arguments in our own day justifying divorce are somewhat different because the law has abandoned most of the injustices of coverture (although amazingly marital rape is still not a crime in some jurisdictions). Yet laws of most Anglo-American jurisdictions allow for divorce, a recognition that the state will not enforce a person's promise to live intimately with another person for life nor prohibit the formation of a new relationship through remarriage. Divorce law reflects in part society's determination that the law cannot permit people to be bound to a promise when they and their relationship have fundamentally changed. Not to allow a woman to revoke her consent during pregnancy or at birth seems to ignore the possibility of a somewhat analogous change that simultaneously affects the self as an individual and as a person-in-relationship. It is possible that persons may also undergo such change, regardless of whether or not they are in relationship with someone else, to justify the judgment that the person's sense of self has changed so significantly that enforcing a contract would do violence to that self.[15]

The arguments prohibiting consensual slavery and justifying divorce are related to the issue of enforcing pregnancy contracts. The potential violation of a woman's self when she has entered a pregnancy contract stems from the months she will spend in relationship with a developing human being. It is this relationship that may change her, and it is this relationship that is severed if a pregnancy contract is enforceable. Defenders of pregnancy contracts argue eloquently and with much truth that intentional parents have also been in a relationship with their child-to-be, imagining the role the child will play in their lives, planning for its care, and loving it as it develops in utero. Marjorie Shultz argues that it is the relationship between intentional parents and fetus that must be protected by enforcing reproductive contracts. "To ignore the significance of deliberation, purpose and expectation—the capacity to envision and shape the future through intentional choice—is to disregard one of the most distinctive traits that makes us human. It is to disregard crucial differences in moral meaning and responsibility. To disregard such intention with reference to so intimate and significant an activity as procreation and child-rearing is deeply shocking." When a surrogate reneges on her promise to relinquish custody, it is wrong "to say to a disappointed parent, 'go get another child.'" Such a judgment "offends our belief in the uniqueness of each individual. It inappropriately treats the miracle and complexity of particular individual lives as fungible. By contrast, surrogacy and other reproductive arrangements transfer the life and parental responsibility for a particular unique child." Hence, argues Shultz, "although it may seem counter-intuitive, the extraordinary remedy, specific performance of agreements about parenthood, in some sense confirms core values about the uniqueness of life" (Shultz 1990, 377–378, 364).

Thus the claims on behalf of both the intentional parents and the gestational mother rest on assertions about the relationship between parent and fetus. Defenders of contract pregnancy like Shultz are deeply disturbed by the prospect that allowing a gestational mother to void her contractual agreement "expresses the idea that the biological experience of motherhood 'trumps' all other considerations. ... It exalts a woman's experience of pregnancy and childbirth over her formation of emotional, intellectual and interpersonal decisions and expectations, as well as over others' reliance on the commitments she has earlier made" (Shultz 1990, 384). Yet even Shultz's eloquent plea and my own commitment to gender-neutral law do not persuade me that promises to relinquish custody should be enforced against the wishes of the gestational mother. Her later judgment based on her experience of the pregnancy does "trump"—it trumps her own earlier promise, upon which the intentional parents' claim to sole custody depends. It trumps because enforcement of a pregnancy contract against the gestational mother's wishes would constitute a legal refusal to recognize the reality of the woman and fetus as beings-in-relationship, which the law should protect as it does many other personal relationships. Yet the biological father or the commissioning couple also have parental claims, which can probably best be recognized by granting and enforcing visitation rights.[16]

I find my thoughts on the importance of the actual embodied relationships of gestational mother and fetus to be akin (with certain significant exceptions) to those of Robert Goldstein, who argues in *Mother-love and Abortion* that most discussions of abortion, whether put forward by regulationists or pro-choice advocates, err in regarding pregnant woman and fetus as distinct individuals with competing rights.[17] As he points out, "rights talk" in this context emphasizes what Ferdinand Schoeman refers to as "the appropriateness of seeing other persons as separate and autonomous agents," whereas "the relationship between parent and infant [or fetus] involves an awareness of a kind of union between people. ... We *share our selves* with those with whom we are intimate" (Schoeman 1980, 35). A correct approach, says Goldstein, would not "define personhood as if it were a solitary achievement of the fetus and its DNA that precedes rather than presupposes participation in the primary community of woman and fetus."

With regard to abortion, respect for this "primary community" requires that the law recognize the pregnant woman as the person who must make decisions about the dyad she and the fetus constitute; she must be accorded "a privileged position as dyadic representative that is superior to that of other would-be dyadic participants," such as the biological father, the state, and potential adoptive parents. In Goldstein's analysis, the privacy and autonomy that *Roe v. Wade* protects, then, belong "not only to the woman as an individual but also to the dyadic, indeed symbiotic, unit of woman and fetus. This dyad constitutes the relevant community for understanding the abortion decision" (Goldstein 1988, 35, 65, x). In the case of surrogacy, the embodied relationship of the gestational mother (who may or may not be the genetic mother) is stronger than that between the commissioning parent(s) and fetus as well as her own "intentional self" and the fetus prior to conception. In Kenneth Karst's expressive phrase, a critically important aspect of the "right of privacy" is not to isolate people from one another but to protect and foster what he calls "the freedom of intimate association" (Karst 1980, 634–683). A legal rule enforcing a pregnancy contract would reinforce notions of human separateness and insularity rather than recognizing that the development of individuality and autonomy takes place through sustained and intimate human relationship.

None of these considerations argues against a woman voluntarily bearing a child for someone else or against adoption. Law in a liberal polity should not force a woman to retain physical custody of her child once it is born, and the woman may decide that placing the child in someone else's care may be best for her, for the child, and for the new custodial parent(s). But adoption and "gift" pregnancy must be distinguished from contract pregnancy: Even though gestational mothers may mourn for children they entrust to others to care for and raise, they have made their decision to separate from an existing human being, not from a potential one. Their actions, which may bring relief as well as (or as much as) sorrow, are not the consequence of an agreement that ignores or dismisses the relevance of the experience of pregnancy and of the human and embodied relationship between woman and fetus to our understanding of human freedom and choice.

Contracts, Human Relationships, and Freedom

Those who argue that respect for women's autonomy necessarily entails allowing and enforcing pregnancy contracts present contract as the paradigmatic bond linking people to one another in human society. Thinking carefully about pregnancy contracts shows what is wrong not only with contract pregnancy but more broadly with certain efforts to enhance women's freedom in family relationships by replacing legal rules based on notions of men's and women's "natural" roles in families with contractual paradigms and rules.

The impetus behind such efforts is quite understandable given the burdens that ascriptive notions about women's "nature" and proper roles have placed upon women seeking equality in both the family and public life. From the mid-nineteenth to the mid-twentieth centuries, feminists found contractual ideas, which emphasize equality, freedom, and volition, to be extremely effective tools for removing the disabilities married women suffered under traditional family law.[18] In place of the common law rules of coverture, which assumed that when a woman married her legal personality was subsumed in that of her husband, advocates of women's rights fashioned statutes that rested upon notions of spousal equality. Gradually the idea that the family was a natural, hierarchical, unitary, and indissoluble association gave way to understandings of families as voluntaristic and egalitarian associations that people could enter and leave at will and in which responsibilities were not prescribed by nature but properly determined by the marriage partners themselves.

Without arguing for a return to earlier notions of natural or ascriptive family roles, I maintain that some of the inadequacies of a contractual paradigm for family relations are evident in the proposals for legal recognition and enforcement of pregnancy contracts. Family relationships involve and affect the self in ways that cannot be fully predicted or provided for in advance and are particularly striking in parent-child relationships. In addition, Martha Fineman has criticized the effects of adopting abstract liberal principles in laws dealing with child custody, property division, and spousal support after divorce. When a court assumes that its aim should be to restore divorcing parents to their former autonomy and independence, it frequently produces grave inequalities in the actual social and economic opportunities of divorced men and women (Fineman 1991).

The dilemmas and difficulties that arise in trying to conceptualize the proper bases of family law should stimulate a rethinking not only of these laws but also of certain aspects of liberal political theory. This article certainly takes exception to the libertarian version of liberalism that understands freedom as the ability to determine and pursue one's goals without interference from government or other individuals and that sees relationships among individuals as the result of specific agreements. This individualistic paradigm ignores the human need to foster the interdependence that is the basis of human development. Although some of the human associations that the liberal state should protect can be understood in voluntaristic or contractual terms, some cannot. The fallacies of a view of political life—as well as family life—that ignores the noncontractual ties among human beings is well captured in Christine Di Stefano's analysis of some passages from Thomas Hobbes's writings. Di Stefano notes that when Hobbes set out to depict those aspects of the state of nature that he hoped would make his prescriptions for civil society seem "welcome and reasonable," he asked his reader to "consider men as if but even now sprung out of the earth, and suddenly, like mushrooms, come to full maturity, without all kinds of engagement with each other." As Di Stefano argues, Hobbes's picture of "abstract man" altogether ignores women's experience of reproduction and early nurturance and falsely assumes that "characteristically human capacities need no particular social life forms in which to develop."[19]

The attempt to justify the enforceability of contracts for pregnancy similarly rests on a model of the autonomous individual that either ignores or takes too little account of the truth that human beings are constituted in part by relationships with others. Men as well as women do not spring like mushrooms from the earth but begin existence in a state of interdependence with and dependence on another human being. As Virginia Held points out, "Western liberal democratic thought has been built on the concept of the 'individual' seen as a theoretically isolatable entity. This entity can assert interests, have rights, and enter into contractual relationships with other entities. But this individual is not seen as related to other individuals in inextricable or intrinsic ways." As Held correctly observes, "at some point contracts must be embedded in social relations that are noncontractual" (Held 1987, 124, 125). This is not to argue, as some do, that all liberal theory is antithetical to women's interests.[20] Indeed, liberalism's very respect for the individual and her freedom, as seen among other places in Locke's and Mill's condemnations of consensual slavery, shapes my conviction that enforceable pregnancy contracts are illegitimate.[21] It is those contractarian theories that ignore the limits to the freely willed self that run the risk of confusing broadly conceived human freedom and dignity with a narrow notion of freedom of contract.

Feminists must look elsewhere than contractual paradigms to find the theoretical basis for the human liberation we seek. One error of the feminist arguments for contract pregnancy is that they conflate the freedom of the individual woman prior to conception with the conditions that preserve her freedom as a person in relationship. Another is that they conceive of market language and mechanisms as morally neutral, whereas market language invokes a particular notion of the person and her relationship to her body and her labor. Further, market transactions occur within social contexts that affect their meanings. In each instance, feminist arguments defending contract pregnancy attribute freedom to the person only as an isolated individual and fail to recognize that individuals are also ineluctably social creatures. Any liberalism worth its salt must protect both individual rights as such and the associations and relationships that shape us and allow us to be who we are. Outlining such a theory is a task well beyond the scope of this essay, but I hope that by showing what is wrong with arguments for contract pregnancy I have also shown that the model upon which it rests—the self-possessing individual linked to others only by contractual agreements—fails to do full justice to the complex interdependencies involved in human procreative activity, family relations, and human social life in general. Attention to women's experiences, so long absent from political theory, must provide us with ways of understanding and conceptualizing the individual-in-relationship that will allow us to speak more effectively about the simultaneity of human autonomy and interdependence, of freedom and commitment in social and political life.

Notes

I wish to acknowledge the help of Nancy ("Ann") Davis, Robert Goodin, Amy Gutmann, Mona Harrington, Virginia Held, Will Kymlicka, Martha Minow, Susan Okin, Kate Tyler, members of the 1990 Mellon Faculty Center at Vassar College, and members of the 1991–1992 Program in Ethics and Public Affairs at Princeton University. The final version of this paper was written while I was a Fellow at the University Center for HumanValues at Princeton University, for whose support I am grateful.

This chapter is revised from Mary L. Shanley, " 'Surrogate Mothering' and Women's Freedom: A Critique of Contracts for Human Reproduction," *Signs* 18(3):618–639 (1993). Reprinted with permission from the publisher, the University of Chicago Press.

1. See, e.g., Lori Andrews, *Between Strangers: Surrogate Mothers, Expectant Fathers, & Brave New Babies* (New York: Harper & Row, 1989); Avi Katz, "Surrogate Motherhood and the Baby-Selling Laws," *Columbia Journal of Law and Social Problems* 20(1):1–52 (1986); Carmel Shalev, *Birth Power* (New Haven: Yale University Press, 1989); Marjorie Maguire Shultz, "Reproductive Technology and Intention-based Parenthood: An Opportunity for Gender Neutrality," *Wisconsin Law Review* 1990(2):297–398 (1990).

2. John Lawrence Hill, "The Case for Enforcement of the Surrogate Contract," *Politics and the Life Sciences* 8(2):157–159 (1990); John Robertson, "Procreative Liberty and the Control of Conception, Pregnancy and Childbirth," *Virginia Law Review* 69:405–462 (1983); John Robertson, "Embryos, Families and Procreative Liberty: The Legal Structures of the New Reproduction," *Southern California Law Review* 59:942–1041 (1986); and Shalev, 1989.

3. See, e.g., Katharine T. Bartlett, "Re-Expressing Parenthood," *Yale Law Journal* 98 (2):293–340 (1988); Carole Pateman, *The Sexual Contract* (Stanford: Stanford University Press, 1988), 209–218; Barbara Katz Rothman, *Recreating Motherhood: Ideology and Technology in Patriarchal Society* (New York: W. W. Norton & Co., 1989); Susan M. Okin, "A Critique of Pregnancy Contracts," *Politics and the Life Sciences* 8(2):205–210 (1990); and Martha A. Field, *Surrogate Motherhood: The Legal and Human Issues* (Cambridge, Mass.: Harvard University Press, 1988) and "The Case Against Enforcement of Surrogacy Contracts, *Politics and the Life Sciences* 8(2):199–204 (1990).

4. Defenses of the practice of contract pregnancy that focus on the "right to procreate" sometimes ignore the ethical issues related to the woman who bears the child. Robertson 1983 and 1986 render the pregnant woman all but invisible. Maura A. Ryan critiques Robertson's work in "The Argument for Unlimited Procreative Liberty: A Feminist Critique," *Hastings Center Report* 20(4):4–12 (1990).

5. See, e.g., *Hoyt v. Florida* 368 U.S. 57 (1961), which held that Florida's automatic exemption of women from jury duty because they might have dependent children at home was not unconstitutionally overbroad. See generally Deborah L. Rhode, *Justice and Gender* (Cambridge, Mass.: Harvard University Press, 1989), 29–50.

6. See, e.g., Andrews, 1989, 252–272; Shalev, 1989, 144; and Hill, 1990, 157–159. In his decision in Orange County (California) Superior Court, Judge Richard N. Parslow awarded cus-

tody to the commissioning parents and "he proposed that all parties to any surrogate agreement undergo psychiatric evaluation, that all agree from the start that the surrogate mother would have no custody rights, that she have previous experience with successful childbirth and that a surrogate be used only in cases where the genetic mother is unable to give birth." Mydans 1990, A14.

7. Judge Parslow said that Anna Johnson had served as a "home" for the embryo she carried, "much as a foster parent stands in for a parent who is not able to care for a child." "Surrogate Denied Custody of Child," Mydans 1990, A14.

8. The debate over whether prostitution should be decriminalized finds feminists on both sides of the issue, sometimes for reasons akin to those that divide them with respect to contract pregnancy. See discussions in Alison Jaggar, "Prostitution," in The *Philosophy of Sex: Contemporary Readings*, ed. A. Soble (Totowa, N.J.: Rowman & Littlefield, 1980); Christine Overall, "What's Wrong with Prostitution?: Evaluating Sex Work," *Signs: Journal of Women in Culture and Society* 17(4):705–724 (1992); Carole Pateman, "Defending Prostitution: Charges Against Ericsson," *Ethics* 93:561–565 (1983); Laurie Shrage, "Should Feminists Oppose Prostitution?" *Ethics* 99:347–361 (1989); Sibyl Schwarzenbach, "Contractarians and Feminists Debate Prostitution," *Review of Law and Social Change* 18:103–130 (1990–1991); and Rosemarie Tong, *Women Sex and the Law* (Totowa, N.J.: Rowman & Allenheld, 1984), 37–64.

9. Two strong critics of gift surrogacy, on the ground that it reinforces gender stereotypes of women as altruistic conduits for fulfilling the needs of others, are Sharyn L. Roach Anleu, "Reinforcing Gender Norms: Commercial and Altruistic Surrogacy," *Acta Sociologica* 33:63–74 (1990); and Janice G. Raymond, "Reproductive Gifts and Gift Giving: The Altruistic Woman," *Hastings Center Report* (November-December 1990): 7–11. Anleu concludes that commercial surrogacy provides an acceptable and desirable challenge to gender norms, whereas Raymond condemns both altruistic and commercial surrogacy. Richard J. Arneson, "Commodification and Commercial Surrogacy," *Philosophy and Public Affairs* 21(2):132–164 (1992) argues "tentatively for the claim that commercial surrogacy should be legally permissible (133)."

10. A few writers propose legalizing commissioned adoption or creating a market in babies but they are in a minority and arrived at their views from considering issues other than contract pregnancy. Richard Posner declares that the objections to the sale of babies for adoption are unpersuasive. Even the poor might do better in a free baby market than under current adoption law because people who did not meet adoption agencies' requirements might, "in a free market with low prices, be able to adopt children, just as poor people are able to buy color television sets." *Economic Analysis of Law*, 3d ed. (Boston: Little Brown, 1986), 141–142. See also Elizabeth Landes and Richard A. Posner, "The Economics of the Baby Shortage," *Journal of Legal Studies* 7:323 (1978); but see Posner, "Mischaracterized Views," letter, *Judicature* 69(6):321 (1986), where he says he "did not advocate a free market in babies". Cited in Radin 1989, at 1850, 1863.

11. Men sell their genetic material through artificial insemination by donor programs, a fact advocates of contract pregnancy often mention to argue that contract pregnancy is the analogous activity for women. The analogy between donating sperm and gestating a human fetus for nine months is extremely strained. Even donating an egg is not comparable to donating sperm, as doing so requires surgery. The logic of commercial contract pregnancy allows the eventual commodification of all procreative activity, where individuals of either sex might purchase sperm from one source, ova from another, and hire a third person to gestate the fertilized egg. This total commodification seems undesirable and at least raises the question of whether the sale and purchase (rather than the donation) of human sperm and ova is bad public policy.

12. Judge Parslow makes a false distinction between gestational mothers who have a genetic relationship to the fetus they bear and those who do not. The absence of a genetic relationship need not alter a gestational mother's experience of pregnancy, and that experience is the basis of her custodial rights. A gestational mother undergoes all the extensive hormonal and physiological changes of pregnancy; her social experience as a pregnant woman will be the same whether she has a genetic tie to the fetus or not. From her perspective, the distinction between "full surrogacy" (in which she donates an ovum) and "partial surrogacy" (in which she bears no genetic relationship to the fetus) may well be immaterial.

13. In recommending the prohibition of payment under any circumstances, Anderson assumes the existence and desirability of mother-fetus bonding; I do not assume that such a bond always develops or that the state should prohibit all payment. When a gestational mother does experience a strong tie with the child she is carrying, however, law and social practice should recognize and protect that bond.

14. Locke only allowed for slavery following capture in a just war, when enslavement was substituted for a death sentence. For an excellent discussion of Locke's views of slavery see James Farr, " 'So Vile and Miserable an Estate': The Problem of Slavery in Locke's Political Thought," *Political Theory* 14(2):263–289 (1986).

15. For example, we might imagine a student who received a college scholarship from the military discovering as she neared graduation that she has become a pacifist and that the person she is now cannot in conscience enter the armed forces as had been promised. To force her to do so would violate her deepest principles concerning the taking of human life and do violence to the "self" she has become since entering into her agreement with the military. On the very complicated problem of whether promises can bind people who experience profound changes in values, see Parfit 1973, 144–146; and Williams 1976. Charles Fried believes that to respect persons we must respect the persistence of their choices over time and that to release them from their promises "infantilize[s]" them. See Fried 1981, 20–21. I am grateful to Robert Goodin of the Australian National University for an insightful letter about the problem of "later selves" (personal correspondence, October 1989).

16. Even if one accepts my argument that a woman's contract to relinquish all custodial claims should not be enforced against her will, the question of how to deal with the custodial claims of the commissioning parent(s) is enormously difficult. One could argue that these claims should be adjudicated on a case-by-case basis, but that would not serve the goal of stabilizing the child's situation as quickly as possible nor give more weight to actual physical relationship and nurturance than to intentionality alone. Yet the claims of the commissioning parents are real and certainly stronger than those of a biological father who "unintentionally" becomes a parent through unprotected intercourse (and who can claim paternal rights and responsibilities in many jurisdictions). This is a large issue that I cannot address adequately here other than to note that society might do well to develop forms of acknowledging the existence of "intentional" and biological, as well as nurturing, parents rather than try to make all families resemble households of two heterosexual parents and their biological offspring. In this regard see Bartlett, 1988.

17. Robert D. Goldstein, *Mother-love and Abortion: A Legal Interpretation* (Berkeley and Los Angeles: University of California Press, 1988). I do not believe all women experience "mother-love" during pregnancy and disagree with Goldstein's assumption that mother-love must continue to privilege a mother's relationship to her child over the father's after birth.

18. For a discussion of nineteenth-century feminist ideology and marriage law reform campaigns see Norma Basch, *In the Eyes of the Law* (Ithaca, N.Y.: Cornell University Press, 1982), and Mary Lyndon Shanley, *Feminism, Marriage and the Law in Victorian England, 1850–1895* (Princeton, N.J.: Princeton University Press, 1989).

19. Christine Di Stefano, "Masculinity as Ideology in Political Theory: Hobbesian Man Considered," *Women's Studies International Forum* 6(6):633–644 (1983); quoting Thomas Hobbes, *The Citizen* [1651] in Bernard Geit, ed., *Man and Citizen* (Garden City, N.Y.: Doubleday, 1972), 205, 638.

20. Barbara Katz Rothman (1989) condemns contract pregnancy as a manifestation of "liberal philosophy [that] is an articulation of the values of technological society, with its basic themes of order, predictability, rationality, control, rationalization of life, the systematizing and control of things and people as things, the reduction of all to component parts, and ultimately the vision of everything, including our very selves, as resources" (63).

21. Alfonso J. Damico, "Surrogate Motherhood: Contract, Gender, and Liberal Politics," in Ethan Fishman, ed., *Public Policy and the Public Good* (Westview, Conn.: Greenwood Press, 1991), intelligently distinguishes liberal values from arguments for contract pregnancy.

References

Anderson, Elizabeth S. 1990. "Is Women's Labor a Commodity?" *Philosophy and Public Affairs* 19:71–92.

Andrews, Lori. 1989. *Between Strangers: Surrogate Mothers, Expectant Fathers, & Brave New Babies.* New York: Harper & Row.

Anleu, Sharyn L. Roach. 1990. "Reinforcing Gender Norms: Commercial and Altruistic Surrogacy." *Acta Sociologica* 33:63–74.

Arneson, Richard J. 1992. "Commodification and Commercial Surrogacy." *Philosophy and Public Affairs* 21(2):132–164.

Bartlett, Katharine T. 1988. "Re-Expressing Parenthood." *Yale Law Journal* 98(2):293–340.

Basch, Norma. 1982. *In the Eyes of the Law.* Ithaca, N.Y.: Cornell University Press.

Brooks, Gwendolyn. 1989. "The Mother" (1945). *The Norton Anthology of American Literature* 2:2505. 3d ed. (New York and London: W. W. Norton & Co).

Damico, Alfonso J. 1991. "Surrogate Motherhood: Contract, Gender and Liberal Politics." In *Public Policy and the Public Good.* Edited by Ethan Fishman. Westview, Conn.: Greenwood Press.

Di Stefano, Christine. 1983. "Masculinity as Ideology in Political Theory: Hobbesian Man Considered." *Women's Studies International Forum* 6(6):33–44.

Farr, James. 1986. " 'So Vile and Miserable an Estate': The Problem of Slavery in Locke's Political Thought." *Political Theory* 14(2):253–289.

Field, Martha A. 1988. *Surrogate Motherhood: The Legal and Human Issues.* Cambridge, Mass.: Harvard University Press.

———. 1990. "The Case Against Enforcement of Surrogacy Contracts." *Politics and the Life Sciences* 8(2):199–204.

Fineman, Martha Albertson. 1991. *The Illusion of Equality: The Rhetoric and Reality of Divorce Reform.* Chicago: University of Chicago Press.

Finley, Lucinda. 1986. "Transcending Equality Theory: A Way Out of the Maternity and the Workplace Debate." *Columbia University Law Review* 86:1118–1182.

Fried, Charles. 1981. *Contract as Promise.* Cambridge, Mass.: Harvard University Press.

Goldstein, Robert D. 1988. *Mother-love and Abortion: A Legal Interpretation.* Berkeley and Los Angeles: University of California Press.

Held, Virginia. 1987. "Non-contractual Society: A Feminist View." In *Science, Morality and Feminist Theory.* Edited by Marsha Hanen and Kai Nielsen. *Canadian Journal of Philosophy,* Suppl. vol. 13. Calgary: University of Calgary Press.

Hill, John Lawrence. "The Case for Enforcement of the Surrogate Contract." *Politics and the Life Sciences* 8(2):147–160.

Hobbes, Thomas. [1651] 1972. *The Citizen*. In *Man and Citizen*. Edited by Bernard Geit. Garden City, N.Y.: Doubleday.

Jaggar, Alison. 1980. "Prostitution." In *The Philosophy of Sex: Contemporary Readings*. Edited by A. Soble. Totowa, N.J.: Rowman & Littlefield.

Johnson, Barbara. 1987. "Apostrophe, Animation, and Abortion." In *A World of Difference*. Baltimore: The Johns Hopkins University Press.

Karst, Kenneth. 1980. "The Freedom of Intimate Association." *Yale Law Journal* 89(4):624–693.

Katz, Avi. 1986. "Surrogate Motherhood and the Baby-Selling Laws." *Columbia Journal of Law and Social Problems* 20(1):1–52.

Landes, Elizabeth, and Richard A. Posner. 1978. "The Economics of the Baby Shortage." Letter. *Journal of Legal Studies* 7:323.

Lawson, Carol. 1990. "Couple's Own Embryos Used in British Surrogacy," *New York Times*, August 12, metropolitan edition, A1.

Littleton, Christine. 1987. "Equality and Feminist Legal Theory." *University of Pittsburgh Law Review* 48:1043–1059.

Locke, John. [1690] 1980. *Second Treatise of Government*. Edited by C. B. Macpherson. Indianapolis: Hackett Publishers.

Mill, John Stuart. [1859] 1975a. *On Liberty*. In *Three Essays*. New York: Oxford University Press.

Mydans, Seth. 1990. "Surrogate Denied Custody of Child," *New York Times*, October 23, metropolitan edition, A14.

_____. [1869] 1975b. *The Subjection of Women*. In *Three Essays*. New York: Oxford University Press.

New York Times. 1990. August 12, metropolitan edition, A1.

Okin, Susan Moller. 1990. "A Critique of Pregnancy Contracts." *Politics and the Life Sciences* 8(2):205–210.

Overall, Christine. 1992. "What's Wrong with Prostitution? Evaluating Sex Work." *Signs: Journal of Women in Culture and Society* 17(4):705–724.

Parfit, Derek. 1973. "Later Selves and Moral Principles." In *Philosophy and Personal Relations: An Anglo-French Study*. Edited by Alan Montefiore. Montreal: McGill-Queens University Press.

Pateman, Carole. 1983. "Defending Prostitution: Charges against Ericsson." *Ethics* 93(3): 561–565.

_____. 1988. *The Sexual Contract*. Stanford: Stanford University Press.

Posner, Richard. 1986a. *Economic Analysis of Law*, 3d ed. Boston: Little Brown.

_____. 1986b. "Mischaracterized Views," letter. *Judicature* 69(6):321.

Radin, Margaret Jane. "Market-Inalienability." *Harvard Law Review* 100:1849–1937.

Raymond, Janice G. 1990. "Reproductive Gifts and Gift Giving: The Altruistic Woman." *Hastings Center Report* 20(6):7–11.

Rhode, Deborah. 1989. *Justice and Gender*. Cambridge, Mass.: Harvard University Press.

Rich, Adrienne. 1976. *Of Woman Born: Motherhood as Experience and as Institution*. New York: W.W. Norton; Bantam Paperback Edition.

Robertson, John. 1983. "Procreative Liberty and the Control of Contraception, Pregnancy and Childbirth." *Virginia Law Review* 69:405–462.

_____. 1989. "Embryos, Families and Procreative Liberty: The Legal Structures of the New Reproduction." *Southern California Law Review* 59:942–1041.

Rothman, Barbara Katz. 1989. *Recreating Motherhood: Ideology and Technology in Patriarchal Society*. New York: W.W. Norton & Co.

Ryan, Maura A. 1990. "The Argument for Unlimited Procreative Liberty: A Feminist Critique. *Hastings Center Report* 20(4):6–12.

Schoeman, Ferdinand. 1980. "Rights of Children, Rights of Parents, and the Moral Basis of the Family." *Ethics* 91(1):6–19.

Schwarzenbach, Sibyl. 1990–1991. "Contractarians and Feminists Debate Prostitution." *Review of Law & Social Change* 18:103–130.

Shalev, Carmel. 1989. *Birth Power.* New Haven, Conn.: Yale University Press.

Shanley, Mary Lyndon. 1989. *Feminism, Marriage and the Law in Victorian England.* Princeton, N.J.: Princeton University Press.

Shrage, Laurie. 1989. "Should Feminists Oppose Prostitution?" *Ethics* 99:347–361.

Shultz, Marjorie Maguire. 1990. "Reproductive Technology and Intention-based Parenthood: An Opportunity for Gender Neutrality." *Wisconsin Law Review* 1990 (2):297–398.

Sklar, Kathryn Kish. 1986. "Why Were Most Politically Active Women Opposed to the ERA in the 1920s?" In *Rights of Passage: The Past and Future of the ERA.* Edited by Joan Hoff-Wilson. Bloomington: Indiana University Press.

Stumpf, Andrea E. "Redefining Motherhood: A Legal Matrix for New Reproductive Technologies." *Yale Law Journal* 96(1):187–208.

Tong, Rosemarie. 1983. *Women, Sex, and the Law.* Totowa, N.J.: Rowman & Allenheld.

Williams, Bernard. 1976. "Persons, Character and Morality." In *The Identities of Persons.* Edited by Amelie O. Rorty. Berkeley: University of California Press.

Williams, Patricia. 1988. "On Being the Object of Property." *Signs: Journal of Women in Culture and Society* 14(11):5–24.

Young, Iris. 1984. "Pregnant Embodiment: Subjectivity and Alienation." In *"Throwing Like a Girl" and Other Essays in Feminist Philosophy and Social Theory.* Bloomington: Indiana University Press, 1990.

The "Gift" of a Child: Commercial Surrogacy, Gift Surrogacy, and Motherhood

UMA NARAYAN

LIKE MANY OTHERS, my interest in the moral and legal problems concerning surrogate motherhood was initially provoked by the Baby M. controversy. Since most of the discussions I read focused on the moral and legal ramifications of the practice of commercial surrogacy under a legally enforceable contract, I gave little thought to gift surrogacy. My unreflective assumption was that it was benign compared to commercial surrogacy, perhaps even a laudable practice.

My moral reservations about gift surrogacy were triggered by overhearing some family gossip about a relative in India, who bore a child for her infertile sister. Although the act was regarded as praiseworthy by those who told the story, I was disturbed that the arrangement was to be kept a "family secret." This incident led me to reflect on the fact that both sisters were middle-class housewives who did not work outside the home and how this made it easier for one's pregnancy (and the other's lack thereof) to be concealed—making it possible to pretend that the infertile sister had given birth. It occurred to me that being able to give birth at home rather than in a hospital (where the name of the child's biological mother would be recorded) made it possible for such exchanges to bypass state scrutiny; I worried about the implications of unregulated exchanges.

As I turned the family gossip over in my mind I made further connections that fueled my moral unease about gift surrogacy. I knew from conversations with workers at Indian adoption agencies that many Indians, higher-caste Hindus in particular, had reservations about adoption since adoptable children were unlikely to be of the "right" caste. I was reminded of arguments here, in the United States, about how it was the shortage of adoptable *white* infants that made commercial surrogacy so attractive to many couples. Adopting a child based on the right caste is likely to be a greater impediment than adopting for race, given many castes and the impossibility of guessing caste background from appearance. My family's incident was undoubtedly motivated by the fact that a genetically related child would also be of the right caste.

I became convinced that many of the moral and legal problems with commercial surrogacy, though often exacerbated by the commercial nature of the transaction and the existence of an enforceable contract, were not really unique to such arrangements. Since much of the literature on surrogacy focuses on commercial surrogacy, it often suggests that the major problems with surrogacy are problems unique to "commercialized and commodified reproduction." I challenge this by suggesting that many of these problems are not *necessarily* connected to the commercial and contractual aspects of paid surrogacy but rather are results of women bearing children under conditions of powerlessness, whether as commercial surrogates, gift surrogates, or simply as women having children within patriarchal relationships. I wish to argue that bearing children within the context of market relationships is not *necessarily* more oppressive and exploitative of women than bearing children within patriarchal familial contexts.

In contrast to the criticisms usually levelled at commercial surrogacy, I argue that gift surrogacy may be as problematic as commercial surrogacy. In my view, many of these problems also arise in the context of women's reproduction within the confines of patriarchal heterosexual relationships within and outside of marriage; I argue that it is a mistake to see surrogacy as radically discontinuous with ordinary motherhood. Placing gift surrogacy in the foreground is useful for two reasons: It helps show that many of the problems with surrogacy are not unique to its commercial version; and because gift-surrogacy often takes place among family members it helps raise questions about the problematic nature of the family relationships in which many women function as gift surrogates and mothers. Understanding these connections is important, particularly since they have received less attention than they deserve.

The connections between commercial surrogacy, gift surrogacy, and women's reproduction within patriarchal relationships must be taken into account in formulating legal proposals for regulating surrogacy in general. The second half of this essay explores some alternative ways in which commercial and gift surrogacy could be legally regulated. I am sympathetic to Mary Shanley's conclusion in Chapter 9 that commercial surrogacy *contracts* ought not to be legally enforceable.[2] Therefore, I shall not deal much with moral or legal issues specifically pertaining to the enforceability of surrogacy contracts. Rather, I shall treat commercial surrogacy as a practice that operates in the absence of a legally enforceable contract.

I consider three legal alternatives: criminalizing commercial surrogacy; treating both commercial and gift surrogacy arrangements like private adoptions;

and handling disputes over children who result from any surrogacy arrangement as custody disputes. I argue in favor of the last alternative, because I believe that a reformed custody approach is the alternative most likely to secure the parental rights of *all* women, not just surrogates, and to protect a range of parental relationships that might be in the interests of children.

Intrusions into Women's Reproductive Autonomy and Privacy

Many of the moral objections to commercial surrogacy are arguments to the effect that commercial transactions involving women's reproductive capacities are exploitative because they permit serious intrusions into women's reproductive autonomy and privacy.[3] Such arguments often focus on the sale of women's reproductive services under an enforceable surrogacy contract, whereby women may be *contractually* bound to refrain from abortion, undergo various intrusive medical procedures such as amniocentesis, be subject to surveillance regarding matters of diet, exercise, and lifestyle, and be subject to other serious intrusions on their autonomy, privacy, and decisions regarding their bodies.

Even where commercial surrogacy contracts are not legally enforceable (currently the case in a number of states), commercial surrogates may well remain vulnerable to intrusions both from the commissioning parents and from legal or psychological professionals hired by them. The degree to which a particular commercial surrogate is vulnerable will depend on the degree of access to her life that the commissioning parents or their hired professionals have, the surrogate's own economic and psychological vulnerabilities, and her capacity to insist on relative autonomy during the process of commercial surrogacy. Given the relative economic powerlessness of commercial surrogates vis-à-vis the commissioning parents, commercial surrogates may be browbeaten into submitting to invasive conditions, even in the absence of an enforceable contract.

Vulnerability is not, however, unique to commercial surrogates. Since gift surrogacy may often take place under circumstances that encourage coercive intrusions, the risk of intrusions may be even greater. Gift surrogates who have prior friendship or kinship ties with the receiving parents may be as economically or psychologically vulnerable as commercial surrogates to intrusive procedures. The gift surrogate, though unpaid, may be economically dependent on the commissioning parents or members of their family. The fact she is unpaid is as likely to be a symptom of the family's power in taking her reproductive services for granted as an indication that she is acting out of uncoerced altruism.

Indeed, the gift surrogate's relationship and emotional ties to the receiving parents—ties the commercial surrogate usually lacks—may make her more vulnerable to emotional pressure and coercion concerning the conditions of pregnancy and childbirth. Further, personal and familial ties may give the commissioning parents greater access to the gift surrogate, making it easier to monitor and impose conditions on her lifestyle. Thus, the gift surrogate may be especially vulnerable to coercive pressures regarding their pregnancy compared to commercial surrogates.

In short, it would be naive to assume that families, which often exercise an oppressive degree of control over women, are necessarily freer spaces for women's choices than commercial relationships.[4] Cases like that of Alejandra Muñoz, a poor, illiterate, nineteen-year-old Mexican illegally brought into the United States by relatives and impregnated with her cousin's husband's sperm, confirm that such worries about familial exploitation are not figments of feminist imaginations. Muñoz was told that the embryo she conceived would be implanted into the womb of her infertile cousin. When this failed to happen she wished to terminate the pregnancy but was threatened with being exposed as an illegal alien and forcibly confined to the house by her relatives until she gave birth.[5]

Many feminists have worried that commercial surrogacy will result in poor women in the United States and Third World countries being reduced to hired "breeders" for better-off couples.[6] Instances like the Muñoz case suggest that in a society like ours, with significant class differences and numerous immigrant communities with ties to relatives in poorer countries, it may be simpler and considerably cheaper to exploit one's poor relatives than hire strangers. Using family members is also an effective way to ensure that the child meets the parents' preferences in terms of race, caste, ethnicity, and appearance.

Keeping it in the family may also make it possible for families to conceal who the child's biological mother is and to pretend that the child is the natural child of the couple raising it. This was clearly attempted not only in my family's case, but also in the Muñoz case, which involved considerably more deceit and coercion than ours. Alejandra's cousin wore a pillow under her clothes to pretend she was pregnant; she and her husband directed Alejandra to use her cousin's name when she went to the doctor and arranged matters so that the cousin's name ended up on the child's birth certificate. Such arrangements run the dangers inherent in concealing such exchanges of children from legal scrutiny; they may also make it impossible for the biological mother to establish that she is the mother of the child (thus making it virtually impossible for her to challenge the parental claims of the commissioning couple).[7]

Risks of coercion and manipulation are not unique to women who are commercial or gift surrogates. Many women around the world who have children in the context of patriarchal families and cultures are subject to severe intrusions into their reproductive autonomy and privacy. There is an extensive literature that documents the extent to which women in many countries give birth under conditions that eradicate their sense of agency, are subjected to unnecessary medical procedures such as cesarean sections, and have their reproductive choices adversely affected by developments in reproductive technology.[8] For many women, the decisions whether to have children, how many children to have, and under what conditions are controlled by the husband and his family or are made in the context of overwhelming cultural pressures.[9] Women in countries like India and China who are under heavy pressures to bear sons feel compelled to undergo amniocentesis and abort the fetus if it happens to be female.[10]

In many cultures women are blamed for infertility and subject to physical and mental abuse as a result. Some U.S. studies also indicate that abusive husbands become more violent when their wives become pregnant, putting both women and fetuses at risk at the point when deciding to leave the marriage may be most difficult.[11] For many women, inability or unwillingness to conform to the reproductive choices of their husbands leads to the breakdown of the marriage. For example, a study of voluntarily childless U.S. couples found that when the wife wanted a child and the husband did not they usually stayed childless; but when the husband wanted a child and the wife did not they often divorced.[12]

Thus, gift surrogates are vulnerable to the same intrusions on autonomy and privacy that commercial surrogates are. Moreover, vulnerability to such intrusions marks, in different degrees, *all* women who bear children under conditions of powerlessness in patriarchal contexts. Commercial surrogacy and the marketplace are not the only contexts in which women are reduced to reproductive vehicles for men to acquire genetically related children. Marriage often suffices, giving men control over wombs they do not have to rent. The class and power differentials that may exist between commercial surrogates and receiving couples often exist between husbands and their wives.

Surrogacy and Gendered Altruism

Commercial surrogacy is also frequently criticized on the grounds that it involves the economic and gender-role exploitation of women. Women's economic vulnerabilities, their emotional training to be caring and self-sacrificing, and their socialization to see their value in terms of motherhood may make them feel that surrogate motherhood is a wonderful undertaking. But these are not problems unique to commercial surrogacy; again, gift surrogacy and ordinary motherhood under patriarchal conditions are subject to the same criticisms.

Clearly commercial surrogacy involves the economic exploitation of women: the average commercial surrogate is paid $10,000, not a generous sum for all the effort and inconvenience involved (artificial insemination, nine months of pregnancy, the risks and pains of childbirth, and the intrusions into privacy and autonomy). But the fact that women enter such arrangements voluntarily does not mean they are not exploitative.[13] Given women's economic marginalization, it is not surprising that $10,000 is an attractive proposition, especially since being a surrogate can be combined with caring for one's own children.

But if commercial surrogacy involves economic exploitation so do many instances of ordinary motherhood. Many mothers do most of the work involved in child care, child rearing, and most other domestic work as unpaid labor. Their domestic and child-rearing activities are often perceived as "gifts of love"—activities done out of a mother's emotional care for her family—and thereby not perceived as unremitting hard work or as "real" economic contributions.[14]

Unlike commercial surrogates, ordinary mothers are not paid to have children. Yet they bear a disproportionate share of the economic costs of having and raising children. They are more likely than fathers to compromise their careers, drop out of the labor force, or opt for part-time work while raising their children. These decisions often reduce their economic earning power, leaving them economically dependent on their spouses and vulnerable to poverty if the marriage breaks up.[15] In many social contexts, motherhood and economic marginalization often work to reinforce each other. Lack of attractive economic and career opportunities makes motherhood an appealing avenue for feeling a sense of achievement; and being a mother, with primary responsibility for children, perpetuates economic marginalization. Again, the fact that women *choose* to be mothers does not make motherhood any less exploitative under such conditions.

Both commercial and gift surrogacy often involve gender-role exploitation. The very aspects of "femininity" used to glorify motherhood—views of women as loving, nurturing, and self-sacrificing—also seem to be deeply involved in motivating women to be surrogates. Rather than drawing a stark contrast between "unnatural" commercial surrogate mothers who bear and give children away for cold cash and gift surrogates who act out of purer motives, we need to develop a more complex and context-sensitive picture of women's motivations to have children, whether for themselves or others.

Sharyn L. Roach Anleu argues that public and legal attitudes favor gift surrogates over commercial surrogates because gender-norms "specify ... that it is unnatural and inappropriate for women to become pregnant for economic reasons."[16] Anleu's point is borne out by numerous news and magazine articles stressing that most commercial surrogates are motivated more by altruistic reasons than by a desire to be paid. One article, "Searching For A Very Special Woman," tells of a study where 150 commercial surrogacy applicants were interviewed[17] and reports with evident satisfaction that "[t]hese women state they are volunteering primarily for reasons other than money."[18] It points out that four surrogates registered with an agency even offered to turn down the fee.[19] The same study reveals that the most prevalent motivation for commercial surrogacy is "quite simply, a love of being pregnant." As one interviewee put it, "[p]regnancy is my highest level of being alive. I feel in touch with the reason I was put on earth as a woman." Several of the women interviewed saw being a surrogate as helping them resolve painful or ambivalent reactions they had had to an abortion or to giving up a child for adoption. Other motivations included what the article called a "need for accomplishment," exemplified in one woman's statement: "I'll never cure cancer or be an astronaut. This is my unique gift, the most important thing I could ever do in my lifetime." Many surrogates wanted to help infertile couples desperate to have a child, and one mother of four stated she felt guilty about having her tubes tied "while someone needed a baby."[20]

The articles implicitly subscribe to the view that only "bad women" would be so crass as to become surrogates for purely commercial motives. In their enthusiastic concern to stress the "altruistic" motivations of commercial surrogates they reveal a frightening failure to attend to the problematic and gendered nature of these motivations. The fact that some women experience their greatest sense of fulfillment in being pregnant or view having a child for strangers as their greatest accomplishment points to the power of gender norms and to the limited opportunities women have for feeling worthwhile and having a sense of achievement in their own right. Nor does it seem wise or efficacious to risk the pain of carrying another child and surrendering it to strangers in order to assuage the grief of an abortion or of putting up a child for adoption.[21] It is not clear to me that noncommercial motivations are any more admirable or indicative of psychological well-being than purely economic motivations would be, though many clearly regard them as being so.

It is also striking how deeply gendered these expressed noncommercial motivations for surrogacy are. Few men are likely to see children as their greatest accomplishment or feel so guilty about having participated in an abortion or adoption decision that they are driven to expiate their guilt through such strenuous acts of self-sacrifice. It seems extremely unlikely that male counterparts would subject themselves to the medical risks, pain, and discomfort associated with pregnancy and childbirth out of a deep desire to help strangers have children. The fact these noncommercial motivations for surrogacy are uncritically taken to be laudable testifies to the degree to which self-sacrificing altruism is part of our cultural definition of what makes women "special."[22]

In fact, men seem less likely than women to submit themselves to physical pain and medical risks—even to help close family members and even in situations where their pain and risk might help to save a life. Studies on kidney donations suggest that women are much less likely than men to be ambivalent about donating kidneys to relatives. The results of studies reveal that "the female appears to take the donation more for granted" and that she is less likely to "perceive the act to be an extraordinary one on her part."[23] The authors conclude: "Perhaps donation seems to the female to be a simple extension of her usual family obligations, while for the male it is an unusual type of gift. In our society the traditional female role is one in which altruism and sacrifice within the family is expected."[24] Although the ability to act altruistically in the interests of others is praiseworthy, the problem is that women are expected to be altruistic in ways men are not, to sacrifice their interests to meet the interests of others without critical assessment, and to minimize the value of what they have done. If gender socialization operates so as to cause some women to feel a strong desire, or even a sense of obligation, to help strangers have children, it is likely to make many women feel an even greater degree of obligation to help infertile friends and relatives have children. Indeed, the gift surrogate's emotional and familial ties may make her feel *obliged* to bear a child for her infertile relatives.

Gift-giving often serves social functions, such as maintaining social bonds or promoting group unity, and is often experienced as prescriptive and exacting.[25] Janice Raymond says of gift surrogacy:

> Family opinion may not force a woman, in the sense of being outrightly coercive, to become pregnant for another family member. However, where family integration is strong, the nature of family opinion may be so engulfing that, for all practical purposes, it exacts a reproductive donation from a female source. And representing a surrogate arrangement as a gift holds the woman in tutelage to the norms of family duty, represented as giving to a family member in need. Within family situations, it may also be considered selfish, uncaring, even dishonorable for a woman to deprive a relative of eggs or her gestating ability.[26]

Such an analysis of gift-giving is useful in shaking our commonplace assumption that gifts are always "freely bestowed" since it points out that gift-giving often takes place in contexts of felt obligation. Building on Raymond's criticisms of gift-surrogacy, I would add that women's sense of obligation to have children also surfaces in the context of their *own* families, where women may feel that they "owe" their husband children and are taught to blame themselves for their failure to be satisfactorily fertile.

The gendered altruism involved in gift-surrogacy can be criticized along other lines as well. Unlike kidney donation, where the life of another person may depend on the gift, the end towards which the gift surrogate makes her sacrifice is arguably less pressing, urgent only to the degree to which one subscribes to the view of infertility as deeply tragic.

Certain cases of gift-surrogacy also involve considerably greater risks than commercial surrogacy. I am thinking especially of cases that involve older women, whose age considerably increases the physical costs and risks of pregnancy, and multiple births, such as the forty-eight-year-old South African woman who had four embryos transplanted into her and gave birth to triplets for her daughter.[27] A recent U.S. case involved fifty-three-year-old Geraldine Weslowski, who had been through menopause and underwent extensive hormone treatment and three embryo transplants so that she could eventually give birth to her grandchild.[28] The sense of priorities involved in such decisions, and the wisdom of making such sacrifices, seem questionable at best. One can imagine few grand*fathers* in their fifties taking such risks to enable their offspring to have a genetically related child.

The contrast between commercial surrogacy and gift surrogacy is also blurred by the fact that many commercial and gift surrogates act in the hope that their sacrifice will lead to acceptance and integration into a surrogate family and sustained emotional bonds with the receiving parents. Phyllis Chessler reports several cases of mothers who expected that being a commercial surrogate would lead to a "wonderful" and "lifelong relationship" with the receiving parents.[29] However, Chessler's analysis suggests that although many receiving parents play up to these expectations while the commercial surrogate is pregnant they "want nothing more to do with her once the baby is safely 'theirs.'"[30]

Some gift surrogates probably do maintain emotionally satisfying bonds with receiving parents and the child. However, previous relationships do not *guarantee* that gift surrogates will find their expectations satisfied. Neither are the motivations of commercial and gift surrogates who see their "gift" as a chance to secure acceptance and emotional integration into a family very different from those of many regular mothers, who may see having a child as an opportunity for securing their relationship to a man and establishing familial bonds that provide a sense of emotional connection and value. Again, all this suggests there are no simple contrasts to be drawn among commercial surrogacy, gift surrogacy, and motherhood within marriage or heterosexual cohabitation. Next I examine some of the moral criticisms of commercial surrogacy that focus on wrongs or harms to the child involved, exploring the degree to which gift surrogacy escapes these problems.

Surrogacy and the Commodification of Children

One general criticism of commercial surrogacy is that it constitutes baby-selling and involves a commodification of human beings akin to slavery.[31] But it is not clear that treating children as entities that can be gifted away is any less objectionable than treating them as entities that can be sold. Neither is it clear that an entity must be subject to market mechanisms to be commodified; being able to gift something seems to imply ownership of that entity just as much as being able to sell it.

Is buying and selling of parental claims to children tantamount to treating children as property rather than persons? Parental claims to children are not strictly analogous to property rights: The receiving father who acquires full parental claims to the child cannot resell it and there are restrictions on how the child may be treated.[32] But even if parental claims to children are claims to maintain a relationship rather than assertions of property rights,[33] buying and selling claims to parental relationships may seem morally objectionable.

Others object to commercial surrogacy because commodifying parental relationships amounts to children being used as means to others' ends. For example, Elizabeth Anderson argues that children "are to be loved and cherished by their parents, not to be used or manipulated by them for merely personal advantage."[34] She goes on to argue against commercial surrogacy on the grounds that the surrogate "deliberately conceives a child with the intention of giving it up for material advantage. Her renunciation of parental responsibilities is not done for the child's sake, nor for the sake of an interest she shares with the child, but typically for her own sake (and possibly, if 'altruism' is a motive, for the intended parents' sakes)."[35]

I agree that it is wrong not to respect persons as ends in themselves and with the contention that persons can thus be wronged even if they are not harmed.[36] However, the Kantian injunction on which such arguments rely merely requires that we do not treat persons *only* as means to our ends. It is not clear that such arguments conclusively apply to commercial surrogacy since the commercial surrogate could claim that she is relinquishing parental responsibilities at least *partly* for the child's sake. She has borne and relinquished the child so that the receiving parents can establish the parental bonds they desire with the child and raise it in a manner that secures its well-being. Where the child is being surrendered to a couple who have the intention and the means to care for it as parents, it is not clear that the child is being used *merely* as a means to others' ends, either in commercial surrogacy or in gift surrogacy.

I suspect that an overly strict notion of "respect for persons" is at work in a number of such arguments—a sense that a child must be desired purely for its own sake if it is not to be treated merely as a means to adults' ends. Although this may constitute an ideal stance towards children, most people who have children seem to do so for a *variety* of motives, some more admirable than others, ranging from economic necessity to the desire to pass on genes, cement a relationship, or experience the pleasures of raising a child. Although none of these desires are purely for the sake of the child, they are compatible with the parents also loving the child and caring for it in ways that do treat it as an end in itself. Thus it is not so clear that a commercial or gift surrogate who brings a child into the world in order to surrender it or that the receiving parents who secure the surrogate's services in order to have a child they plan to care for and raise are necessarily treating the child merely as a means.

Anderson is also troubled by receiving parents in commercial surrogacy contracts who seek to "specify the height, I.Q., race, and other attributes of the surrogate mother, in the expectation that such traits will be passed on to the child." She thinks children are thereby "valued as mere use-objects" by parents who seek to select the child's genetic makeup to accord with their own wishes.[37] Although I personally find obsessive concern with the child's potential traits distasteful and narcissistic, such concerns are hardly peculiar to parents who seek a child via commercial surrogacy. Parents often manifest interest in the child's actual or potential traits, whether in gift surrogacy, adoption, or in choosing the attributes of the person with whom they might have children.

Children who result from commercial surrogacy arrangements may indeed experience "feelings of abandonment, insecurity and incomplete identity," even when they know they are loved and wanted by their receiving parents.[38] But the same risks are borne by adopted children. Children may also experience such feelings if they are products of gift surrogacys, if their parents undergo a divorce, and if they are subject to emotionally distant parenting by their natural parents. In fact, children worldwide, especially girls in cultures where daughters are seen as burdens and sons are highly prized, go through life knowing that they were not particularly desired by their parents—even when parents do not subject them to other forms of mistreatment. Thus psychological risks are not unique to surrogacy nor do they constitute an especially compelling moral argument against commercial or gift surrogacy. I do not see why surrogate mothers or commissioning parents should be held to higher standards than regular parents.

Many who object to surrogacy seem to believe that adoption is a morally preferable solution to infertility, a view that becomes more problematic if one considers the social context in which the practice of adoption occurs. Although genetic narcissism and racist attitudes about adopting nonwhite children may explain why some people do not choose adoption as a solution to infertility, other factors may be at work. Same-sex couples usually are not allowed to adopt children. And, as Barbara Berg points out, adopting children of other races and ethnic backgrounds may seem problematic to those who believe that this deprives the children of access to their cultural heritage and who do not feel confident of their abilities to provide it.[39] Berg also points out that unwillingness to adopt older children or children with special needs is not necessarily a result of selfishness or bias but may be based on an honest evaluation that one will not be able to cope with the additional challenges and responsibilities such adoptions pose.[40]

When we consider the social factors that cause children to be put up for adoption the arguments for preferring adoption to surrogacy become even more suspect. Women's lack of access to contraception, women's economic powerlessness, and cultural attitudes that stigmatize unwed mothers and their children are part of the context in which women make choices to relinquish children for adoption. Often women's families, pregnancy counselors, and social workers concentrate on separating young unwed mothers from their children. Chessler cites numerous incidents where pregnancy counselors have warned women that they will probably abuse their children, that their initial grief will quickly subside, and that they are exceedingly "selfish" in wanting to keep their children.[41] Chessler also points out that in a context where the mother has no job, housing prospects, legal advice, or counsel from family and friends there is duress involved in adoption agencies offering hospital care and living expenses in exchange for her child.[42]

Thus, it is problematic to tout adoption as a feminist alternative to surrogacy since patriarchal attitudes and treatment of women are implicated in inducing many women to surrender children for adoption. The more successful a society is in empowering women with regard to reproductive choices the less likely women will risk unwanted pregnancies; and it is more likely that women will find it economically and socially feasible to raise the children they bear. As a result, the pool of children available for adoption will shrink, making adoption even less available as an alternative solution for infertility.

As we have seen, arguments that commercial surrogacy commodifies children and poses specific harms to them point to problems that are not unique to commercial surrogacy. Not only are there many instances of commercial surrogacy that do not manifest these problems, but there are also many cases of gift surrogacy, of women reproducing as wives in patriarchal families, and of adoption that *are* problematic in these ways. In my view, none of these problems provides adequate justification for legally prohibiting commercial surrogacy, gift surrogacy, or traditional patriarchal marriages. They do, however, testify to the urgency of legal, social, and cultural changes that will empower women and promote less morally problematic stances towards children.

Given that commercial and gift surrogacy arrangements continue to occur and may sometimes be unproblematic, the practice of surrogacy needs to be legally regulated in ways that will help empower women. What legal alternative might best protect the multiplicity of interests at stake in surrogacy arrangements? I explore the three most viable alternatives that have been proposed as means to regulate surrogacy, parenthood, and the custody of children. The first option is to permit gift surrogacy but criminalize commercial surrogacy. The second is to permit both forms of surrogacy and regulate the exchanges of children in ways that are similar to private adoption. The third is to permit both commercial and gift surrogacy and to treat all disputes over children who result from surrogacy arrangements as custody disputes.

Criminalizing Commercial Surrogacy

Many have argued that commercial surrogacy should be legally prohibited under penalty of a criminal sanction.[43] Although I am not an advocate of surrogacy in any form, I find criminalization of commercial surrogacy problematic on several grounds.

One objection has to do with the intended targets and purported effects of the penalties. Most proponents of criminalization argue that criminal penalties should apply only to the middlemen involved in surrogacy transactions.[44] Although moral antipathy toward brokers is understandable, it does not seem fair to subject only middlemen to criminal penalties. If it is legal for two parties to enter the commercial transaction, why should it be illegal for someone to engage in the business of making the transaction possible?

Most who would criminalize surrogacy find it unpalatable to extend criminal penalties to the surrogate mother and the commissioning parents. This position is morally inconsistent. If the practice is worthy of criminal prohibition on the grounds of the harms involved (the commodification of children and the exploitation of women) it would seem appropriate to penalize *any* party who engaged in such harmful transactions. It should not matter that, in Mary Gibson's words, parents "act in response to personal vulnerability, pain and desperation"[45]: such factors are not usually grounds for refraining from punishing those culpable of premeditated criminal conduct. The argument that criminal penalties should not apply to parents because it is not in the best interests of the child is equally problematic, since the effects on children of having parents incarcerated are not usually grounds for withholding criminal penalties on parents.[46]

Furthermore, criminalizing the conduct of middlemen alone is unlikely to deter the practice and may even have the opposite effect. On average, middlemen are paid at least as much as the surrogate mother.[47] Criminalizing the conduct of middlemen without penalizing nonmediated commercial surrogacy arrangements may decrease the costs involved and make the practice more affordable. Ousting middlemen would also enable commissioning parents to offer higher fees to surrogates, thus increasing the financial incentives for women. Criminalizing commercial surrogacy might also drive the practice underground, leaving the women and children involved even more vulnerable and devoid of legal protection.

Another objection to applying criminal prohibitions and sanctions to surrogacy is rooted in the argument made in the first half of this essay. As we have seen, the moral concerns aroused by commercial surrogacy are not unique to that situation but are often present in gift surrogacy and reproduction within the confines of patriarchal relationships, families, and culture. Focusing only on commercial surrogacy suggests that commercialized reproduction is profoundly different from reproduction in noncommercial contexts. However unwittingly, this tends to reinforce the cultural ideology that sees the family as a "haven in the heartless world" and commercial relationships alone as the site of alienation, commodification, and exploitation. Yet we know that families are not free from coercion, inequality, and alienation.[48] In short, since none of the dangers outlined above are unique to commercial surrogacy, they cannot provide a justification for criminalizing commercial surrogacy alone while we continue to permit other relationships that might manifest the same problems. There is no reason to privilege some potentially problematic relationships over others.

Recognizing the extent to which the moral problems with commercial surrogacy extend to a variety of other possible relationships within which women reproduce should give us pause about suggesting legal prohibitions that single out commercial surrogacy. The argument that prohibiting commercial surrogacy at least gets rid of one problematic practice is not much comfort. If we routinely permit people to enter into some alienating and exploitative relationships and transactions, but prohibit others that have exactly the same features, that raises questions of fairness. Why should certain choices—entering into surrogacy contracts through middlemen—be denied the protection routinely accorded others, such as surrogacy agreements arrived at without the help of mediators or reproduction within oppressive marriages?

Surrogacy Arrangements as Private Adoptions

Some believe that noncommercial surrogacy should be handled the same way as private adoption, arguing that there is little difference between arranging to adopt a mother's baby soon after it is conceived and arranging to do so prior to conception.[49] Under this view, it would only be legal to pay the mother "reasonable medical expenses" and the mother would have a period of time after birth in which to decide whether she really wished to relinquish the child. Further, the birth mother would be regarded as the legal mother of the child, regardless of whether she is the genetic mother.[50] Since I think commercial and gift surrogacy arrangements are morally similar, I consider here the benefits and burdens of treating *all* cases of surrogacy in this manner. (I should note at the outset that some states forbid private adoptions; this proposal would not be legally viable in those contexts.)

An attractive feature of this proposal is that it seems to restrict the amount of money paid to the surrogate and the reasons for payment, thus making the transaction seem less like baby-selling. I think this difference is more apparent than real, especially in contexts where the commissioning parents are legally permitted to pay the birth mother's hospital and medical expenses and other "provable necessary expenses" such as food and rent. Given that the average commercial surrogate receives $10,000, surrogacy arrangements that work as private adoptions will not necessarily involve a smaller amount of money changing hands under the rubric of "necessary expenses." And even if it limited payment to surrogate mothers, the private adoption approach would still be lucrative to middlemen, especially lawyers, who would continue their crucial roles in these arrangements.

This proposal would protect the parental claims of gestational mothers and provide them time for a reflective assessment about whether to surrender the child. (See Mary Lyndon Shanley's powerful essay in Chapter 9.) But it raises the question of whether treating surrogacy as adoption is fair to the genetic commissioning father or couple, who would have no valid legal claims to the child until the birth mother surrendered it for adoption. How seriously should such genetic connections be taken? This is a difficult question to answer. However, it is clear that in most societies genetic connections are taken seriously and valued—and not only in the case of children. Many of us maintain ties with relatives whom we do not necessarily like or with whom we have little in common because we perceive them to be "family"—because we are genetically related. The deep desire of some adopted children to know their family of origin, especially their birth mothers, even where they have been well cared for by their adoptive parents, is undoubtedly linked to the cultural weight most societies as-

current UK position.

sign genetic relationships. The social weight given to genetic ties does benefit individuals in that people feel a degree of responsibility for and accept obligations to assist relatives in situations where they might not act to help strangers or acquaintances. Such explanations point to the fact that we live in a world where genetic connections are valued, but do not provide a *reason* for valuing such connections.[51]

Given how important genetic connections are to many people, one might question the fairness of treating surrogacy arrangements as private adoptions, where genetic mothers and fathers would have no recognized basis for parental claims to the child even though they might in other contexts. Why, for instance, should genetic paternity constitute a basis for legal claims to a child within the institution of marriage but not in surrogacy? Why should women who have gestated their children within the institution of marriage have *less* of an exclusive claim to their children than surrogate mothers? I am dubious about proposals that provide ad hoc solutions that secure the desired result in one area but do not comport with general principles that ought to determine valid bases for parental claims to children.

The proposal to treat surrogacy as private adoption needs to justify treating gestation as the sole basis for parental claims. The gestational relationship is certainly a unique one; no one else stands in that particular relationship to a child. However, if gestation is seen as a basis for parental claims on the grounds that it involves providing care for the child before birth, spouses or partners who support the mother economically and psychologically during her pregnancy (thus indirectly providing for the care of the child) may have a basis for parental claims on grounds not altogether different from the gestational mother.[52] Unlike anonymous sperm donors and genetic fathers who desire no contact with or responsibility for their children, the commissioning genetic father or couple have manifested a strong desire to have parental connections to the child and may have assisted the gestational mother in providing for the child's well-being. Even greater risks and efforts can be expended by genetic commissioning mothers. Producing ova for in vitro fertilization involves hormonal treatment to ripen the woman's eggs and surgical procedures to remove the eggs from her body. Such considerations make it harder to justify the position that commissioning parents have no parental claim until they secure the child through adoption.[53]

Favoring the gestational relationship in surrogacy cases makes some feminists nervous. Treating gestational ties as special and unique may become grounds for holding pregnant women to more stringent standards of behavior than others, an issue other essays in this volume explore in depth.[54] As Lori Andrews puts it, "The other side of the gestational coin … is that with special rights come special responsibilities. If gestation can be viewed as unique in surrogacy, it can be viewed as unique in other areas. Pregnant women could be held to have responsibilities that other members of society do not have—such as the responsibility to have a Ceasearean section against their wishes in order to protect the health of a child."[55]

On the one hand, lack of respect for genetic ties and failure to recognize the risk, support, and effort expended by commissioning parents makes me reluctant to endorse treating surrogacy disputes under private adoption standards. On the other hand, I also think gestation should provide a basis for parental claims since the gestatory mother has invested more effort and risk in securing the child's existence than the genetic parents. Thus, I am not sure considering the gestational relationship to be the *sole* basis for parental claims in surrogacy cases is any wiser than refusing, as courts have done, to see it as *a valid basis at all*. I am reluctant to privilege *any* of the possible bases for parental claims to children—genetic ties, gestation, or the provision of social care—as the *sole* basis for parental claims to children. A general rule that may yield appropriate results in some cases may fail to yield satisfactory results in others.

Surrogacy and Custody

Now I consider the option of legally permitting both commercial and noncommercial surrogacy, handling disputes between surrogate mother and commissioning father or couple not as contract violations but as regular custody disputes, which would be decided on the basis of the "best interests of the child." I begin with commercial genetic and gestational surrogacy and then consider noncommercial cases of genetic and gestational surrogacy.

In contexts where the surrogacy contract is regarded as unenforceable, disputes between genetic commercial surrogates and commissioning parents are handled as regular custody disputes. But commercial *gestational* surrogates who are not genetically related to the child are often regarded as having no valid legal basis for parental claims. This disparity in treatment is unjust: Why should genetic connections be privileged over gestational ones as bases for parental claims to children, especially given the fact that the gestational mother has expended more effort and risk in securing the child's existence than anyone else? Treating disputes over children who result from commercial surrogacy arrangements as custody disputes would give gestatory as well as genetic surrogates recognized bases for asserting parental claims to the child.

Legal disputes over children are also likely in cases of gift surrogacy since gift surrogates also might change their minds about relinquishing the child. I think cases of noncommercial genetic or gestatory surrogates who change their mind about relinquishing the child should also be treated as custody disputes.

One problem with this approach is that courts often award custody to the parent who can provide the child with a higher standard of living. Since commercial surrogate mothers, genetic or gestatory, are usually poorer than the contracting father or couple, this is likely to work to their disadvantage.[56] Genetic or gestatory gift surrogates who are less affluent than the commissioning father or couple might also be disadvantaged in custody decisions.

Of course the use of economic criteria in determining the best interests of the child also works to the disadvantage of women who have children within the institution of marriage and who face a custody battle because of divorce. The pervasive use of economic criteria to ascertain the child's best interests underscores the need to limit the importance assigned to such criteria since they work to disadvantage women *in general* and in contexts where women are usually less well-off than men.

Surrogate mothers face other disadvantages in the criteria used to determine the best interests of the child. For example, commercial surrogates may run the risk of being stigmatized as unfit mothers merely by virtue of the fact that they entered such a commercial transaction in the first place. For instance, Judge Sorkow felt that Mary Beth Whitehead had proved her unfitness as a mother the day she signed the contract with the Sterns.[57] This seems sexist and unfair, given that the commissioning parents signed the same contract and were not perceived as unfit parents even though their desire and fee generated the transaction in the first place.

Divorced women fighting for custody of their children are also subject to sexist (and heterosexist) double-standards that lead to their being regarded as unfit mothers.[58] Such practices point to the need to ensure that morally problematic and sexist criteria are not used to determine a child's best interests in order to empower all women who seek custody of their children. Thus, although I favor treating disputes over children who result from surrogacy arrangements as custody disputes, I also favor *reforming* our legal practices involving custody to enable non-genetic gestational mothers to assert parental claims and to eradicate the use of problematic criteria such as financial security that disadvantage women in determining the best interests of their children. Such an approach has the advantage of treating genetic and gestational and commercial and noncommercial surrogates as women who have valid bases for asserting parental claims to a child.

I would reform our current custody practices in two other ways. First, I would recognize caring for a child as a basis for asserting parental claims. Surely any sustained efforts at caring for the child and functioning as a *social parent* can create emotional ties that are valued by the adult as well as the child involved—ties that deserve to be given legal weight. Such legal recognition would benefit a variety of people. For instance, gay men and lesbian women who work at parenting children who are biologically related only to their partner would have a basis for maintaining parental bonds with that child, even if the relationship with their partner broke up, instead of being treated as a person with no legal standing with respect to that child. Unmarried heterosexual partners who are not genetically related to the children they help raise would also have legally recognized claims to maintain their parental bonds to those children, as would married partners who help raise children from their partner's previous relationships. In cases of surrogacy, where a dispute over the child results in custody being shared between the commissioning father and the surrogate mother, the wife of the commissioning father who helps raise the child would also have parental claims by virtue of that fact. Currently, she is not recognized has having any legal standing as a parent of that child.

Second, I support moving in the direction of recognizing that it is in the child's best interests to maintain as many of these parental connections with willing, caring adults as is practically feasible. Recognizing that children may have a stake in maintaining relationships with their genetic and gestational parents, as well as with those who have socially cared for them, would require us to rethink our current legal practice (where no more than two persons at any given time are granted legal recognition of their parental claims to a particular child, which is clearly anachronistic given the complexity of contemporary marital, partnering, reproductive, and parental relationships). The policy I recommend also has the virtue of privileging a child's interests above those of competing parents, treating children more as ends in themselves, and less as objects of property disputes between contending parents.

In sum, I favor a reformed custody approach over the private adoption approach for a number of reasons. The private adoption approach, despite its advantages, is still all or nothing. The gestatory mother has *all* the parental claims before ceding the child for adoption and *no* claims whatsoever after she changes her mind. The commissioning parents have *no* parental claims until the child is ceded for adoption and thereafter have the *only* recognized parental claims to it. The reformed custody approach potentially allows for a wider range of parental relationships to be preserved through shared custody and visitation rights. A surrogate mother who did not wish to relinquish her parental claims to the child would have a good chance of maintaining parental bonds to the child by sharing in its custody.

This might be a welcome alternative to being forced to choose between the burdens of assuming full responsibility for the child and surrendering all ties to it, as the private adoption model requires. It would give the surrogate mother and the commissioning parents the option of agreeing beforehand that the surrogate would not totally surrender all parental claims but legally share custody or maintain visitation rights in a way that does not prevent the genetically unrelated wife of the commissioning father from acquiring legally recognized parental claims to the child she helps raise. This would be a significant improvement over the current situation, where prevailing custody and adoption practices make it impossible for her to acquire parental claims except via adoption or to adopt the child unless the surrogate mother completely relinquishes her parental claims. This makes it impossible to protect the parental interests of both women simultaneously and raises the commissioning parents' stake in making sure that they have "exclusive possession" of the child.

Conclusions

My essay begins by pointing out that many of the moral problems raised by commercial surrogacy also pertain to gift surrogacy and to women's reproduction under conditions of powerlessness. I conclude by considering the deep-rooted similarity of women's experiences with regard to childbearing, arguing that the reformed custody model is the legal approach most consistent with paying attention to the overlapping nature of these problems.

As I have argued, commercial surrogacy, gift-surrogacy, and regular motherhood in patriarchal contexts have much in common. I want to examine a commonality that is particularly perplexing. For every mother (surrogate or not) who acknowledges that her reproductive experience involved exploitation, coercive intrusions, and alienation, there are many who sincerely deny that they have experienced any of these problems and are willing to make the same choices over again.

The degree to which coercion, exploitation, and alienation manifest themselves in particular cases of commercial or gift surrogacy, or in cases of what one might call ordinary motherhood, vary widely. Take gift surrogacy, for instance. For every horrible instance involving outright coercion and exploitation, such as the Alejandra Muñoz case, there are undoubtedly instances that are genuinely benign and unproblematic.[59] Although it would be a mistake to see any of these reproductive contexts as devoid of problems, it would also be a mistake to ignore significant differences in the degree to which these problems manifest themselves in different cases.

Even many women who do recognize that their reproductive experiences have taken place in contexts of coercion, exploitation, or alienation might decide nevertheless that their reproductive decisions were, all things considered, ones they *wanted* to make, even given the constraints on their choices. The effects of women's inequality in sexist cultures is so pervasive that few of us are able to make choices that are entirely egalitarian, nonexploitative, and unmarked by power. Relationships and reproductive decisions that involve gender inequality and exploitation are, for many of us, also sites of meaningfulness, significance, and value and these elements are inextricably intertwined in the grain of many lives. Autonomy is exercised in the context of the choices we have, yet even the desires and values that structure our choices are affected by the contexts that have formed us. The fact that people do not always choose freely or wisely does not necessarily detract from the value of preserving choices.

This suggests that areas such as surrogacy, where not only our experiences but our understandings of our experiences vary widely, are not good areas for prohibitory state legislation. Rather, we need to regulate the potential problems and harms involved in surrogacy arrangements in ways that the individuals subjected to these harms—surrogate mothers (genetic and gestatory, commercial and gift), commissioning parents (genetic and unrelated), and children—have avenues of recourse. Let me use an analogy that I believe is appropriate. More women are injured, and often very much more grievously so, as a result of domestic violence than as a result of surrogacy. Yet the extent of domestic violence, and the serious harms that accrue to women as a result, do not motivate us to legally prohibit marriage or domestic partnerships. What we aim to do instead is to provide as many legal avenues and social structures as we can to enable women to leave battering relationships and seek redress for their injuries or to provide access to therapy that might stop the battering.

Similarly, what I propose in the case of surrogacy is not legal prohibition but a variety of policies that will warn women of the risks involved, make it possible for them to seek redress if their rights are violated during the process of functioning as a surrogate, help secure parental claims they do not wish to relinquish, and see that the interests of resulting children are protected.

Because I believe that both the benefits and the burdens of women's reproductive choices, whether as commercial or as gift surrogates or in the context of patriarchal relationships, are more alike than different, I think we should seek to devise legal solutions that would empower *all* women who are mothers. I believe that reforming our legal practices regarding custody in the ways I have suggested, and treating disputes over children who result from surrogacy arrangements as custody disputes, is a fair and principled way to protect the variety of parental claims that may arise and also the interests of the children involved. Legally recognizing a plurality of parental relationships may go a long way toward valuing and validating a variety of relationships coveted by both adults and children and away from viewing children as entities over whom adults should be driven to seek exclusive possession.[60]

Notes

1. It has been pointed out there are problematic connotations to the term "surrogate" mother since it implies she is not the "real" mother. See for instance, Hilde Lindemann Nelson and James Lindemann Nelson, "Cutting Motherhood in Two: Some Suspicions Concerning Surrogacy," *Hypatia* 4(3) (Fall 1989). However, the common alternative, "contract motherhood," does not serve my purposes very well, since I intend to focus on commercial surrogacy *without* an enforceable contract. The alternative terms for "gift surrogacy" in the literature are terms like "altruistic surrogacy" and "noncommercial surrogacy," all terms that include the problematic word "surrogacy." In the absence of satisfactory semantic alternatives, I shall use the terms "commercial surrogacy" and "gift surrogacy."

2. For similar views, see Katherine T. Bartlett, "Re-Expressing Parenthood," *Yale Law Journal* 98(2):293–340 (1988); Martha A. Field, "The Case Against Enforcement of Surrogacy Contracts," *Politics and the Life Sciences* 8(2):199–204 (1990); Mary Gibson, "Contract Motherhood: Social Practice in Social Context," *Women and Criminal Justice*, Vol. 1 & 2, (1991), also published in *Criminalization of a Woman's Body*, ed. Clarice Feinman (New York: The Haworth Press, 1992), 55–99; Susan Muller Okin, "A Critique of Pregnancy Contracts," *Politics and the Life Sciences* 8(2):205–210 (1990).

3. Besides exploitation arguments, there are arguments that the sale of reproductive services is *intrinsically* wrong. Sara Ann Ketchum argues that "some activities that are close to our personhood ... should not be for sale." See "Selling Babies and Selling Bodies," *Hypatia* 4(3):120 (Fall 1989). Although interesting, such arguments are not easy to clearly spell out and so I shall not address them here.

4. For similar arguments see Sharyn L. Roach Anleu, "Reinforcing Gender Norms: Commercial and Altruistic Surrogacy," *Acta Sociologica* 33(1):63–74 (March 1990), and Janice Raymond, "Reproductive Gifts and Gift Giving: The Altruistic Woman," *Hastings Center Report* 20:7–11 (November-December 1990).

5. For a discussion of the Muñoz case see, Phyllis Chessler, *Sacred Bond* (New York: Times Books, 1988), Chapter 3, and Raymond, "Reproductive Gifts and Gift Giving: The Altruistic Woman."

6. Sarah Boone, "Slavery and Contract Motherhood: A Racialized Objection to the Autonomy Arguments," in *Issues in Reproductive Technology I: An Anthology*, ed. Helen B. Holmes (New York: Garland Press, 1992); Gibson, "Contract Motherhood: Social Practice in Social Context"; and Barbara Katz Rothman, "Cheap Labor: Sex, Class, Race—and 'Surrogacy,'" *Society* 25(2):21–23 (March-April 1988).

7. Phyllis Chessler, *Sacred Bond,* Chapter 3.

8. Rita Arditti et al. (eds.), *Test-Tube Women: What Future for Motherhood?* (London: Pandora Press, 1989); Gena Corea et al. (eds.), *Man Made Women: How New Reproductive Technologies Affect Women* (Bloomington: Indiana University Press, 1987); Barbara Katz Rothman, *Recreating Motherhood: Ideology and Technology in a Patriarchal Society* (New York: Norton, 1989); Michelle Stanworth (ed.), *Reproductive Technologies: Gender, Motherhood and Medicine* (Oxford: Polity Press, 1987).

9. Martha Gimenez has argued that most cultural contexts are what she calls "pronatalist," meaning there are structural and ideological pressures that strongly depict parenthood as an adult norm and that childlessness is often subject to economic, social, and psychological sanctions. See Martha E. Gimenez, "Feminism, Pronatalism and Motherhood," in *Mothering: Essays in Feminist Theory*, ed. Joyce Trebilcot (Totowa, N.J.: Rowman and Allenheld, 1983).

10. Elizabeth Bumiller, *May You Be the Mother of a Hundred Sons* (New York: Fawcett, 1990), Chapters 5 and 11; Viola Roggencamp, "Abortion of a Special Kind: Male Sex Selection in India," in *Test-Tube Women: What Future for Motherhood?*, ed. Rita Arditti et al. (London: Pandora Press, 1989).

11. It is reported that pregnant women's risk of violence is 60.6 percent greater than that of nonpregnant women. See Murray A. Strauss and Richard J. Gelles (eds.), *Physical Violence in American Families* (New Brunswick, N.J.: Transaction Publishers, 1990), 282.

12. It has been argued that the dominant partner in a relationship controls a variety of reproductive decisions and that, in our sorts of society, the dominant partner is likely to be a man. See Judith Lorber, "Choice, Gift, or Patriarchal Bargain: Women's Consent to In Vitro Fertilization in Male Infertility," *Hypatia* 4(3):32 (Fall 1989).

13. Sara Ann Ketchum also argues that we cannot assume that "the presumed or formal voluntariness" of the arrangement makes it nonexploitative. See "Selling Babies and Selling Bodies," 121. We need to think about the contexts that makes such transactions attractive to women. For one such discussion, see Margaret Radin, "Market-Inalienability," *Harvard Law Review* 100(8):1849–1937 (1987).

14. Anleu, "Reinforcing Gender Norms."

15. For an extended analysis of the economic, social, and personal price women pay for mothering, see M. Rivka Polatnick, "Why Men Don't Rear Children: A Power Analysis," in *Mothering: Essays in Feminist Theory*, 21–40, ed. Joyce Trebilcot (Totowa, N.J.: Rowman and Allenheld, 1983).

16. Anleu, "Reinforcing Gender Norms," 71.

17. It is pertinent to note that the study was conducted by Dr. Betsy Aigen, founder and director of the Surrogate Mother Program in New York City, who herself had a daughter with the assistance of a commercial surrogate.

18. Arking, "Searching for a Very Special Woman," *McCalls*, June 1987, 55–57.

19. They were urged to accept it and give it to their favorite charity by the director of their surrogate agency, who is reported as saying, "I think it makes the contract more binding. It also gives them a chance to do *two* wonderful deeds." Arking, "Searching for a Very Special Woman," 57.

20. Ibid., 56–57. There are also some less common personal reasons. Arking reports one woman wanted to be a surrogate because she had been told that a pregnancy could help cure her endometriosis and prevent infertility at the point she wanted to start her own family. One woman reportedly wanted to become a nun, but first wished to experience child birth without sexual contact. See *The Sunday Star Ledger* (Newark, N.J.), 23 November 1986, 54.

21. Phyllis Chessler reports conversations with several commercial surrogate mothers who were emotionally devastated at the thought of surrendering the child in *Sacred Bond*. Reports indicate that roughly 10 percent of surrogate mothers experience serious grief, requiring therapy, upon surrendering the child. See Elizabeth S. Anderson, "Is Women's Labor a Commodity?" *Philosophy and Public Affairs* 19:83 (1990).

22. Similar arguments are made by Anleu, "Reinforcing Gender Norms"; Radin, "Market-Inalienability"; and Raymond, "Reproductive Gifts and Gift Giving."

23. Lorber, "Choice, Gift, or Patriarchal Bargain," 27.

24. R. G. Simmons, S. Klein Marine, and R. L. Simmons, *Gift of Life: The Effect of Organ Transplantation on Individual, Family and Societal Dynamics* (New Brunswick, N.J.: Transaction Books, 1987), cited in Lorber, "Choice, Gift, or Patriarchal Bargain," 27.

25. Marcel Mauss, *The Gift* (Glencoe, Illinois: Free Press, 1954).

26. Raymond, "Reproductive Gifts and Gift Giving," 10.

27. Eric Levin, "Motherly Love Works a Miracle," *People*, October 19, 1987, 43.

28. Lindsey Gruson, "A Mother's Gift: Bearing Her Grandchild," *New York Times*, 16 February 1993, B1, B4. It is also interesting to note that the article blurb describes her considerable efforts as "lending her womb."

29. Chessler, *Sacred Bond*, 57.

30. Ibid.

31. See for instance, Anderson, "Is Women's Labor a Commodity?"; Boone, "Slavery and Contract Motherhood"; Gibson, "Contract Motherhood: Social Practice in Social Context"; and Ketchum, "Selling Babies and Selling Bodies."

32. John Robertson, "Surrogate Mothers: Not So Novel After All," *Hastings Center Report* 13 (October 1983).

33. Ketchum recommends such a view in "Selling Babies and Selling Bodies," 119–120.

34. Anderson, "Is Women's Labor a Commodity?" 75.

35. Ibid., 76.

36. Gibson, "Contract Motherhood: Social Practice in Social Context," 78.

37. Anderson, "Is Women's Labor a Commodity?" 77.

38. Gibson, "Contract Motherhood: Social Practice in Social Context," 79.

39. Barbara Berg, "Listening to the Voices of the Infertile," in *Reproduction, Ethics and the Law: Feminist Perspectives*, ed. Joan C. Callahan (Bloomington: Indiana University Press, 1995).

40. Berg, "Listening to the Voices of the Infertile."

41. Chessler, *Sacred Bond*, 119–121.

42. Ibid., 122.

43. See Rosemarie Tong, "The Overdue Death of a Feminist Chameleon: Taking A Stand On Surrogacy Arrangements," *Journal of Social Philosophy* 12(2 & 3):50 (Fall-Winter 1990); and Gibson, "Contract Motherhood: Social Practice in Social Context," 85.

44. Thus, Gibson argues that only commercial brokering should be a criminal offense, "Contract Motherhood: Social Practice in Social Context," 85. The Surrogacy Arrangements Act in the United Kingdom penalizes lawyers, physicians, and social workers who serve as middlemen in commercial surrogacy negotiations as well as publishers and managers of publications that accept ads offering or seeking surrogacy services; but the law withholds penalties from the surrogate mother or contracting parents. Department of Health and Social Security, United Kingdom, *Report of the Committee of Inquiry into Human Fertilization and Embryology,* London, HMSO, July 1984, 47.

45. Gibson, "Contract Motherhood: Social Practice in Social Context," 99, n. 97.

46. Department of Health and Social Security, United Kingdom, *Report of the Committee of Inquiry into Human Fertilization and Embryology,* London, HMSO, July 1984, 47.

47. Whereas surrogates are usually paid $10,000, it has been estimated that the total cost of the fees paid to the surrogate, the commercial broker, the physicians, psychiatrists, and attorneys involved in many surrogacy arrangements range from $30,000 to $50,000. See Alta Charo, "Legislative Approaches to Surrogate Motherhood," in *Surrogate Motherhood: Politics and Privacy,* ed. Larry Gostin (Bloomington: Indiana University Press, 1990), 92.

48. See for instance, Michele Barrett and Mary McIntosh, *The Anti-Social Family* (London: Verso Editions/NLB, 1982) and Joyce Trebilcot (ed.), *Mothering: Essays in Feminist Theory* (Totowa, N.J.: Rowman and Allenheld, 1983).

49. See Lori B. Andrews, "Alternative Modes of Reproduction," in *Reproductive Laws for the 1990's,* ed. Sherill Cohen and Nadine Taub (Clifton, N.J.: Humana Press, 1989), 384. Rosemarie Tong ultimately supports this approach, Tong, "The Overdue Death of a Feminist Chameleon: Taking A Stand On Surrogacy Arrangements."

50. George J. Annas, "Regulating the New Reproductive Technologies," in *Reproductive Laws for the 1990's,* ed. Sherill Cohen and Nadine Taub (Clifton, N.J.: Humana Press, 1989), 414.

51. In my view, the ways we value genetic connections cannot be reduced to men valorizing genetic connections so that they can appropriate their genetic offspring.

52. For such a view developed in the context of questions about unwed fathers' parental rights, see Mary Lyndon Shanley, "Fathers' Rights, Mothers' Wrongs," paper presented at the American Political Science Association Annual Meeting, Washington D.C., September 1993.

53. These problems are acknowledged in Tong, "The Overdue Death of a Feminist Chameleon: Taking a Stand on Surrogacy Arrangements," 52.

54. See the essays in this volume by Patricia Richard (Chapter 2), Deirdre Condit (Chapter 3), Ruth Ann Strickland and Marcia Whicker (Chapter 4), and Iris Young (Chapter 6).

55. Lori B. Andrews, "Surrogate Motherhood: The Challenge for Feminists," in *Surrogate Motherhood: Politics and Privacy,* ed. Larry Gostin (Bloomington: Indiana University Press, 1990), 179.

56. Tong, "The Overdue Death of a Feminist Chameleon: Taking A Stand On Surrogacy Arrangements," 44.

57. Chessler, *Sacred Bond,* 38.

58. For some details on this issue see Ruthann Robson, *Lesbian (Out)law* (Ithaca, N.Y.: Firebrand Books, 1992), Chapter 11.

59. For instance, see some of the Dutch cases of gift surrogacy mentioned in Juliette Zipper and Selma Sevenhuijsen, "Surrogacy: Feminist Notions of Motherhood Reconsidered," in *Reproductive Technologies: Gender, Motherhood and Medicine,* ed. Michelle Stanworth (Oxford: Polity Press, 1987), 118–138.

60. I would like to thank Pat Boling for her painstaking attention to various drafts of this paper. I would also like to thank Jennifer Church, Jesse Kalin, Elizabeth Kelly, James Hill, and Mary Shanley for their generous assistance and helpful comments.

References

Anderson, Elizabeth S. "Is Women's Labor a Commodity?" *Philosophy and Public Affairs* 19:71–92 (1990).

Andrews, Lori B. "Alternative Modes of Reproduction." In *Reproductive Laws for the 1990's.* Edited by Sherill Cohen and Nadine Taub. Clifton, N.J.: Humana Press, 1989.

———. "Surrogate Motherhood: The Challenge for Feminists." In *Surrogate Motherhood: Politics and Privacy.* Edited by Larry Gostin. Bloomington: Indiana University Press, 1990.

Anleu, Sharyn L. Roach. "Reinforcing Gender Norms: Commercial and Altruistic Surrogacy." *Acta Sociologica* 33(1):63–74 (March 1990).

Annas, George J. "Regulating the New Reproductive Technologies." In *Reproductive Laws for the 1990's.* Edited by Sherill Cohen and Nadine Taub. Clifton, N.J.: Humana Press, 1989.

Arditti, Rita et al., eds. *Test-Tube Women: What Future for Motherhood?* London: Pandora Press, 1989.

Arking, Linda. "Searching for a Very Special Woman." *McCalls'.* June 1987, 55–57.

Barrett, Michele, and Mary McIntosh. *The Anti-Social Family.* London: Verso Editions/NLB, 1982.

Bartlett, Katherine T. "Re-Expressing Parenthood." *Yale Law Journal* 98(2):293–340 (1988).

Berg, Barbara. "Listening to the Voices of the Infertile." In *Reproduction, Ethics and the Law: Feminist Perspectives.* Edited by Joan C. Callahan. Bloomington: Indiana University Press, 1995.

Boone, Sarah. "Slavery and Contract Motherhood: A Racialized Objection to the Autonomy Arguments." In *Issues in Reproductive Technology I: An Anthology.* Edited by Helen B. Holmes. New York: Garland Press, 1992.

Bumiller, Elizabeth. *May You Be the Mother of a Hundred Sons.* New York: Fawcett, 1990.

Charo, Alta. "Legislative Approaches to Surrogate Motherhood." In *Surrogate Motherhood: Politics and Privacy.* Edited by Larry Gostin. Bloomington: Indiana University Press, 1990.

Chessler, Phyllis. *Sacred Bond.* New York: Times Books, 1988.

Corea, Gena et al., eds. *Man Made Women: How New Reproductive Technologies Affect Women.* Bloomington: Indiana University Press, 1987.

Department of Health and Social Security, United Kingdom. *Report of the Committee of Inquiry into Human Fertilization and Embryology.* London, HMSO, July 1984.

Field, Martha A. "The Case Against Enforcement of Surrogacy Contracts." *Politics and the Life Sciences* 8(2):199–204 (1990).

Gibson, Mary. "Contract Motherhood: Social Practice in Social Context." *Women and Criminal Justice,* Vol. 1 & 2, 1991. Also published in *Criminalization of a Woman's Body,* 55–99. Edited by Clarice Feinman. New York: The Haworth Press, 1992.

Gimenez, Martha E. "Pronatalism and Motherhood." In *Mothering: Essays in Feminist Theory.* Edited by Joyce Trebilcot. Totowa, N.J.: Rowman and Allenheld, 1983.

Gruson, Lindsey. "A Mother's Gift: Bearing Her Grandchild." *New York Times,* 16 February 1993, B1, B4.

Ketchum, Sara Ann. "Selling Babies and Selling Bodies." *Hypatia* 4(3):116–127 (Fall 1989).

Levin, Eric. "Motherly Love Works a Miracle." *People*, 19 October 1987.

Lorber, Judith. "Choice, Gift, or Patriarchal Bargain: Women's Consent to In Vitro Fertilization in Male Infertility." *Hypatia* 4(3):23–36 (Fall 1989).

Mauss, Marcel. *The Gift*. Glencoe, Illinois: Free Press, 1954.

Nelson, Hilde Lindemann, and James Lindemann Nelson. "Cutting Motherhood in Two: Some Suspicions Concerning Surrogacy." *Hypatia* 4(3):85–94 (Fall 1989).

Okin, Susan Moller. "A Critique of Pregnancy Contracts." *Politics and the Life Sciences* 8(2):205–210 (1990).

Polatnick, M. Rivka. "Why Men Don't Rear Children: A Power Analysis." In *Mothering: Essays in Feminist Theory*, 21–40. Edited by Joyce Trebilcot. Totowa, N.J.: Rowman and Allenheld, 1983.

Radin, Margaret. "Market-Inalienability." *Harvard Law Review* 100(8):1849–1937 (1987).

Raymond, Janice. "Reproductive Gifts and Gift Giving: The Altruistic Woman." *Hastings Center Report* 20:7–11 (November-December 1990).

Robertson, John. "Surrogate Mothers: Not So Novel After All." *Hastings Center Report* 13 (October 1983).

Robson, Ruthann. *Lesbian (Out)law*. Ithaca, N.Y.: Firebrand Books, 1992.

Roggencamp, Viola. "Abortion of a Special Kind: Male Sex Selection in India." In *Test-Tube Women: What Future for Motherhood?* Edited by Rita Arditti et al. London: Pandora Press, 1989.

Rothman, Barbara Katz. "Cheap Labor: Sex, Class, Race—and 'Surrogacy.'" *Society* (March-April 1988), 21–23.

_____. *Recreating Motherhood: Ideology and Technology in a Patriarchal Society*. New York: Norton, 1989.

Shanley, Mary Lyndon. "'Surrogate Mothering' and Women's Freedom: A Critique of Contracts for Human Reproduction." *Signs* 18(31):1–22 (Spring 1993), reprinted in this volume.

Stanworth, Michelle, ed. *Reproductive Technologies: Gender, Motherhood and Medicine*. Oxford: Polity Press, 1987.

Strauss, Murray A., and Richard J. Gelles, eds. *Physical Violence in American Families*. New Brunswick, N.J.: Transaction Publishers, 1990.

Tong, Rosemarie. "The Overdue Death of a Feminist Chameleon: Taking a Stand on Surrogacy Arrangements." *Journal of Social Philosophy* 12(2 & 3):50 (Fall-Winter 1990).

Trebilcot, Joyce, ed. *Mothering: Essays in Feminist Theory*. Totowa, N.J.: Rowman and Allenheld, 1983.

Zipper, Juliette, and Selma Sevenhuijsen. "Surrogacy: Feminist Notions of Motherhood Reconsidered." In *Reproductive Technologies: Gender, Motherhood and Medicine*, 118–138. Edited by Michelle Stanworth. Oxford: Polity Press, 1987.

About the Contributors

Patricia Boling teaches political science and women's studies at Purdue University. She has recently completed a manuscript on feminist democratic theory and the transition from private to public, *Privacy and the Politics of Intimate Life*, and published articles on public-private distinctions, maternal thinking, and constitutional protections for privacy.

Lisa C. Bower teaches political science at Arizona State University. She is currently working on two book-length manuscripts, *(Trans)Forming the Legal Field: Feminist Theories, Legal Feminisms and Law* and *Law, Culture and the Politics of 'Direct Address': Raced/Sexed Subjects as Agents of Cultural and Legal Transformation*.

Deirdre Moira Condit teaches political science and women's studies at Virginia Commonwealth University. Her work explores the body in political theory, with specific interest in the pregnant body, the fetal form, and the sex/gender distinction through the lens of pregnancy.

Nancy Hartsock teaches political science at the University of Washington. She is the author of a number of works in feminist theory, including *Money, Sex, and Power*. She is currently working on a collection of her essays to be published as *The Feminist Standpoint Revisited and Other Essays* and a book-length critique of postmodernism in feminist theory.

Phillip E. Johnson is the Jefferson E. Peyser Professor of Law at the University of California, Berkeley. He has written law school casebooks in criminal law and criminal procedure, *Darwin on Trial*, a skeptical account of Darwinian evolution, and numerous scholarly articles on law, including several challenging orthodox theories in the areas of evolution and HIV/AIDS.

Uma Narayan was educated in India and the United States (B.A. from Bombay University, M.A. from Poona University, Ph.D. from Rutgers University, all in philosophy). She teaches philosophy at Vassar College, where her major areas of interest are philosophy of law, social and political philosophy, applied ethics, and feminist theory. She has published articles on a wide range of topics, including affirmative action, immigration laws, ethnic food and identity, punishment, and nonwestern legal frameworks.

Paul Peretz teaches political science at the California State University, Fullerton. His primary research interests lie in political economy. He has written numerous articles and the following books: *The Political Economy of Inflation* and *The Politics of Economic Policy-Making*. He is currently working on a book about political economy for the University of Michigan Press.

Patricia Bayer Richard is dean of University College at Ohio University where she is also a professor of political science. She has written extensively on reproductive rights issues and about elections and campaigns. Her current research investigates gender differences in political participation and support for democratic values in Central America.

Jean Reith Schroedel teaches at the Center for Politics and Economics at the Claremont Graduate School. Her primary research and teaching interests are gender politics and congressional politics. Schroedel has written *Alone in a Crowd: Women in the Trades Tell Their Stories, Congress, the President and Policy-Making: A Historical Analysis,* and numerous articles.

Mary Lyndon Shanley holds the Margaret Stiles Halleck Chair in Political Science at Vassar College. She is author of *Feminism, Marriage and the Law in Victorian England* and editor, with Carole Pateman, of *Feminist Interpretations and Political Theory.* Her essay, "Fathers' Rights, Mothers' Wrongs? Reflections on Unwed Fathers' Rights and Sex Equality," *Hypatia* 10(1):74–103 (Winter 1995) continues the examination of parental rights begun in her chapter in this book. She is currently working on a book on ethical issues in contemporary family law.

Ruth Ann Strickland teaches political science at Appalachian State University. Her general research and teaching interests include public policy analysis, judicial process, women's issues in public policy, and American government and institutions. She has published numerous articles in scholarly journals.

Marcia Lynn Whicker is professor of public administration at the Graduate School at Rutgers, Newark. Her publications include thirteen books and numerous articles in the areas of public policy, American politics, and public administration. Her interests include using computer simulation models to test the effectiveness and representativeness of governmental structures and systems.

Iris Marion Young teaches ethics and political philosophy in the Graduate School of Public and International Affairs at the University of Pittsburgh. She is author of *Throwing Like a Girl and Other Essays* and *Justice and the Politics of Difference.* Her articles have appeared in a variety of philosophical and feminist journals. She is currently working on a book on democratic theory.

About the Book

THE GROWING AVAILABILITY of unprecedented reproductive technologies has raised equally unprecedented moral and political questions, not only for pregnant women but for all those who wish the state to act humanely and wisely in this extraordinarily sensitive arena. In this timely and provocative volume a group of distinguished feminist scholars explore the ethics and the politics of issues such as surrogacy, genetic testing, in utero surgery, genetic intervention, in vitro fertilization, and fetal endangerment.

Expecting Trouble is essential reading for scholars and students of women and politics, women and public policy, sexual ethics, and medical ethics.

Index